Labour's second lan

MANCHESTER
UNIVERSITY PRESS

Labour's second landslide

The British general election 2001

edited by
Andrew Geddes and Jonathan Tonge

MANCHESTER UNIVERSITY PRESS
Manchester and New York

distributed exclusively in the USA by Palgrave

Published by Manchester University Press
Oxford Road, Manchester M13 9NR, UK
and Room 400, 175 Fifth Avenue, New York, NY 10010, USA
www.manchesteruniversitypress.co.uk

Distributed exclusively in the USA by
Palgrave, 175 Fifth Avenue, New York,
NY 10010, USA

Distributed exclusively in Canada by
UBC Press, University of British Columbia, 2029 West Mall,
Vancouver, BC, Canada V6T 1Z2

British Library Cataloguing-in-Publication Data
A catalogue record for this book is available from the British Library

Library of Congress Cataloging-in-Publication Data applied for

ISBN   0 7190 6265 9 *hardback*
       0 7190 6266 7 *paperback*

First published 2002

10 09 08 07 06 05 04 03 02   10 9 8 7 6 5 4 3 2 1

Typeset by Ralph J. Footring, Derby
Printed in Great Britain
by Biddles Ltd, Guildford and King's Lynn

Contents

Tables, figures and boxes

Contributors

John Benyon is Professor of Political Studies at the University of Leicester, where he is also Director of Lifelong Learning. From 1987 to 1999 he was Director of the Scarman Centre for the Study of Public Order. He has published widely on crime, public order, policing and ethnic relations.

Jonathan Bradbury is Lecturer in Politics at the University of Wales, Swansea. He is convenor of the PSA British Territorial Politics Group. Publications include *British Regionalism and Devolution* (HMSO, 1997). He researches in the areas of British public policy and sub-national government, and contemporary British politics and devolution.

Philip Cowley is a Lecturer in the Department of Politics at the University of Hull. One of life's deputies, he is the Deputy Director of the Centre for Legislative Studies and Deputy Editor of the *Journal of Legislative Studies*. His publications include *Conscience and Parliament* (ed.) (1998) and over 40 articles and chapters.

David Denver is Professor of Politics at Lancaster University and has been co-convenor of EPOP since 1993. He has written extensively on elections and, with colleagues, has recently completed ESRC-supported research projects on the 1997 Scottish referendum and on candidates in the Scottish Parliament and Welsh Assembly elections. The former is reported in *Scotland Decides* (Frank Cass, 2000).

David P. Dolowitz is a Lecturer in Politics at the University of Liverpool.

Steven Fielding is a Senior Lecturer in the School of English, Sociology, Politics and Contemporary History, and a member of the European Studies Research Institute, at the University of Salford. He is author of *The Labour Party. Continuity and Change in the Making of New Labour* (Palgrave, 2002) and is also working on a study of the Labour Party and social change during the 1960s for Manchester University Press, which is due for publication in 2003.

Justin Fisher is Lecturer in Political Science at Brunel University and co-convenor of EPOP.

Andrew Geddes is a Senior Lecturer in the School of Politics and Communication Studies at the University of Liverpool. His recent work has focused on comparative European immigration policy and politics. Recent publications include: *Immigration and European Integration* (Manchester University Press, 2000) and (as co-editor) *Immigration and Welfare: Challenging the Borders of the Welfare State* (Routledge, 2000). He is currently completing two book projects: *The European Politics of Immigration* (Sage) and *The EU and British Politics* (Palgrave).

James Mitchell is Professor of Politics at the University of Strathclyde. He is the author of various books and articles on Scottish politics.

Stuart Quayle is completing a PhD in the Department of Politics at the University of Bristol. His research focuses on the organisation of the Conservative Party and the role and influence of members within it.

Jonathan Tonge is Professor of Politics at the University of Salford. He is the author and editor of various works on Northern Ireland and British politics. Recent books include *Northern Ireland: Conflict and Change* (Pearson, 2001, 2nd edition); *Peace or War: Understanding the Peace Process in Northern Ireland* (Ashgate, 1997), edited with Chris Gilligan; *The New Civil Service* (Baseline, 2000); and *Labour's Landslide: The British General Election 1997* (Manchester University Press, 1997), edited with Andrew Geddes.

Rachel J. Ward is a doctoral student in the School of Politics at the University of the West of England, Bristol.

Stephen Ward is a Lecturer in Politics and Contemporary History, European Studies Research Institute, at the University of Salford. He has published widely in the fields of environmental politics and the politics of the Internet. His publications include *British Environmental Policy and Europe: Politics and Policy in Transition* (edited with Philip Lowe, Routledge, 1998).

Mark Wickham-Jones is Senior Lecturer in Politics at the University of Bristol.

Dominic Wring is Lecturer in Communication and Media Studies and a member of the Communication Research Centre at Loughborough University. He has published widely on the historical development of election campaigning.

Acknowledgements

The editors would like to thank the authors of each chapter for the prompt submission of contributions. Production of this book has incurred a number of debts and we wish to thank the following: Andrew Mycock, Research Assistant at the University of Salford, for his sterling work in preparing the manuscript; Bill Jones, University of Manchester, for being supportive of the idea of election studies; Stephen Ward (Salford) for the additional Penrith constituency profile; Steven Fielding (Salford), for several perceptive comments; and Richard Delahunty at Manchester University Press for his support throughout the project. On a personal note, we say thanks to Federica, Maria, Connell and Anita.

Abbreviations

AMS	additional member system
AV	alternative vote
AWS	all-women short-lists
BES	British Election Study
BNP	British National Party
CPF	Conservative Policy Forum
CSR	Comprehensive Spending Review
DUP	Democratic Unionist Party
EAZ	Education Action Zone
EiC	Excellence in Cities
EMU	Economic and Monetary Union
ERM	Exchange Rate Mechanism
ES	Employment Service
EU	European Union
FoE	Friends of the Earth
GDP	gross domestic product
ICD	International Commission on Decommissioning
IFS	Institute of Fiscal Studies
IMF	International Monetary Fund
IRA	Irish Republican Army
LEA	local education authority
MAFF	Ministry of Agriculture, Forestry, and Fisheries
MPC	Monetary Policy Committee
NATO	North Atlantic Treaty Organisation
NEC	National Executive Committee
NHS	National Health Service
NI	National Insurance
NICE	National Institute for Clinical Excellence
OECD	Organisation for Economic Co-operation and Development
PEB	party election broadcast
PFI	Private Finance Initiative

PPC	prospective parliamentary candidate
PPP	public–private partnership
PUP	Progressive Unionist Party
RUC	Royal Ulster Constabulary
SDLP	Social Democratic and Labour Party
SDP	Social Democratic Party
SLP	Socialist Labour Party
SNP	Scottish National Party
SSP	Scottish Socialist Party
STV	single transferable vote
UKIP	United Kingdom Independence Party
UKUP	United Kingdom Unionist Party
UUP	Ulster Unionist Party
VAT	value added tax
WFTC	working families tax credit

Introduction

Andrew Geddes and Jonathan Tonge

It is appealing to begin a book about British general elections by drawing an analogy to the breaking of new dawns. This has both a metaphorical and a literal resonance because the method used for counting votes means that the election result usually becomes known as day breaks. After his second landslide victory, Tony Blair was thus able to claim victory in the half-light of the new dawn on 8 June 2001, when a combination of euphoria and exhaustion easily steers oratory towards cliché.

This analogy also has appeal because it allows a connection to be made between the Labour Party's victory celebrations in 1997 and 2001. Daybreak on 2 May 1997 was certainly a good time to be a supporter of the Labour Party after a landslide victory that had ended eighteen years in opposition, during which time its ability ever to win again had been questioned. Daybreak on 8 June 2001 could well have been a time for equal celebration. Not only had Labour managed to secure a second term in government, but it had done so with a second consecutive landslide victory, unprecedented in the Party's history. Yet the mood at Labour's Millbank headquarters in central London was relatively downbeat. A great victory had been secured, but turnout at the election had slumped to 59.2 per cent, the lowest in any general election since 1918, while the election campaign had revealed public dissatisfaction with the government's record, particularly concerning the delivery of improved public services.

On this basis two equally plausible scenarios can be sketched to introduce a book that focuses on the 2001 general election. The first concentrates on the second consecutive landslide victory enjoyed by Tony Blair's Labour government at the expense of a Conservative Party that made no significant electoral gains during the four years in opposition following its calamitous 1997 defeat. The second addresses the precipitate fall in turnout. For instance, it can be asked to what extent a government that received the support of only 25 per cent of the electorate can claim a mandate? Clearly the first scenario focuses on Labour's great victory while the second injects a note of caution. Labour did secure a landslide victory, but the endorsement was

1

lukewarm. This was a decidedly apathetic landslide. Taken together, both scenarios provide complementing themes that underpin this book's attempt to explain Labour's second landslide.

The landslide

To begin with, the dimensions of this landslide can be sketched. It needs to be remembered that no Labour government had ever before managed to secure a second full term in office. In 2001, Labour secured 42 per cent of the vote, down 2.3 per cent from 1997. The workings of the British electoral system meant that this share of the vote translated into 64 per cent of the seats in the House of Commons and a crushing Labour majority of 167, down 12 from 1997. The situation on the government benches had hardly changed since 1997. Most of those Labour MPs who had been surprised to be elected in 1997 in what used to be safe Conservative seats were re-elected in 2001, often with increased majorities. Labour fought a defensive campaign that emphasised the long-term nature of their plans with the slogan 'The work goes on'. Labour's victory had a hollow ring. New Labour still has much work to do and must be seen to 'deliver' on its promises in the second term.

The picture was correspondingly bleak for William Hague's Conservative Party, which effectively stood still. The Conservative campaign played hard on three issues: opposition to European integration, tax cuts and a tough stance on asylum seekers. This right-wing populism failed to reap electoral dividends. The Conservatives saw their share of the vote rise by only 1.1 per cent, to 33 per cent, an increase securing just one more seat in the House of Commons. These disastrous results rendered Hague's position untenable and he resigned as Conservative Party leader on the morning after the election. At such a rate of progress and assuming elections every five years, the Conservatives could hope to return to power some time in the twenty-seventh century. As David Denver points out in his chapter surveying the results, the Conservatives are in search of a Moses to lead them to the promised land of electoral revival. That said, even if such a leader were to be found the Conservatives face major difficulties: the average age of their members is sixty-seven, they have very few women elected representatives and were seen by many at the 2001 election as out of touch with the concerns of the electorate.

The Liberal Democrats could lay claim to being the success story of the 2001 election. Under their new leader, Charles Kennedy, whose laidback style was in marked contrast to that of his hyper-energetic predecessor, Paddy Ashdown, the Liberal Democrats increased both their share of the vote and their number of seats. The Liberal Democrat vote rose from 17 per cent to 19 per cent while the number of seats won by Liberal Democrat candidates increased from forty-six to fifty-two. The rules on equal coverage of the

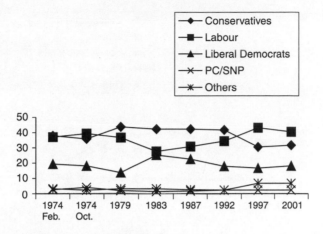

Figure 0.1. Main parties' percentage share of the vote in general elections, 1974–2001. (PC, Plaid Cymru; SNP, Scottish National Party.)

parties during election campaigns in the broadcast media gave the Liberal Democrats a rare opportunity to expose their ideas and leaders to the wider scrutiny of the public and escape the effects of the Westminster two-party duopoly.

The overall outcome of the 2001 election is shown in its recent historical context in Figures 0.1 and 0.2. Figure 0.1 shows the shares of vote obtained by the main parties since 1974 while Figure 0.2 shows the number of seats won. Taken together, the two figures also indicate the disproportionality of the British electoral system by demonstrating a skewing effect that can lead to Labour receiving 42 per cent of the vote but 64 per cent of the seats, as it did in 2001.

The extent of Labour's victory in 2001 almost exactly reflected its 1997 triumph in terms of share of the vote and the number of seats won. The difference this time, of course, was that, unlike in 1997, very little changed. In 2001 only twenty-nine seats changed hands. Despite the deployment of election-night technical wizardry by the television channels, assisted by psephologists who apparently require no sleep, there was very little to report. This might help explain why the election-night television audiences in 2001 peaked at only 7.3 million, compared with 12.7 million in 1997. Broadcasters threw a few teasers to their drowsy audience. Would the result in ultra-marginal Torbay herald the Conservative fight-back? Actually, the Liberal Democrat candidate increased his share of the vote and turned a knife-edge marginal into a safe Lib Dem seat. Would Schools Minister Estelle Morris lose her Birmingham Yardley seat? As it turned out, Morris won quite comfortably. Perhaps former Conservative cabinet minister Gillian Shephard would be vulnerable in South West Norfolk? Wrong again – she actually managed to

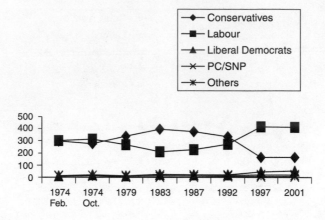

Figure 0.2. Main parties' numbers of seats in the House of Commons, 1974–2001. (PC, Plaid Cymru; SNP, Scottish National Party.)

increase her share of the vote by more than 10 per cent. The night's biggest casualty was perhaps the Liberal Democrats' Jackie Ballard, but the cry of 'Were you still up for Jackie Ballard?' was hardly likely to adorn the cover of a big-selling post-election paperback book.[1] Never had so much television time been expended in the pursuit of so little drama. This is best represented by the BBC's use of a virtual reality William Hague standing at the bottom of a staircase of seats that, if won, would lead him to the door of Number 10 Downing Street. When the polls closed at 10 p.m. he was stood at the bottom of this staircase. When all the results were in, he was still stood at the bottom, staring forlornly at the electoral mountain that he had manifestly failed to climb.

The apathy

The second key feature of the 2001 general election was the sharp fall in turnout (see Figure 0.3). How can this be explained? Low turnout might be indicative of a lack of faith in political institutions and the democratic process. It could be construed as a rational response to an election that appeared to be a foregone conclusion. It might also be linked to the perception that there is very little real choice between parties that seem alike and focus on 'spin' rather than substance. Or, perhaps, it reflected disillusion with both the Labour government and the Conservative alternative. When considering these explanations, it is useful to distinguish between *structural* and *contingent* explanations for low turnout.

One set of *structural* explanations focus on the democratic and political processes themselves and try to identify causes for disaffection, disengagement

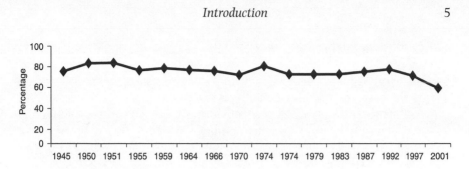

Figure 0.3. Turnout at general elections, 1945–2001.

and apathy. It has been argued that 'globalisation' and the power of multi-national corporations have led to a sense of powerlessness, with an associated feeling that politics – as represented by national elections – no longer matters.[2] The perception is that choices expressed through the ballot box make little difference in the face of powerful global corporations and remote international institutions, such as the World Trade Organisation and the European Union (EU). As a perspective on the internationalisation of politics and the current wave of anti-capitalist protests, this view presents a powerful critique of politics in a post-ideological era; but as an explanation for low turnout in the British general election of 2001 its utility is less evident. An emphasis on all-conquering globalisation neglects the ability of political choices expressed at the ballot box to make some difference. Students of European politics may observe that elections can revolve around real choices about levels of taxation and the provision of public services and distinctly different visions of the national future. It is also worth remembering that the British government still spends 44 per cent of gross domestic product (GDP), which gives significant room for manoeuvre. In a sense, the low turnout in 2001 election may have shown that how that money is spent on education, health and public transport still matters. Consequently, while the relative power of the nation state in a globalised world can be questioned, it is misleading to suggest that low turnout can be attributed to the ideas that national governments have become powerless in the face of global capitalism and international organisations, and that national politics has become irrelevant.

The second structural explanation is equally sweeping. In the aftermath of victory, some government ministers were moved to remark that the low turnout reflected satisfaction with the job done by Labour in its first term. Thus, a 'culture of contentment' with Labour's economic competence and commitment to delivery of improved public services could explain low turnout. However, as Steven Fielding points out in his chapter on Labour's 'hollow' victory, if contentment underpins low turnout then inner-city Liverpool must be a very happy place indeed. At the very least, the precipitate decline in turnout in Britain's inner cities and evidence of structural disengagement from the political process by many of the country's poorest people must give pause for thought to a government that preaches the language of social cohesion.

Contingent explanations focus on those factors related to the 2001 campaign. Of these, the most important was the fact that the result of the 2001 election appeared to be a foregone conclusion. Close elections produce high turnouts, but anticipated landslides produce low turnouts.[3] As David Denver shows in his chapter analysing the results, Labour had enjoyed a constant opinion-poll lead – aside from a blip during the September 2000 fuel tax protests – since April 1992. It is also worth recalling that turnout in 1997 was the lowest since the Second World War. Perceptions of the 1997 general election can be warped by memories of flag-waving people greeting Tony Blair as he entered Downing Street as Prime Minister. These 'spontaneous' outpourings actually came from Labour Party supporters bussed in for this purpose. Research into low turnout at the 1997 general election suggests that the main reasons for it were that many people saw the outcome as a foregone conclusion and that many discerned little choice between parties with relatively similar policies. After all, it is commonly supposed that voters are nowadays more rational and more prone to act as consumers rather than as loyal party identifiers. If so, then why bother to vote in an election when the outcome is already clear?

Another factor also appeared to influence the 2001 campaign: the perception that Labour had failed to deliver improved public services. One of the most difficult moments for Tony Blair on the campaign trail was when he was confronted by Sharon Storrer outside a Birmingham hospital. Ms Storrer was extremely unhappy at the standards of care received by her partner in a Birmingham hospital. The way that this issue was covered by the media helped reinforce the idea that politicians were remote from 'ordinary people' and unable to deal with a situation that had not been scripted by spin-doctors. Perhaps fortunately for Blair, his discomfort was overshadowed when his Deputy, John Prescott, punched a young man who had thrown an egg at him from short range. The sight of the Deputy Prime Minister grappling with a voter is likely to become an abiding image of a not particularly memorable campaign.

Despite Labour's vulnerability on the issue of public service delivery, the Conservatives chose to centre their campaign on cutting taxes, opposition to European integration and a tougher regime for asylum seekers. This meant that in 2001 the public were faced three choices: a Labour government that some saw as having failed to deliver, or at least not matching the expectations raised in 1997 when, for instance, Labour spoke of '24 hours to save the NHS'; a Conservative Party with an unpopular leader that had veered to the right with its espousal of tax cuts, Euroscepticism and tough policies on asylum; or Charles Kennedy's Liberal Democrats, who admitted that they could not win, but offered an 'honest' form of anti-populism, with calls for increased taxes to fund improvements in public services.

Plan of the book

The conventional wisdom is that elections are not won and lost in the campaign itself. Rather the election result is a product of developments over the lifetime of a parliament. In the case of the 2001 election, this means that the period we are surveying starts in effect on 2 May 1997, after Labour's first landslide. The first five chapters of the book pay attention to the campaign and to the development of party strategies over the four years of the parliament, as well as to the media's role in the campaign. We then analyse key campaign issues. We show how Labour in office managed to exorcise what Mark Wickham-Jones calls the ghost of economic incompetence that had lingered from previous administrations. This is followed by an analysis of what was probably the key issue in the 2001 campaign, the provision of public services, and an outline of the many challenges facing a re-elected Labour government, not least lingering fears about 'privatisation'. Other issues did not have such decisive effects on the election outcome, but did have important repercussions before the election, during the campaign or both. Europe is a good example of just such an issue. William Hague was determined to turn the 2001 general election into a mini-referendum on the euro. We explain why this strategy failed. We then analyse the (lack of) impact of environmental issues on the campaign. Given the parlous state into which Britain's rail system has fallen and increased congestion on the roads, the environment was a dog that did not bark. Law and order, on the contrary, was a much discussed campaign theme. The Conservatives' policy for the detention of asylum seekers caused some controversy, while outbreaks of urban disorder in northern England drew attention to the poor state of race relations in some English towns. The 2001 general election was the first post-devolution general election (albeit devolution had taken different forms in different parts of the United Kingdom). We analyse the campaigns in Scotland and Wales, and in Northern Ireland. There were few female politicians who became prominent campaign figures. We examine the representation of women and the attention devoted to gender issues by the main political parties.

At the end of each chapter will be found a brief constituency profile that injects some local colour into the coverage of national politics. It may appear that elections are fought out in television studios in London, but much of the hard work is done in villages, towns and cities across the country. Our constituency profiles aim to provide an insight into some key contests. They have been selected not only for the colour they provide but also because they can at times help relate the national political debate to the local context. Thus, for instance, we profile Wyre Forest, where Dr Richard Taylor, standing for the Kidderminster Hospital and Health Concern Party, won with a massive 26.2 per cent swing against the sitting Labour MP.

The conclusion addresses the key themes underpinning the election campaign, notably the dominance of Labour and the lack of interest of the electorate. We consider the electoral futures of the each of the main parties. We then raise some issues for further discussion in relation to what might be done about the decline of interest in politics, reflecting upon what David Denver rightly labels a 'catastrophic' decline in turnout.

Notes

1 Unlike B. Cathcart, *Were You Still Up for Portillo?* (London: Penguin, 1997).
2 See, for example, G. Monbiot, *The Captive State: The Corporate Takeover of Britain* (London: Macmillan, 2000); N. Hertz, *The Silent Takeover* (London: William Heinemann, 2001).
3 See, for example, A. Heath and B. Taylor, 'New sources of abstention?', in G. Evans and P. Norris (eds), *Critical Elections: British Parties and Voters in Long-Term Perspective* (London: Sage, 1999); C. Pattie and R. Johnston, 'A low turnout landslide: abstention at the British general election of 1997', *Political Studies*, 49:2 (1999), pp. 286–305.

1

The results: how Britain voted (or didn't)

David Denver

Introduction

In terms of trends in party support, the period between the 1997 and 2001 general elections was a remarkable one. It was remarkable because this was the first inter-election cycle since regular polling began in which the governing party never once lost its lead in monthly voting intentions (on the basis of the average of all published polls in a given month). As Figure 1.1 shows, the Conservatives very slowly improved their position after the 1997 election, without ever really threatening Labour's lead. They did come within hailing distance of the governing party in September and October 2000, during the protests over petrol prices – indeed, five individual polls put the Tories in the lead at this time – but this proved a temporary boost. In the last polls before the 2001 election was called, the Conservatives stood at 32 per cent of voting intentions – almost identical to their vote share in the disastrous 1997 election.

Liberal Democrat support declined somewhat after 1997 but thereafter was very consistent, only twice straying outside a very narrow band of 13–16 per cent. The party also benefited from government unpopularity at the time of the fuel protests but, as with the Conservatives, this proved to be temporary and from November 2000 until the election was called Liberal Democrat poll ratings were around the level that had been sustained from late 1997.

For a governing party, Labour's support between the two elections was remarkably strong and consistent. It hit 60 per cent of voting intentions three times during its 'honeymoon' with the electorate in the second half of 1997 and its worst rating was 39 per cent in September 2000. After that, it improved steadily and in the last few pre-election polls stood at 51 per cent. This was well up on Labour's 1997 vote share and seemed to presage another stunning victory. There is a conventional wisdom, after all, that elections are not won and lost in the four weeks of the official campaign but in the four years that have gone before.

While many factors affect the popularity of the parties – their policies, their performance in government or opposition, their success in creating a

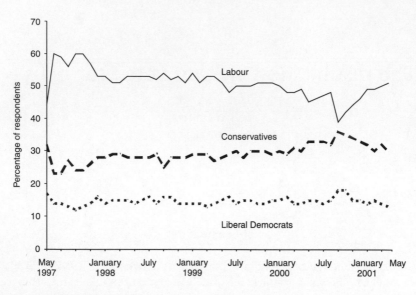

Figure 1.1. Monthly voting intentions, 1997–2001.
Source: Published polls reported on the MORI website.
Note: The figures are means of results in all published polls in the month concerned. The data for May 2001 are derived from four polls undertaken before the date of the election was announced.

positive image, the general economic situation and so on – most commentators agree that over the past twenty years or so voters' judgements about the party leaders have become an increasingly important influence on their choice of party. Labour's dramatic recovery of popularity began in earnest when Tony Blair became party leader in 1994, and support for the parties between 1997 and 2001 closely reflected the electorate's reactions to the party leaders. Figure 1.2 shows which leader was thought the best person to be Prime Minister from July 1997 (i.e. after William Hague took over as Conservative leader) to April 2001. Throughout the period Blair was the preferred Prime Minister by large margins. Hague made little impact initially, but his ratings improved slightly during 2000, without ever making a serious dent in Blair's huge lead. While Paddy Ashdown was leader of the Liberal Democrats he was consistently rated a more likely Prime Minister than Hague but when Charles Kennedy took over in August 1999 the latter trailed in the prime ministerial stakes.

Campaign opinion polls

The changing pattern of party support during the campaign itself is charted in Figure 1.3, which is based on the results of national polls conducted by

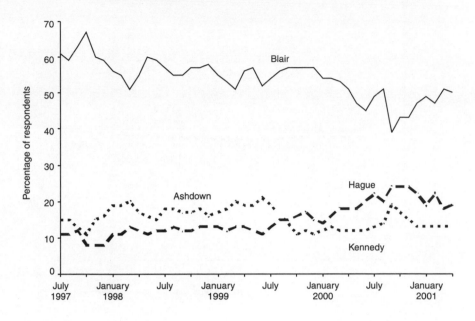

Figure 1.2. Party leader thought to be the best person for Prime Minister, 1997–2001.
Source: Gallup Monthly Index.

the four major polling companies (Gallup, ICM, MORI and NOP). Four pre-election polls at the beginning of May constitute the starting point and the chart then shows the average share of voting intentions in each week of the campaign, the results of the two exit polls conducted on polling day and the parties' actual shares of the vote in Great Britain in the election itself.

As can be seen, the polls were unremittingly gloomy for the Conservatives. No matter what they tried, William Hague and his party were unable to provoke a significant positive response from the electorate. Although some individual polls suggested a glimmer of light, the overall story is that the level of Conservative support hardly moved from around the 30 per cent mark throughout the campaign. On the other hand, there was some slippage in Labour's fortunes – having had more than 50 per cent of voting intentions in early May, support fell, according to the polls, to around 45 per cent in the last week of the campaign. Even this proved to be an underestimate of the decline in Labour support during the campaign, as the party ended up with 42 per cent of the vote.

In contrast, there was a clear upward trend in support for the Liberal Democrats. A similar trend had occurred in 1997 (although not in 1992) and in part this simply reflects the fact that general election campaigns give the party (and its leader) more exposure than they can get between elections.

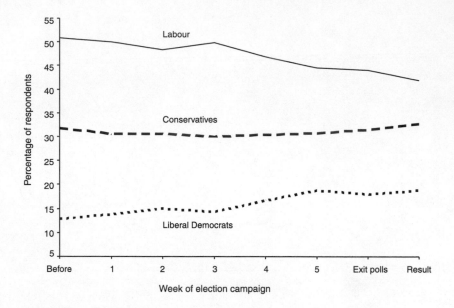

Figure 1.3. Voting intentions in campaign polls.
Source: Results of published national polls reported on the MORI website.
Note: The calculations – the simple mean in each case – are based on the 'headline' figures reported by the polls, whether these were adjusted or unadjusted. Each poll is assigned to the week in which the majority of the fieldwork was carried out.

In part also, however, the 2001 figures probably reflect a positive response on the part of the public to Charles Kennedy's energetic campaign and to the party leader himself. During the campaign, Gallup conducted a rolling series of polls on behalf of the British Election Study (BES) in which respondents were asked to indicate how much they liked each of the party leaders by giving them a score on a scale running from 0 (Strongly dislike) to 10 (Strongly like). When the series began on 14 May, Hague's mean score was 3.9, Blair's 5.6 and Kennedy's 4.9. By the end of the campaign Hague was still on 3.9 and Blair had increased to 5.9 but Kennedy made the biggest advance, scoring 5.4. The Liberal Democrat leader's affability was effectively communicated to the electorate and the voters also seem to have warmed to Kennedy's attempt to portray himself and his party as straight-talking and honest, in contrast to the endless 'spin' employed by the others.

Media reporting of the election generated a widespread impression that the campaign made no difference to the outcome. While it is true that Labour won easily, as expected, and the Conservatives 'flatlined', Figure 1.3 makes clear that it is wrong to suggest that nothing changed over the weeks leading up to polling day.

The election outcome

The overall results of the election in Great Britain (i.e. excluding Northern Ireland, which is discussed in Chapter 12) and changes as compared with 1997 are shown in Table 1.1.[1]

Table 1.1. Outcome of the 2001 election and changes from 1997 (Great Britain)

	Share of vote (%)	Change, 1997–2001	Number of seats	Change, 1997–2001
Conservatives	32.7	+1.2	166	+1
Labour	42.0	−2.3	413	−5
Liberal Democrats	18.8	+1.6	52	+6
Other	6.5	−0.6	10	0
Turnout	59.2	−12.3		

Note: The Speaker is counted as a Labour candidate although he was not opposed by the Conservatives or Liberal Democrats.

Turnout

The most striking change – and perhaps the 'big story' of the 2001 election – is the very sharp decline in turnout, from 71.5 per cent in 1997 to 59.2 per cent. Despite the fact that it had been made easier to claim a postal vote (and the number claimed was around double the usual figure) this was the lowest turnout in a general election since 1918 and the largest fall between any two elections in modern times. Turnout fell in every region and in every constituency, the biggest decline being in Liverpool Wavertree (−18.6 per cent) and the smallest in Hackney North and Stoke Newington (−3.9 per cent from an already low figure). The widespread nature and extent of the change is illustrated by the figures in Table 1.2, which shows the number of constituencies with various levels of turnout in the two elections. In 1997 the great majority of constituencies had a turnout in excess of 70 per cent, eight exceeded 80 per cent and none fell below 50 per cent. In 2001, however, sixty-eight constituencies fell below 50 per cent and only eleven managed a turnout above 70 per cent.

Table 1.2. Constituency turnouts in the 1997 and 2001 general elections

	Below 40%	40–49%	50–59%	60–69%	70–79%	Above 80%
1997	0	0	33	163	437	8
2001	3	65	258	304	11	0

What accounts for this widespread and steep fall in electoral participation? Various hypotheses can be suggested. First, reporting of the opinion polls discussed above gave rise to a widespread impression that the result of the election was a foregone conclusion and this might well have depressed interest in it. Second, it could be argued that there was actually very little difference between the major parties in policy terms and so they failed to arouse traditional passions. Third, it might be that Labour supporters in particular had been disillusioned by the party's rightward drift when in office. Fourth, it could be suggested that many voters were disillusioned by all parties – in particular by what they perceived as cynicism and the overuse of 'spin' – and by politics in general. Finally, it could be suggested that a 'culture of contentment' had grown up. People were broadly satisfied with, if not enthusiastic about, how things were going in the country and saw no need to get excited about the election. These various suggestions require further examination and in most cases survey evidence to investigate them.

On the basis of the election results, however, it appears that disillusion with the government did contribute to the fall in turnout. In seats that were Labour-held, the mean change in turnout was –13.1 per cent as compared with –11.3 per cent in Conservative-held seats and –10.9 per cent in those held by the Liberal Democrats. In addition, the safer the seat for Labour the greater was the turnout decline. While the change averaged –10.6 per cent in seats held with a majority of less than 5 per cent, it was –13.5 per cent in those held by a majority of more than 20 per cent. The relationship between change in turnout and previous party strengths can be measured more exactly by correlation coefficients. Relating Labour share of the vote in 1997 to change in turnout between 1997 and 2001 gives a coefficient of –0.421. That is, the stronger Labour was in a constituency in 1997 the greater was the decline in turnout. This evidence can be interpreted in another way, however. In general, turnout declined less in more marginal seats – the correlation between the percentage majority in 1997 and the change in turnout between 1997 and 2001 was –0.340 (which means that the larger the majority the greater the fall in turnout) – and it could be argued that this shows that the electorate have 'rumbled' the electoral system. Voters know that most seats are safe (or hopeless) for one party or another but turn out to vote in greater numbers where it matters, that is in seats where the competition between the parties is close.

It is striking, however, that the variations in the absolute levels of turnout across constituencies remain strongly related to their social make-up. On the basis of figures from the 1991 census, it is apparent that turnout was higher (correlation coefficients are in parentheses) in constituencies with more owner occupiers (0.670), more professional and managerial workers (0.538) and more people employed in agriculture (0.486). On the other hand, turnout was lower in areas with more households without a car (–0.802) (which is an indicator of the level of poverty), more ethnic minority voters (–0.412), more council tenants (–0.592), more manual workers (–0.376) and more persons per hectare (–0.629) (which is a measure of how urban a constituency is). The 1991 census was, of course, ten years out of date at the time of the election, but up-to-date 'lifestyle' data used in commercial marketing[2] confirm the general pattern. In the 10 per cent of constituencies with the most 'wealthy achievers living in suburban areas' the mean turnout was 64.3 per cent and in those with the most 'comfortable middle managers in mature home-owning areas' it was 62.7 per cent, whereas in the 10 per cent of constituencies with the most 'council estate residents with high unemployment' turnout averaged only 51.1 per cent.

It is worth noting, however, that analysis of the results shows that there was no systematic relationship between change in turnout and change in Labour's share of the vote. On the other hand, there was a slight (but statistically significant) relationship with the Conservative vote share (correlation coefficient = 0.110) – the smaller the decline in turnout the bigger the increase in the Conservative vote. It should be emphasised, however, that this is only a slight tendency.

Votes and seats

In terms of party support, the overall results in 2001 show little change from 1997. There was a swing of 1.8 per cent from Labour to Conservative and a small increase in the Liberal Democrats' share of the vote. In broad terms, this pattern of change was repeated around the country, as the three right-hand columns of Table 1.3 show. The Conservatives declined further in Scotland and dropped back a little in Greater London, but advanced in all other regions. Labour lost support everywhere but more heavily in heartland areas of Wales, the North and Yorkshire than in the South East and South West. The Liberal Democrats declined a little in their strongest region (the South West) but otherwise improved on their 1997 performance everywhere. The nationalist parties experienced mixed fortunes. In Scotland, the Scottish National Party (SNP) stayed in second place to Labour with 20.1 per cent of the votes but this was a drop of 2 per cent on its 1997 vote. In Wales, on the other hand, Plaid Cymru's support rose from 9.9 per cent in 1997 to 14.3 per cent in 2001 – the party's highest-ever vote in a general election.

There was also little net change in the number of seats each party won in the House of Commons. The Conservatives gained nine seats (five of them from Labour) but also lost eight (seven to the Liberal Democrats and one to Labour), leaving them with a net gain of just one. Labour gained two seats but lost seven, while the Liberal Democrats advanced to their largest-ever representation – fifty-two seats – having gained eight and lost two. The effect was to leave Labour with a huge majority of MPs.

Table 1.3 also shows that, with the exception of Greater London, there remains a broad north–south division in terms of party support, although

Table 1.3. Party shares of votes (percentages) in 2001 and changes (percentage points) from 1997, by region

	Conservatives	Labour	Liberal Democrats	SNP/ Plaid Cymru	Other	Change, 1997–2001 Conservatives	Labour	Liberal Democrats
Scotland	15.6	44.0	16.3	20.1	4.0	−1.9	−1.6	+3.3
Wales	21.0	48.6	13.8	14.3	2.3	+1.4	−6.1	+1.5
North	24.7	55.7	17.1	–	2.5	+2.5	−5.2	+3.8
North West	28.3	51.8	16.5	–	3.4	+1.2	−2.4	+2.2
Yorkshire and Humberside	30.2	48.6	17.1	–	4.0	+2.2	−3.3	+1.1
West Midlands	35.0	44.8	14.7	–	5.5	+1.3	−2.2	+0.9
East Midlands	37.3	45.0	15.4	–	2.2	+2.4	−2.8	+1.8
East Anglia	41.6	35.8	19.0	–	3.5	+2.9	−2.5	+1.1
South East	42.6	31.7	21.6	–	4.1	+1.2	−0.2	+0.2
Greater London	30.5	47.3	17.5	–	4.7	−0.7	−2.2	+2.9
South West	38.5	26.3	31.2	–	4.0	+1.8	−0.1	−0.1

Table 1.4. Number of seats won in 2001 and changes from 1997, by region

| | Conservatives | Labour | Liberal Democrats | SNP/ Plaid Cymru | Other | Change, 1997–2001 | | |
						Conservatives	Labour	Liberal Democrats
Scotland	1	56	10	5	–	+1	0	0
Wales	0	34	2	4	–	0	0	0
North	3	32	1	–	–	0	0	0
North West	7	60	3	–	–	0	0	+1
Yorkshire and Humberside	7	47	2	–	–	0	0	0
West Midlands	13	43	2	–	1	–1	–1	0
East Midlands	15	28	1	–	–	+1	–2	+1
East Anglia	14	7	1	–	–	0	–1	+1
South East	73	35	9	–	–	0	–1	+1
Greater London	13	55	6	–	–	+2	–2	0
South West	20	16	15	–	–	–2	+1	+1

Table 1.5. Changes in party shares of the vote in individual constituencies, 1997–2001

	Best (%)	Worst (%)	No. of constituencies in which support was:	
			up	down
Conservatives	+11.4	−17.1	380	258
Labour	+12.7	−26.6	198	440
Liberal Democrats	+23.5	−17.6	448	189
SNP	+6.9	−13.0	17	54
Plaid Cymru	+11.9	−7.4	35	5

Note: The constituencies of West Bromwich West (former Speaker), Glasgow Springburn (current Speaker) and Tatton (not contested by Labour or Liberal Democrats in 1997) are excluded in all cases and Wyre Forest (not contested by the Liberal Democrats in 2001) from the Liberal Democrat figures.

the gap narrowed a little. The Labour share of the vote was greater and the Conservative vote smaller in Scotland, Wales and the three northernmost English regions than they were in East Anglia, the South East and the South West.

The north–south divide is even more apparent in terms of seats won (see Table 1.4). In Scotland, Wales and northern England the Conservatives won only eighteen seats, compared with 229 won by Labour. In Scotland, however, the Conservatives broke their duck by regaining Galloway and Upper Nithsdale from the SNP (the only seat to change hands in Scotland). In Wales the Conservatives remain without a seat. The notable Liberal Democrat gain in the East Midlands (Chesterfield) was a first for the party in the region and meant that for the first time it held a seat in every region of Britain.

Although changes in party support were broadly similar across regions this was not true across individual constituencies. At this level change was far from uniform, as the data in Table 1.5 indicate. The difference between each party's best and worst performances is huge and all parties managed to increase their support in some seats while declining in others. This reflects the important part that local factors play in elections – including the role of incumbency, variations in campaigning intensity and, of course, the pattern of electoral competition in the constituency.

The influence of incumbency and of varying tactical situations is illustrated in Table 1.6. It is a well established feature of British election results that when an MP defends a seat for the first time then he or she benefits from an incumbency effect. When that MP first won the seat at the previous election, he or she would usually have been replacing a sitting MP and would be relatively unknown to the local voters. By the time of the second election the new MP would have had a chance to become established and to have

Table 1.6. Changes in party shares of votes related to 'first-time incumbency' and according to tactical situation in constituency

	Number of seats	Mean change in vote share		
		Conservatives	Labour	Liberal Democrats
All seats	638	0.8	−2.0	1.5
Conservative first-time incumbents	49	3.1	−0.3	−0.9
Labour first-time incumbents	195	−0.1	−0.8	1.0
Liberal Democrat first-time incumbents	26	−1.6	−2.3	5.3
Tactical situation from 1997				
Conservatives first, Labour second	92	2.9	−0.3	−0.9
Conservatives first, Liberal Democrats second	72	2.1	−0.5	−0.0
Labour first, Conservatives second	339	0.5	−2.6	2.0
Labour first, Liberal Democrats second	32	−0.7	−3.5	1.8
Liberal Democrats first, Conservatives second	39	−0.4	−1.3	2.5
Liberal Democrats first, Labour second	6	0.9	−5.1	5.1

Notes: For the reasons explained in the notes to Table 1.5, West Bromwich West, Glasgow Springburn and Tatton are excluded. Incumbents are candidates who first won their seats in 1997 and stood again in 2001 except that Romsey, which was won in a by-election, is also included for the Liberal Democrats. The tactical situation is based on the 1997 results but in this case Romsey is excluded.

made a name in the constituency. Table 1.6 shows how first-time incumbents performed. The theory finds some support, since Labour declined less and the other parties did worse where a first-time incumbent was the Labour candidate. The incumbency effect is even clearer, however, in the case of the Conservatives and Liberal Democrats.

While there is little evidence of widespread tactical voting in these figures, they do show variations in how the parties' votes changed in different electoral contexts. The Conservatives did best in seats that they already held – and in that sense consolidated their position – but lost support where they were in second place to the Liberal Democrats and in seats where the latter were second to Labour. Labour had its worst performances in the seats where it was in contention with the Liberal Democrats. The biggest Liberal Democrat improvements came in seats that they already held.

The fact that the swing was not uniform across constituencies had important consequences for the election outcome. It explains one of the puzzles of the results, namely why the Conservatives did not win more seats given that there was a small but clear movement in their favour nationally. On a uniform swing of 1.8 per cent from Labour to the Conservatives the latter would have taken fifteen Labour-held seats. In fact they took only three of these and in nine of them there was actually a swing to Labour against the national trend. Labour's ability to hold on to its vote where it mattered is also shown by the fact that in the sixty-three seats that it held by a majority of less than 5 per cent, the Labour share, on average, *increased* by 1.8 per cent whereas it fell by an average of 3.9 per cent in seats that the party held with a majority of more than 20 per cent. Similarly, the Liberal Democrats sharply improved their performance in the ten seats that they held most narrowly from the Conservatives, increasing their vote share by an average of 8.8 per cent – well above the national figure – so that the Conservatives were unable to cash in on their small overall increase in support.

Voting behaviour

Measuring electoral change by means of 'swing' figures or changes in the parties' shares of the vote can be useful for analysis. But swing indicates only the net change in the positions of two parties relative to one another and, as the British party system has become more complicated, the usefulness of the measure has declined. In addition, the figures for net changes in support tell us nothing about the behaviour of the voters which brought about the change – how many switched between the major parties, how many switched from abstention to voting, and so on. For this we need a 'flow of the vote' table based on survey data. At the time of writing, the only survey data available for analysis come from opinion polls conducted during the campaign and in this section I make use of a poll conducted by ICM Research for the BBC during the last week of the campaign.[3] Given that this is a pre- rather than post-election poll, the figures for party support relate to voting intentions rather than actual votes cast and it is not possible to investigate the sources and effects of non-voting. Nonetheless, in Table 1.7, which shows the flow of the vote, poll respondents who said that they had decided not to vote are taken at their word and shown as non-voters.

Despite being derived from a campaign poll the figures shown in the table are intuitively plausible. Given that in 1997 the Conservatives were already down to their core supporters it is not surprising that they did not lose many more to other parties – they have, indeed, the largest 'retention rate' (69 per cent) among the major parties. They also suffered less from abstentions. Almost a quarter of 1997 Labour voters did not intend to vote in 2001 – a further indicator of disillusion – and they also lost 9 per cent to the Liberal

Table 1.7. The flow of the vote, 1997–2001

2001 vote	1997 vote (%)				
	Too young	*Did not vote*	*Conservatives*	*Labour*	*Liberal Democrats*
Conservatives	12	8	69	6	11
Labour	23	8	5	58	6
Liberal Democrats	8	3	8	9	55
Other	3	1	1	4	3
Non-voter	54	80	18	24	24
(No. of respondents)	(125)	(395)	(279)	(478)	(123)

Source: ICM/BBC campaign poll. The data are weighted to the outcome of the 2001 election.

Democrats (which may reflect tactical voting) and 4 per cent to 'other' parties. In contrast to 1997, more Liberal Democrat defectors went to the Conservatives (11 per cent) rather than to Labour (6 per cent) but it is indicative of the fragility of Liberal Democrat support that a large proportion of their 1997 voters (24 per cent) did not intend to vote in 2001.

Non-voters usually explain their failure to cast a ballot by reference to what might be called 'accidental' factors, such as being away or ill on the day. The data in Table 1.7 suggest, however, that consistent non-voters are emerging as a significant section of the electorate. Fully 80 per cent of those who did not vote (although eligible) in 1997 did not intend to attend the polling station in 2001. Whether this is due to deep-seated alienation from the political system or is a temporary reaction to the alternatives on offer in this particular election is a subject that remains to be investigated. Similarly, parties and pundits have been wringing their hands over the failure of young people to turn out in the election. In fact there is nothing new in this phenomenon and the proportion of abstainers among the young (54 per cent) is not radically different from that found in previous general elections. As is normal, first-time voters supported Labour rather than the Conservatives by almost two to one, although the Liberal Democrats also made a relatively strong showing among this group.

Focusing now on party choice, Table 1.8 shows voting patterns on the basis of occupational class, age, sex and housing tenure. The class basis of British party politics continued to decline in 2001. Although the working class (manual workers) gave almost half of its votes (of those who voted) to Labour, the party was also in the lead among the middle class. Moreover, while there was a clear movement away from the Conservatives among middle-class voters, there was an even stronger movement away from Labour among the working class. The same story is told by the data on housing

Table 1.8. Party support in 2001 by social group (percentages) and change (percentage points) from 1997

	Conser-vatives	Labour	Liberal Democrats	Change, 1997–2001		
				Conser-vatives	Labour	Liberal Democrats
Occupational class						
Non-manual workers	33	37	24	–4	0	+4
Manual workers	32	48	13	+8	–10	0
Age (years)						
18–24	25	45	24	(+3)	(–12)	(+7)
25–34	25	53	13	–	–	–
35–44	26	43	22	(0)	(–7)	(+5)
45–64	37	38	19	+4	–5	+1
65+	42	37	16	–2	+3	–1
Sex						
Men	33	43	17	+2	–3	0
Women	33	41	20	+1	–4	+3
Housing tenure						
Owner occupiers	34	39	20	–1	–2	+3
Council tenants	22	61	8	+9	–4	–7
Other renters	35	36	21	+11	–18	+5

Sources: ICM/BBC campaign poll 2001; BBC/NOP exit poll 1997.
Notes: Data have been weighted to the election result. The rows do not total 100 because votes for 'others' are not shown. The figures for change compare the 2001 campaign poll with results from the 1997 exit poll. The age groups used in the two polls are different and the change figures shown in parentheses are based respectively on those aged 18–29 and 30–44 in 1997.

tenure, with council tenants showing a significant swing from Labour to the Conservatives while there was little change among owner occupiers. The voting of the different age groups displays a largely familiar pattern. Support for the Conservatives generally increased and that for Labour declined with age and it is only among the over-65s that the Conservatives were the most popular party. As noted previously, however, support for the Liberal Democrats was unusually strong among the youngest age group. Finally, there was little difference in the party choice of men and women. The latter were slightly less likely to vote Labour and more likely to support the Liberal Democrats but the differences are not large.

While party choice continues to be structured to an extent by social and demographic variables, most commentators would now lay more stress on voters' opinions and judgements when explaining voting behaviour. When these are examined the reasons for Labour's victory in the election become perfectly clear. First, the voters' opinions on important election issues were closer to those advocated by Labour (and the Liberal Democrats) than they were to those of the Tories. The whole question of tax and public services was central to voters' concerns, for example, and the Conservatives made much of their plans for tax cuts (which implied cuts in some services) but only 4 per cent of ICM respondents said that they favoured cutting taxation and spending less on health and education. More than half (57 per cent) favoured increased taxation and more spending on these services, while 34 per cent wanted taxation and spending to remain as they were (with 5 per cent having no opinion on the matter). It is true that public opinion was hostile to Britain joining the euro and the Conservatives made much of this issue in their campaign. On the other hand, only 26 per cent of respondents to MORI's final poll chose 'Europe' as an important issue affecting their vote (as compared with 73 per cent choosing health care and 62 per cent education). In addition, voters simply did not believe the Conservative claim that a Labour government would somehow rig a referendum on the euro: the final NOP campaign poll for the *Sunday Times* reported that 55 per cent of respondents said that it would not happen and only 35 per cent said that it would.

Second, in 2001 as in 1997, Tony Blair personally had a commanding lead over his rivals in being thought the best person to be Prime Minister. Every campaign poll which asked about this reported William Hague trailing far behind Blair in this respect. A typical set of results, taken from Gallup's final poll on 6 June, is shown in the first part of Table 1.9. For all his efforts and debating skills in the House of Commons, Hague could barely muster any support among intending Labour and Liberal Democrat voters and only 69 per cent of Conservative supporters thought he would be the best Prime Minister (interestingly, 11 per cent of Conservatives diplomatically answered 'Don't know' to this question, compared with only 5 per cent of Labour supporters). Blair's lead over Hague (+32 per cent) was much wider than the lead he had enjoyed over John Major in 1997 (+14 per cent).

Finally, Table 1.9 also presents some data relating to what we might call the image of the Conservative Party. Even if many voters cannot easily distinguish the precise policies being put forward by a party or have no clear ideas about how the parties have been performing, they often form vague general impressions that may be influential in determining their vote. As can be seen, the party leadership again has an impact here, with a huge 81 per cent of all voters – and 69 per cent of Conservative supporters – agreeing that the Conservative Party did not have a strong team of leaders. In the other cases Conservative voters were less critical. Nonetheless, sizeable

Table 1.9. Party leader thought to be the best person for Prime Minister and images of the Conservative Party (percentages)

	All	Conservative voters	Labour voters	Liberal Democrat voters
Best Prime Minister				
Tony Blair	52	12	90	36
William Hague	20	69	1	6
Charles Kennedy	15	8	4	50
The Conservative Party				
Does not have a strong team of leaders	81	69	88	83
It is hard to know just what they stand for	76	45	88	84
Gives the impression of being out of touch with modern Britain	69	34	86	84
Goes on too much about Europe	65	36	81	71

Source: Gallup polls, 6 June and 8–9 June 2001.
Note: The figures for best Prime Minister do not total 100 because 'Don't knows' are not shown. The second part of the table shows the percentages agreeing with each statement.

minorities agreed that it was hard to know what the party stood for, that it seemed out of touch with modern life and that it talked too much about Europe. These propositions were supported by very large majorities of Labour and Liberal Democrat supporters, at least some of whom need to be won over by the Conservatives if they are to mount a serious challenge at the next election.

Overall, then, the electorate tended to favour Labour policies, thought that Labour had by far the best leader and had a poor image of the Conservatives. With all that stacked up against the opposition it is no surprise that, even if the voters were not greatly enamoured with Labour, they proved unwilling to vote the government out of office.

Conclusion

The Labour government could not have been entirely happy with the outcome of the 2001 general election. To be sure it was re-elected with a large majority in the House of Commons, but it had presided over a catastrophic decline in turnout – especially marked in Labour's strongest areas – which suggested that the electorate was less than enthusiastic about how the government had performed in its first term. The Liberal Democrats, on the other hand, could be forgiven for reacting to the results with some euphoria. They increased their vote share nationally and also picked up some of their target seats. It remains the case, however, that in the great majority of seats the Liberal Democrats trail well behind the other parties. Although a total of fifty-two seats is far from negligible, it still represents a relatively poor return in seats (8.1 per cent of the British total) for almost 19 per cent of the votes. As ever, some form of proportional representation remains the key to a genuine breakthrough for the Liberal Democrats but the size of Labour's majority in the new parliament means that even with fifty-two seats the party will have little leverage on government policy in this respect.

In 1997 the Conservatives were cast out into the electoral wilderness to wander for a time. Like the Israelites in the Old Testament, they needed a leader – a Moses – to take them to the promised land (electoral revival). William Hague did not prove to be such a leader and in recognition of this he resigned the Conservative leadership on the morning after the general election. A party election to choose his successor got under way almost immediately. For observers of British parties the response of the Conservatives to their second consecutive landslide defeat will prove almost as interesting as the performance of New Labour in office. In the light of their poor image discussed above – as well as other problems, such as an ageing membership, the paucity of females among their elected representatives and disagreements over European policy – the party must seek to renew and reinvent itself. Parties which fail to adapt to a changing electorate are frequently consigned to history – or at least to the sidelines – as Labour realised during the 1980s and early 1990s. In the past the Conservatives have proved adept at changing – embracing the welfare state and the mixed economy in the 1950s, for example – and the challenge facing the new leader, whether a Moses or even a Joshua, will be to embark upon a set of changes which will revamp the party so that it can once again have appeal across a broad swathe of the British electorate.

Notes

1 The source used for the analysis of election results in this chapter is *The British Parliamentary Constituency Database 1992–2001*, prepared and made available by Pippa Norris.
2 The data referred to here were provided by CACI Ltd and are included in *The British Parliamentary Constituency Database 1992–2001*.
3 These data were kindly made available by Nick Sparrow of ICM Research.

Hartlepool

To resign once from the cabinet could be seen as unfortunate. To resign twice establishes a rather unfortunate pattern. As Peter Mandelson put it, his greatest achievement was 'joining the government (twice)'. He resigned from the Department of Trade and Industry in December 1998 following revelations about a substantial undeclared home loan from a fellow minister, Geoffrey Robinson. His political resurrection was swift when he returned in October 1999 as Secretary of State for Northern Ireland, but also short-lived when he resigned in January 2001 after becoming embroiled in the Hinduja brothers passport scandal.

Mandelson's political reputation was established by his success as Labour's campaign guru and the *éminence grise* of the dark arts of electoral politics. Mandelson was an architect of 'New Labour' and a key supporter of Tony Blair when he became Labour Party leader in 1994. The legacy of this was a simmering feud with Gordon Brown, who stood aside to clear Blair's path to the leadership. It was for these reasons and others that Mandelson inspired as much fear and loathing within the Labour Party as he did in Labour's political opponents. After his second resignation, his political opponents were keen to write his political obituary, but he was determined to defy them and returned to Hartlepool in an attempt to shore up his political base.

The Conservative candidate, Gus Robinson, played on his local roots by arguing that people should vote for him because he was 'one of us', as opposed to 'one of them', presumably. He was assisted by the ubiquity of his property development company, which meant that his name was evident all round the town. This could be a double-edged sword. One local was reported by the *Guardian* as saying that he knew Gus Robinson well, so that ruled him out. Mandelson also enticed one of 'Old Labour's big beasts' to enter the fray. Arthur Scargill stood for the Socialist Labour Party (SLP), but was rarely seen in the constituency and lost his deposit.

Despite fears that he might be vulnerable, Mandelson easily retained the seat. What was most interesting was his victory speech, in which he lambasted his political opponents (within the Labour Party, doubtless) and said that they had had their pound of flesh and then, in one of the most surreal moments of the campaign, stunned the viewing audience by shouting that he was 'a fighter not a quitter'.

Result

Hartlepool		
	No. of votes	% of vote
Mandelson, P. (Labour)	22,506	59.2
Robinson, G. (Conservative)	7,935	20.9
Boddy, N. (Liberal Democrat)	5,717	15.0
Scargill, A. (SLP)	912	2.4
Others	981	2.5
Labour majority	14,571	38.3
Labour hold		
Turnout		56.3

2

'No one else to vote for'?
Labour's campaign

Steven Fielding

Introduction

Labour won the 2001 general election – and, in terms of seats, won it well. This was a historically unprecedented achievement: the party had in all its 101 years failed to secure two working Commons majorities in a row – and in 2001 Tony Blair had practically repeated his 1997 landslide. As one Millbank worker claimed, Labour's success was demonstrated 'in the number of seats we won.... It tells its own story'.[1] Yet the success or failure of the party's campaign should not be judged by that single criterion. As was also the case in 1997, Labour's haul of seats was vastly disproportionate. While the party gained 64 per cent of Commons seats, this position was based on but 42 per cent of votes cast and, given the low turnout, the support of only 25 per cent of those registered to vote. Labour won nearly three million fewer votes than in 1997: its tally of 10.7 million was lower than that gained by the party at any election since 1945 – apart from 1983 and 1987. If this was not sobering enough, some commentators speculated that the dire state of the Conservative Party – and the cautious nature of Labour's own message – meant the result was more of a vote against William Hague than in favour of Tony Blair. For these reasons, the extent to which Labour had won the 'radical' mandate to improve public services sought by the Prime Minister was highly questionable.

The campaign outlined

Labour's campaign did not get off to the best of starts. The outbreak of foot-and-mouth disease during March put paid to long-standing plans to hold the election on 3 May. Blair's reluctant decision to delay it scuppered a carefully constructed timetable of policy announcements which had culminated in the spring budget. Blair realised the public was troubled by pictures of huge piles of burning farm animals and upset by the farmers' anguished response.

Many saw holding an election in that context as highly inappropriate. Labour also had fifteen rural seats with majorities of 10 per cent or less: Blair did not want to throw these away. Furthermore, opinion polls suggested that one in six voters would be less likely to vote Labour if the poll were held in May. Thus, when the Prime Minister claimed that, by delaying the election, he was placing the country's interests before those of his party he was putting a statesmanlike gloss on what was a highly partisan decision.

Had he not resigned from the cabinet for a second time, Peter Mandelson would have resumed his 1997 double act with Chancellor Gordon Brown at the heart of Labour's national campaign in Millbank Tower. Mandelson's absence was felt – but it hardly affected the result. As in 1997, Brown was charged with establishing strategy. Mandelson would have been responsible for coordination; in his stead was Douglas Alexander, a young Scottish MP and protégé of the Chancellor. Placing the campaign effectively in Brown's hands enabled him to act as he did in the Treasury: do as much as possible himself without consulting others and relying only on trusted aides who acted solely under his remit, thereby sidelining supposedly influential officials. To temper Brown's influence, Alastair Campbell, in contrast to 1997, was based in Millbank to ensure that the Prime Minister's views were represented while he made daily visits to what seemed like every single improving school and refurbished hospital in the land.

If the personnel in charge of the campaign were little different to those of the previous election, neither was the technology they employed. Excalibur II, the computerised information retrieval system, allegedly fifteen times more powerful than the 1997 original, helped Labour speakers rapidly rebut Conservative attacks. The party again used telephone banks to canvass up to 14,000 voters a day and supplemented these calls with hundreds of thousands of direct mailings. Taking account of the spread of home computers and mobile phones since the last campaign, Labour sent out emails and text messages, with 30,000 of the former and 100,000 of the latter being dispatched on polling day alone. Videos were also delivered to those in marginal constituencies to illustrate what a difference a Labour MP had made to their area. Plans had even been prepared to transmit a life-size holographic image of the Prime Minister from Downing Street simultaneously to six meetings in marginal constituencies every day. Blair would have appeared in front of audiences and taken questions, apparently looking his interlocutors in the eye thanks to the presence of hidden cameras. It is probably fortunate that this scheme was abandoned due to technical difficulties. Less innovatively, John Prescott travelled the country in his very own battle bus with the aim of enthusing activists and mobilising core voters. Millbank hoped – vainly as it turned out – that this would keep the unpredictable Deputy Prime Minister out of the media spotlight.

The campaign, as previously, was structured around a detailed grid on which Brown had mapped the subjects to be tackled, when they were to be discussed and by whom. Allegedly, even the intervention of Margaret Thatcher mid-way through the contest had been accounted for. However, when the Conservatives launched their manifesto unexpectedly early, the disadvantages of inflexible planning became evident – and the Chancellor found himself severely criticised as a result.

Brown's overall strategy was extremely cautious. He assumed Labour could win on the basis of the government's – or more specifically his – economic record while arousing fears of the consequences of Conservative tax cuts on public services. Echoing his mentor, Alexander considered the economy central to victory; another Millbank worker stated that it was the 'key to the whole campaign'.[2] As in 1997, to entrench its reputation for economic probity Labour sought endorsements from business people and arranged for fifty-eight of them to sign a letter of support to *The Times*. Labour also launched another business manifesto but did not feel it necessary to devote an election broadcast to the subject – as it had done in the previous campaign. Parallel with this emphasis on the economy, Labour made a variety of claims about by how much the Conservatives would cut public spending. Pre-election posters said £16 billion would go, although Hague stated it would be only half that amount. Comments made by the Conservative frontbencher Oliver Letwin early in the campaign meant that Labour could subsequently cite the figure of £20 billion with some legitimacy – at one point £25 billion was even mentioned.

Labour drew these two themes together in its treatment of William Hague. The party presented Hague in a series of unflattering images that, taken together, denigrated him in a manner that put to shame the *Sun*'s demolition of Neil Kinnock a decade earlier. Along with Michael Portillo, Hague appeared in pastiches of film posters: they were, for example, 'Mr Boom and Mr Bust' starring in *Economic Disaster II*. Each advertisement was derived from the same proposition: the Conservatives were economically incompetent. This was rather unfair: the last years of the Major government laid the basis of the growth enjoyed by Chancellor Brown. However, in politics, impressions matter more than facts. Labour during the 1980s had been castigated for the much-exaggerated consequences of the Callaghan government's 'winter of discontent'. It was now the Conservatives' turn to cry foul. Labour's website even used downloadable computer games to make its points: one had Hague intone 'cut, cut, cut' as he attempted to find enough public service savings to finance his tax reductions. If such methods were juvenile, their effectiveness was less obvious.

The guarded nature of Brown's strategy was reflected in his reluctance to allow the party to make what he considered to be unnecessary spending commitments. If such caution appeared excessive given Labour's opinion poll lead, it at least avoided own goals. One such, from 1997, was Labour's famed pledge card. This had made a splash at the time because it recorded promises to, for example, reduce hospital waiting lists and school class sizes. It was, opponents gleefully pointed out, unfortunate that four years later only three of the five pledges had been met. Thus, while it was decided to issue a new card, its significance was diminished by containing pledges that were banal, had already been announced or were extremely modest. Brown was, however, unable to prevent the Prime Minister making a positive speech on Europe towards the end of the campaign. Blair wanted to help prepare the ground for a possible post-election referendum on Britain's entry into the European single currency. Brown's grid made no mention of Labour taking the initiative on this issue. The Chancellor feared it might alienate voters – and, possibly more importantly, was less enthusiastic about joining the euro than was his leader. The normally risk-averse Blair was, nonetheless, willing to take a chance – it was one of the few he took during the campaign.

Having established Labour's economic competence and the Conservative threat to public services, during the last week of the campaign the party's focus fell on motivating core supporters and those – like women and the young – considered less likely to vote. During the previous year, local Labour parties should have identified various categories of voters and constructed databases to help them get out the vote. Given the fall in membership to 280,000 – about 120,000 less than in 1997 – and the disenchantment of remaining activists with some of the government's policies, it is uncertain how many parties actually undertook this preparatory work.

If those entitled to vote could not be motivated to exercise their franchise by the promise of better schools and hospitals, Labour tried to scare them. To that end, one last poster, showing Margaret Thatcher's hair superimposed on Hague's head, stated 'Get out and vote or they get in'. This illustrated in vivid form the Conservative leader's ideological affinity with his predecessor-but-one – that it also made a sly dig at Hague's baldness was probably not unintentional.

The last few days before 7 June were more fraught than they might have been after the Conservatives unexpectedly raised the prospect of another Labour landslide. Hague asked voters disturbed by the prospect to 'lend' him their votes to keep down Blair's majority. This was not as desperate as it might at first appear. In the mid-1990s in the Australian state of Queensland a party trailing badly in the polls had made a similar appeal and won. Labour strategists rightly feared that talk of an inevitable landslide would only encourage potential non-voters to stay at home and so diminish the party's chances of winning a 'positive' mandate.

Women and the young

Two groups Millbank considered worthy of special attention were women and younger voters: both had been important parts of Labour's winning coalition in 1997; both were thought most likely not to vote in 2001.

Labour had closed the gender gap in 1997: after generations of more women than men supporting the Conservatives, they had voted for the parties to the same degree. However, studies made during the government's mid-term purported to show that women were more dissatisfied than men with Labour's performance in office.[3] Labour's early decision to cut benefits to single parents was not forgotten. Yet the government later introduced a variety of family-friendly policies. Moreover, being disproportionately employed in low-paid occupations, women benefited most from the minimum wage as well as the working families and children's tax credits.

Before the campaign began, focus had fallen on the lack of female representation in the party. In 1997 Labour had 101 female MPs, a historic high, largely because of a form of positive discrimination later judged illegal. According to the ex-Minister for Women, Joan Ruddock, after 1997 local Labour parties simply 'reverted to type'.[4] As a result it was predicted that fewer Labour women would be returned to the new parliament and so it proved: six fewer were elected. Yet this still left Labour in a much better position than any of its rivals. To improve matters, however, before the election the government had promised to pass legislation that would permit all parties to use positive discrimination to ensure a gender balance among their representatives. Less significantly, Labour was also criticised during the campaign for the lack of women presenting the party's daily press conferences; again, the party was better in this respect than the Liberal Democrats and Conservatives. At the height of this particular storm in a teacup – mainly generated by female journalists with columns to write – Alastair Campbell was heard to bark down his mobile phone to a Millbank lackey: 'We must have a woman on the platform – even if she's just in the chair'.[5] Labour's attempts to impress female voters were not always so superficial.

The party's main problem in addressing younger voters was that their interests were as diverse as those of their older counterparts. Labour's website for younger voters, named 'ruup4it', mentioned issues that ranged from the environment to pub closing times. As its own polling demonstrated, the party was also hindered by the fact that Blair's government had introduced university tuition fees, which were naturally loathed by prospective students. In addition, while Labour had established a minimum wage, the full rate was applicable only to workers over twenty-one years of age. The extension of the full rate to twenty-one-year-olds was mooted during the campaign but Brown vetoed the concession.

Some of Labour's attempts to engage young voters were frivolous at best. To encourage them to visit its youth website, scratch cards were distributed which held out the possibility of winning a prize. The party's exploitation of celebrity endorsements was also unfortunate. The use of the out-of-fashion Chris Evans indicated that some Millbank address books required updating; Geri Halliwell's appearance on the party's first election broadcast suggested that more than a few needed throwing away.

Much of Labour's effort went into convincing young people of the importance of simply voting. Significantly, Labour's final election broadcast featured a young couple voting for the party and then being congratulated by those whose lives had been transformed as a result. Just in case the message had not got across, 150,000 letters were sent to first-time voters in marginal seats, ostensibly written by a variety of minor television celebrities, which urged them to vote – even if not necessarily for Labour.

Blair's 'radical' agenda

The former Labour frontbencher Bryan Gould echoed the views of many commentators before the campaign when he predicted that Blair's party would win, 'not because it is loved, but because there is no one else to vote for'.[6] Labour's private research confirmed that the party's substantial opinion poll lead was largely due to the unpopularity of their opponents.[7] Floating voters especially were, moreover, unclear what Labour ultimately sought to do – except, possibly, become more like the Conservatives. Party differences were not, then, immediately obvious to most.[8] Thus, as sympathetic columnists pointed out, if Labour failed to make a positive case for its policies during the campaign, Blair's would be a hollow victory.[9] As the Prime Minister himself conceded, in 1997 the people had been desperate to be rid of the Conservatives: as many said at the time, Labour's was a largely negative mandate. Given that the construction of 'New' Labour was Blair's attempt to stress his party's accommodation with key components of the Thatcherite economic legacy, this was perhaps none too surprising.[10] In 2001, however, he wanted to 'win a mandate for change on our own terms'.

Well before the campaign, the Number 10 Policy Unit had searched for the means to encapsulate Labour's ambition effectively, to give the government's disparate policies a unity that could be communicated to the people. It was hoped such a compelling narrative would break through the public's apparent cynicism by convincing them that Labour was fundamentally different to the Conservatives and stood for something they could enthusiastically endorse at the polls. The intention was, thereby, to allow Blair to claim a 'positive' mandate for his second term – a strategy somewhat at odds with Brown's more prosaic approach. The Prime Minister consequently promised that during the campaign he would set out his 'basic values and philosophy' and 'go right back to the founding basis of my political beliefs and New Labour'. If the first term was about winning the trust of ex-Conservative supporters, the second would be about establishing a 'radical, modern social democratic' agenda. As his still trusted adviser Mandelson pointed out, Blair's first term had fostered a change in the political climate and so Labour could now, for example, talk of achieving 'full employment', mention of which he had once discouraged.[11]

In a series of keynote speeches the Prime Minister sought to establish the basis for what he described as a 'fresh mandate for radical change' so that he could draw a firm line under the transitional character of Labour's first term. This was a strangely old-fashioned means of delivering such an important message. Moreover, while his words hardly acquired the grandeur of Gladstone's archetypal Midlothian campaign, the message was only partly communicated via predigested sound-bites. The whole enterprise, in fact, belied Blair's reputation for superficiality and cynicism. Despite the fact that he must have known his chances of making a deep impact on most people's minds were severely limited, Blair nonetheless claimed to believe that the election would be 'a chance to explain, to engage in a sustained argument about the big issues'. He accepted that most people normally paid little heed to politics but hoped the campaign would cause them to listen to his arguments.

'New Labour's big idea', Blair revealed to members of the Sedgefield party on his formal adoption as their candidate, 'is the development of human potential, the belief that there is talent and ability and caring in each individual that often lies unnurtured or discouraged'. To achieve this end, he stated, the party wanted to establish a society 'in which everybody gets the chance to succeed, to go wherever their talents take them', where opportunities would be spread 'to every part of the country, to every family, and every community'. This would be a 'strong society where work is rewarded; where success is prized, but also possible for all; where none are written off without the hope or the help they need; where aspiration and ambition become the expectation of the many, not the birthright of the few'. To do this, a Labour government would 'break down every barrier, every impediment', for 'no outdated idea, no vested interest, public or private' could be allowed to prevent any individual from developing to her or his full potential. 'We are', he asserted, 'meritocrats', motivated by a 'notion of equality that is not about outcomes or incomes; but equal worth'.

The government, Blair admitted, had gone only part of the way to achieving this society. In its first term Chancellor Brown had established economic stability: if such an achievement was a prerequisite it was still only the 'foundation' to progress. The more specific means of manifesting Labour's 'big idea' was 'sustained investment and far-reaching reform in our public services', for without 'world-class services' – or at least those which matched the standards of other members of the Organisation for Economic Co-operation and Development (OECD) – Labour would not be able to provide 'genuine opportunity for all'.

While Blair stated that 'inadequate investment and poor standards' went 'hand in hand', extra investment would not by itself improve public services. There also had to be 'real reform' of the means by which these services were managed and delivered, in which there would be 'no predisposition towards public or private' provision. 'We need', he stated, 'to break decisively with the tradition of monolithic, centrally driven public services'; instead, the services had to 'mobilise the small battalions, and give them freedom to innovate and change'. In particular, health and education had to be rebuilt 'around consumers'. As the Prime Minister reiterated many times: 'pupils do not exist for state schools; but state schools for pupils. The patient doesn't exist for the NHS, but the NHS for the patient'. The public had to be given greater choice and enjoy guaranteed minimum standards.

Blair claimed he was beginning to 'exorcise the old Tory fatalism that things wouldn't really get better; that extra spending was money down the drain' and called on the people to 'seize the chance to move beyond Thatcherism and set a new course for our country'. Irritated by the charge that he was a 'crypto-Thatcherite', the Prime Minister criticised Thatcherism for its lack of 'compassion'; a 'social indifference it seemed almost to rejoice in'; and a 'selfish individualism that failed to acknowledge the vital role of society in helping individuals to succeed'. Following an 'iron law of individualism' during the 1980s, the Conservatives had opened up opportunities only to a small minority and excluded too many because of their ideological refusal to fund collective provision adequately. The talents Labour sought to unlock consequently remained unnecessarily idle. It was, therefore, 'time to draw a line under the era of Thatcher'. Consequently, Blair claimed, voters were faced with a 'more fundamental choice between the two main parties' since 1983. 'This election', he asserted, 'is about a radical vision of lifting barriers and liberating people's potential in a decent society, where everyone gets the chance to make the most of their God-given talent'. In contrast the Conservatives wanted to go back to the 1980s, cut public services and constrain the development of individual potential.

While the Prime Minister liked to describe his agenda as exemplifying a 'new politics', he was – as he occasionally conceded – really outlining an updated social democratic outlook. Thus he argued that a suitably modified state could improve people's lives and that, without such intervention, many lives would suffer. Within this schema, Blair wanted to appeal to the party's established supporters in the declining working class, those for whom adequately funded public services offered the only real hope of improvement. Yet, as he knew only too well, his outlook had to be couched in terms that would win the approval of more affluent voters, who had once embraced Thatcherism. These residents of 'middle England' also claimed to want better public services but had doubted that higher 'investment' – Blair had converted 'spending' to the more prudent-sounding 'investment' – would necessarily improve them, especially if undertaken by a Labour government.[12]

Blair wanted to keep his 1997 coalition of working class and middle class together but he also sought to move on from his 'negative mandate'. Throughout Labour's first term, therefore, the Prime Minister endeavoured to find a language and concepts that would allow him convincingly to bridge these two groups' interests in terms which were also consistent with his party's precepts. The admittedly nebulous 'Third Way' was one such effort, for which

Blair was unjustly ridiculed: most voters simply did not understand what it signified.[13] His speech to the 1999 Labour Party conference, which notionally pitted the 'forces of conservatism' against those of 'modernity and justice', was another. Blair's focus on public service investment and reform slowly emerged during 2000 and promised to imbue his rhetorical labours with a tangible quality they had previously lacked.

Despite the fervency of his message, Blair did not get through to many voters. For the continued existence of popular cynicism or apathy, the Prime Minister blamed the media's preoccupation with the process of campaigning – in particular an obsession with supposed 'spin' or presentation – rather than the substance of policy. There was, Blair claimed, a 'real hunger out there for understanding what the basic policy issues are' but journalists were not covering the real issues.[14] Blair's outrage was probably genuine – although some commentators suspected that his comments were themselves motivated by 'spin'. Yet one of the factors promoting the very cynicism against which the Prime Minister railed was the popular belief that Labour's – and in particular his – fixation with superficial image making had turned the party into an unprincipled machine that would say anything to win votes.

Labour's association with compulsive image manipulation was actually strengthened at the start of the campaign. Blair announced the election date at an inner-city London girls' school that, in 1997, had been seen to be failing, but four years on had markedly improved. Blair's advisers wanted the location to underline the party's message about the possibility of improving public services. However, this was overshadowed by many journalists' irritation with the accompanying, undoubtedly crass, images. When Blair sang hymns and prayed in front of a choir and stained-glass window it looked like he was parading his personal piety for electoral gain. This, and other staged events, provoked journalists fed up with being forced to write about such banalities to infuse their copy with a heavy dose of scepticism.

Why, journalists asked, did the Prime Minister not meet 'real' people? This question exploded on the second Wednesday of the contest. On that day Labour launched its manifesto, an event that should have been the centrepiece of the party's campaign, a moment when the public would be listening most attentively. Instead, the manifesto was banished from the front pages after Blair was berated outside a hospital by Sharon Storrer, the distraught, but politically confused, partner of a cancer patient whose treatment within the National Health Service (NHS) had been less than ideal. More spectacularly, on the same day John Prescott responded to an egg being thrown at close quarters by punching his assailant. This latter event dominated the headlines for at least two days while the swinging of the punch was replayed on numerous television broadcasts. If these two events made no impact on Labour's electoral position, they nonetheless overshadowed the party's more serious message made earlier in the day. According to Blair, this was just the most extreme example of the media's trivialisation of the election.

Tax and spend

Labour's own handling of the crucial issue of taxation and spending was probably a more important cause of the failure of Blair's rhetoric to provoke a powerful resonance among the electorate. The Prime Minister and his Chancellor refused to countenance the possibility that taxes might have to rise to finance improvements in public services. This was despite the apparent fact that many members of the public – including former Conservatives – already accepted the need to increase taxes.

Labour claimed to favour tax cuts when possible, at least to those on lower incomes, but stated that there had to be a 'balance' between such cuts and the need for increased public spending. The preference was, nonetheless, clear: increased 'investment' in public services. Plans announced before the campaign indicated that, if elected, over its first three years a Labour government would increase spending on health and education by 6 per cent in real terms and nearly double that on transport. This would be financed by the massive surplus accumulated during Blair's first term – not, it was implied, through increasing taxes. In 1997 Labour promised to keep the top rate of direct tax at 40 per cent, something established by the Conservatives at the height of Thatcherism. This had largely been at Blair's behest as he hoped, thereby, to entrench Labour's position among voters still suspicious of its alleged propensity to 'tax and spend' irresponsibly. Four years later, the Prime Minister wanted to reiterate the pledge. Many wondered how necessary such a promise now was, not the least of these being Labour members; it was nonetheless made.

The leadership's extreme caution was further revealed when, within days of the campaign starting, the Conservatives launched their first attack on Labour's taxation and spending plans. The Institute of Fiscal Studies (IFS) had discovered a 'black hole' in Labour's projections. If Brown wanted to continue to invest in public services ahead of economic growth after the next Labour government's first three years, the IFS suggested, he would have to increase taxes. Alternatively, public spending rises would have to be curtailed. The Conservatives claimed that Labour would choose the former option. Forced on to the back foot, Brown seemed to imply he would follow the latter course – even though that contradicted Blair's stress on the need for sustained investment – but refused to make a definitive statement. Consequently, the issue did not go away.

For much of the campaign's second week, the Conservatives again had Labour on the run, this time in relation to Brown's plans for National Insurance (NI). During the 1992 election campaign John Smith, then Labour's shadow Chancellor, stated that he wanted to abolish the ceiling on NI contributions. Over a certain income, the rate at which NI contributions were paid remained static: Smith claimed it was fairer to eliminate this anomaly so that the rich would pay more. John Major's Conservatives infamously converted Smith's pledge into what they described as a 'tax bombshell' and thereby – the likes of Blair and Brown believed – stopped many affluent voters supporting Labour. In 1997 Brown promised to maintain the NI ceiling, although in power he craftily raised it higher than was needed to keep up with inflation – this was one of a number of the Chancellor's 'stealth taxes'.

The Conservatives claimed that, having promised not to raise direct taxes, one of the few means by which Brown could fill the notional 'black hole' was by abolishing the NI ceiling. As the Labour manifesto did not promise to maintain the limit, they accused Brown of wanting to abolish it. Should Labour do so, four million taxpayers earning over £29,900 – the current ceiling – would be affected. It would, they calculated, be the equivalent of Labour imposing a 50 per cent top rate of income tax. This was a clear attempt to revive the 1992 'bombshell'. Indeed, using very similar language, the *Daily Mail* – supposedly the voice of middle England – produced a front-page headline referring to Brown's 'Ticking NI time bomb' and highlighted his 'explosive new threat to middle-class incomes'. Consistent with his strategy of avoiding unnecessary commitments, Brown refused to comment but was eventually forced to make some sort of response to close down the issue. Thus he announced that 'there will be no fifty per cent tax rate'. This was seen as a retreat, as the Chancellor appeared to suggest that Labour would not abolish the NI ceiling. However, he was, instead, denying something of which the Conservatives had not accused him: they had claimed only that abolishing the ceiling would be the equivalent of a 50 per cent top tax rate. Brown's dissembling, however disingenuous, did the job.

Evidence for the impact of the Conservative assault was inconclusive. NOP indicated that, during the week in which Labour's NI plans were scrutinised, the party's lead among middle-class voters declined slightly, from 12 to 8 per cent – well within the margin of error. In any case, floating voters in the crucial marginal of Enfield Southgate did not believe Brown would abolish the ceiling – although they thought he would raise the threshold above £30,000, which many considered actually rather low. Overall, most voters found the entire 'black hole' debate confusing but did not generally believe Conservative claims.[15] Other evidence suggested that floating voters at least were aware that taxes had gone up under Labour and imagined they would rise again. In 1997 MORI discovered that 63 per cent of all voters had expected Labour to put up taxes; in 2001, 11 per cent more held this view. What the public really resented was the 'underhand' way in which Brown had raised taxes, through 'stealth' – not the fact that the overall tax 'burden' had increased.[16]

Many electors saw through the Chancellor's refusal to admit that it might be necessary to raise taxes to improve public services. The public, it seemed, were now prepared to countenance an increase in tax, as they believed a Labour government would spend the money wisely. One MORI poll taken in the last week of the campaign even discovered that over half the electorate wanted the top rate of tax increased to 50 per cent. Brown and Blair simply did not trust such evidence. They presumably recalled that during the 1980s opinion polls regularly suggested that the public supported tax rises in return for better public services – but when general elections came around they voted Conservative. Thus, if Labour was – in contrast to 1992 and possibly even 1997 – virtually bombproof on tax, the party's leaders were, on this defining issue, reluctant to appear to be moving out of Thatcher's shadow.

Problems in St Helens

Blair's claim that Labour had moved on to a 'post-Thatcherite' agenda was further compromised by events in St Helens. Two Conservative MPs defected to Labour after 1997. Of these, Shaun Woodward, wanted to stay in the Commons. Yet, under party regulations, no sitting MP could become a candidate for a safer seat. Woodward was exempted from this 'chicken run' rule as it was considered that finding him a berth would be a positive signal to voters, described by Blair as 'decent one nation Tories', who might still be weaned from Hague's party.

Despite Millbank's best efforts, Woodward was not adopted by any Labour constituency party – local members did not want to be represented by the man who helped mastermind Major's 1992 campaign. Once an election had been called, however, the party's National Executive Committee (NEC) possessed powers to impose a shortlist on parties that had not selected a candidate. Rather suspiciously, immediately after Blair made known the polling date, the MP for St Helens South announced his retirement. Suspicions deepened when the NEC drafted a shortlist that included Woodward but excluded the names of the strongest local candidates. Yet when those selected presented themselves to St Helens members, they chose Woodward, albeit by a majority of only four, after a second ballot. Formally in accordance with the party's rules, the process was criticised for effectively imposing an ex-Conservative – and one, to boot, married to a millionairess and enjoying the services of a butler – on poor working-class voters who had suffered the ill-effects of policies Woodward had once promoted.

Enemies to the left, right, north and west

Events in St Helens gave Blair's far-left critics further ammunition to attack the direction in which he had taken the party since 1994: they seemed to vindicate the claim that Labour had become a pale shadow of Thatcher's Conservatives.

Arthur Scargill's Socialist Labour Party (SLP) was established in 1996 after Labour's old Clause 4 had been abolished; it supported leaving the EU as well as the North Atlantic Treaty Organisation (NATO) and embraced a massive nationalisation programme. The Socialist Alliance, which united the Trotskyist groups of Militant and the Socialist Workers' Party, along with a variety of disenchanted ex-Labour members, supported a strikingly similar programme: it sought to ban public schools and abolish the monarchy. Each attempted to benefit from disillusion within the Labour left and discontent among public sector workers. To advance their cause the SLP and the Alliance stood in seats held by leading Labour figures – but often against each other. Only succeeding in diminishing their collective interest, both parties stood in St Helens, where the Alliance candidate was a Labour member who had resigned in protest at Woodward's selection. The combined far-left vote in the constituency came to 11 per cent, with the Alliance managing to save only its second deposit of the night. Despite this modest success, neither party could claim much from the election: on average SLP candidates won 1.4 per cent of votes while the Alliance garnered 2.4 per cent – although the Scottish Socialist Labour Party did rather better north of the border, with 4 per cent. Such groups, nonetheless, tapped into the real discontent of Labour activists and voters who were neither Trotskyists nor Stalinists. While many remained unconvinced by Blair's rhetoric, the overwhelming majority saw no point voting for parties which harked back to policies that had once condemned Labour to the wilderness. Moreover, rather than the far left, the far right seemed best equipped to profit from disillusion in poverty-ridden white working-class constituencies. Taking advantage of local ethnic tensions, the British National Party (BNP) won 16.4 per cent of votes in Oldham West and 11 per cent in Oldham East and nearby Burnley. Nationally, BNP candidates won 3.9 per cent of votes cast – far better than the SLP and Socialist Alliance combined.

Labour easily repelled nationalist threats in Scotland and Wales. The SNP and Plaid Cymru presented themselves as the only genuine voice of their respective nations; they also claimed to be more willing than Labour to tax and spend. At one point, this left-wing nationalism appeared to pose a real threat. The Scottish and Welsh elections held in 1999 gave the nationalists hope of making a strong challenge for Labour's Westminster seats: Plaid Cymru had even won in the hitherto impregnable South Wales valleys. Yet, possibly because this was a Westminster election, rather than one for the devolved legislatures, Labour did much better than expected. In the end, the party's position remained unchanged in Scotland. While the party lost a seat to Plaid Cymru, this was offset by taking one from them, that of Ynys Mon, in the province's north, long a nationalist stronghold.

Labour suffered a well publicised, if localised, reverse in Wyre Forest. The party's candidate was defending a decent majority and should have been confident of re-election. However, he faced a challenge from an independent who stood in protest at the downgrading of Kidderminster Hospital, a parochial cause célèbre for which many blamed the government's reliance on private finance within the NHS. That Labour's candidate was a junior minister did not help: he was obliged to rigidly defend the proposals. His prospects were worsened when the Liberal Democrats declined to stand: Labour's vote collapsed and the independent won.

Given their action in Wyre Forest, it was clear that not all Liberal Democrats wanted to ease Labour's path back to power. Indeed, the party took Tony Benn's old seat in Chesterfield and ran Labour close in Yardley. Under Charles Kennedy, the Liberal Democrats offered a programme promising to raise direct taxes to finance better public services. If, on that basis, slightly to Labour's left, the party's target seats were predominantly Conservative-held. Thus, while Liberal Democrats criticised Blair for going in the right direction too cautiously, they castigated Hague for taking entirely the wrong journey. Consequently, despite the cooling of relations between them since Paddy Ashdown's retirement – after Blair failed to enact electoral reform – both parties remained true to what amounted to an open relationship. Blair and Kennedy even managed to keep the prospect of electoral change on the agenda by agreeing to review the matter mid-way through the next parliament. Labour, after all, could only benefit from a good Liberal Democrat performance in Conservative seats it had no hope of winning. In turn, Kennedy needed anti-Conservative tactical votes in his target seats. As Labour subsequently held on to marginal constituencies which, even given the modest swing to the Conservatives, it should have lost, the party had a similar interest in implicitly promoting tactical voting.

A hollow victory?

On the morning of 8 June, Labour's Commons majority was confirmed as 167, while its share of votes cast exceeded that of the Conservatives by 9 per cent: the party's campaign, on these grounds, was clearly a success. Yet, if the Conservatives had been defeated, had Labour triumphed? Did Blair win his 'radical' mandate?

The effect of Labour's attempt to encourage electors presumed most likely not to vote was mixed at best. Despite the party's alleged lack of 'female friendliness', women once again voted Labour to the same degree as men. Yet it was doubtful how far the party had convinced women of the merits of its family-orientated policies.[17] Similarly, the party's efforts to win the support of younger voters worked, to the extent that 47 per cent of those between 18 and 24 who entered the polling booth chose Labour – 18 per cent more than the Conservatives. However, they failed insofar as only two-fifths of that age cohort bothered to vote.[18]

Overall, non-voters almost matched the number of Labour voters. Ministers' responses to this fact betrayed a fatalism that did not bode well for the future. Young people had so many other 'lifestyle choices', one said, it was no wonder they were uninterested in politics. Gordon Brown stated that declining turnout was an international phenomenon: nothing much could be done. Lord Falconer even claimed it was due to popular 'contentment' – in which case inner-city Liverpool, where only one-third of the population voted, must be a very happy place indeed. Only David Blunkett considered that Labour needed to address its failure to 'engage' the public. It is true that the decline in voting, most apparent in Labour's safest seats, did not prevent the party winning them. Yet it was accompanied by a fall in Labour's share of support among those unskilled and semiskilled manual workers who did vote, double that evident across society as a whole. Again, the shedding of Labour support among the poorest members of the working class made little impact on the overall result – and was partly offset by a slight increase in the party's share of middle-class votes. It nonetheless raised questions about the extent to which those who remained part of what was still Labour's core vote had endorsed Blair's 'post-Thatcherite' vision for the future.

Furthermore, many Labour voters, not least those in marginal seats, were prepared to give the party only the benefit of the doubt. Frustrated by the poor state of public services, they appreciated that four years was too short a time to allow for improvements. There was, however, a sense that their patience was being tested and would soon run out. Labour was fortunate that the Conservatives had not tried to exploit this sentiment more – although, given the low esteem in which Hague and his followers were held, that would probably not have made much difference.[19]

Still, just because the Prime Minister had the money to invest did not mean that public service improvements were guaranteed to come painlessly, quickly or even at all. His suggestion that, should they be deemed more efficient, private means of delivering health and education would be used had antagon-ised public service unions and professionals alike, the very people meant to deliver those services. As was evident as soon as the polls had closed, these groups – many of them already low-paid and overworked – thought private involvement threatened their interests. Certain unions began to murmur that if they did not get their way on this matter they might cut financial support for Labour. As many party members were also employed in the public sector, it was clear that the Prime Minister would have to tread carefully. Influential observers also suggested that if the private sector could, in some instances, improve the performance of public services, it was hardly a panacea and posed some real dangers if not employed with care.[20] It was also likely that increased investment in public services would entrench the Chancellor's influence vis-à-vis the Prime Minister and so further test their flawed relationship. The Treasury not only generated the money to be invested but it also negotiated agreements with spending departments that tied further funds to specified outcomes. Just as in the first term, Blair would have to be prepared to rein in Brown's overweening ways.

By the time it seeks a third term, Labour will have to show that the public services have markedly benefited from its policies. Blair's direct link between more spending and such an improvement was an advance on his earlier, vaguer rhetoric. However, it still lacked clarity insofar as he refused to state that taxes might have to rise. Blair's was a profoundly cautious 'radicalism': he had identified the problem but was unwilling to admit what many people already appreciated – to make public services better direct taxes would probably have to, indeed possibly should, rise. He nonetheless realised that the stakes were high – not just for himself or his party but for the very idea of state-funded collective provision. As someone described as 'one of the most senior figures in Downing Street' privately warned some time before the campaign:

> If we cannot show the public services can be made to work over the next Parliament then we will not only have failed as a Government but the whole post-war development of the public services will have failed. That will be it. The public will not give you a third chance to get it right.[21]

One of the purposes behind the creation of 'New' Labour was to wean wavering Conservative supporters from a Thatcher-inspired fatalism about public services and towards a positive appreciation of what could be achieved through collective provision under the direction of a 'modernised', economic-ally competent Labour Party. Before 1997 those on the left, impatient for change, often castigated Blair and Brown for advancing their cause too gingerly – and sometimes appearing to go in the wrong direction. The two men considered their caution absolutely necessary if they were to secure the sustained support of voters living in Conservative bastions such as Enfield, Edgbaston and Wellingborough. Such areas fell to Labour in unprecedented numbers in 1997; they remained in the party's grasp in 2001. Yet, having been persuaded of Thatcher's failings, and that Labour could tackle them, middle England now appeared to have edged further away from the politics of the 1980s than the Prime Minister and his Chancellor. It was as if Blair and Brown were still fighting the 1992 general election and trying to defuse a tax bombshell, long rendered safe by their own painstaking efforts. It would, then, be wrong to see Labour's as a hollow victory: 2001 registered a shift and solidification in the public mood in 'New' Labour's favour compared with 1997. However, due to the campaign's failure to build on the 'radical' implications of the vision the Prime Minister had presented to the people, Blair's was a triumph more inconclusive than it might have been.

Notes

1 *Guardian*, 9 May 2001.
2 *Observer*, 20 May 2001.
3 See, for example, H. Harman and D. Mattinson, *Winning for Women*, Fabian pamphlet 596 (London: Fabian Society, 2000); B. Gill, *Where is Worcester Woman?* (London: Fawcett Society, 2001).

4 *Guardian*, 22 April 2001.
5 *Independent*, 24 May 2001.
6 *Guardian*, 4 May 2001. Unless otherwise stated, the remainder of this section is based on speeches made available during the campaign from Labour's website, www.labour.org.uk, and *Sunday Telegraph*, 6 May 2001; *Observer*, 13 May 2001; *The Times*, 1 June 2001.
7 *Sunday Times*, 6 May 2001.
8 *Financial Times*, 9 May 2001.
9 *Independent on Sunday*, 6 May 2001.
10 For an important study of Labour's relationship to Thatcherism in this early period, see S. Driver and L. Martell, *New Labour. Politics After Thatcherism* (Cambridge: Polity, 1998).
11 *Independent*, 14 May 2001.
12 For the views of such voters, see S. Fielding, 'Labour's path to power', in A. Geddes and J. Tonge, *Labour's Landslide. The British General Election 1997* (Manchester: Manchester University Press, 1997).
13 C. Bromley and J. Curtice, 'Is there a Third Way?', in R. Jowell *et al.* (eds), *British Social Attitudes. The 16th Report* (Ashgate: Aldershot, 1999).
14 *Guardian*, 7 May 2001; *Independent*, 24 May 2001.
15 *Sunday Times* and *Sunday Telegraph*, 27 May 2001.
16 *Daily Telegraph*, 11 May 2001; *Sunday Telegraph*, 13 May 2001.
17 *Daily Telegraph*, 23 May 2001.
18 *Observer*, 10 June 2001.
19 *The Times*, 2 June 2001.
20 Commission on Public Private Partnerships, *Building Better Partnerships* (London: Institute for Public Policy Research, 2001).
21 *Observer*, 3 June 2001.

St Helens South

In 1997 the Labour candidate, Gerry Bermingham, held St Helens South with over two-thirds of the votes cast. As such a safe Labour seat, the constituency would have attracted virtually zero attention in a normal election. The situation was transformed by the retirement of Bermingham at the outset of the campaign. Although Labour Party headquarters could have imposed a candidate, it permitted a contest, but a seemingly artificial one. The short-list was devoid of obvious local choices and it was clear that Labour's favoured candidate was Shaun Woodward. Such a choice was not universally welcomed. Woodward's defection from the Conservative Party was fresh in the memory. He was married to a millionairess and apparently employed a butler. His presence in a northern, mainly working-class constituency was seen as grotesque by critics, unconvinced by Woodward's public displays of enthusiasm for rugby league.

Woodward argued that the Conservative Party had changed, not he. He also claimed that there was no local shortage of enthusiasm for his candidature, highlighting the presence of 'seventy to eighty' campaign volunteers, compared to 'about four' for his predecessor (*Guardian*, 4 June 2001). Any slight hope among left-wing constituents that Woodward might face a significant challenge vanished with the decision of the Socialist Alliance and Socialist Labour to compete against each other, in addition to the new Labour candidate. Socialist Labour used part of its election broadcast to attack Woodward. The Socialist Alliance candidate, Neil Thompson, was a former councillor who left the Labour Party after Woodward was chosen. A former St Helens rugby league player, the actor Michael Murphy, joined, then left, the Labour Party within the same week, then announced his decision to stand as an independent, as a protest against the selection of Woodward, described as an 'impostor' (*Guardian*, 23 May 2001).

The furore over Labour's choice of candidate had a marked effect on the vote but not the result. The size of the majority was reduced by almost two-thirds. Nonetheless, almost half the votes cast were for the imported candidate, who promised to fulfil election pledges to bring investment to a town suffering above-average employment.

Result

St Helens South		
	No. of votes	% of vote
Woodward, S. (Labour)	16,799	49.7
Spencer, B. (Liberal Democrat)	7,814	23.1
Rotherham, L. (Conservative)	4,675	13.8
Thompson, N. (Socialist Alliance)	2,325	6.9
Perry, M. (Socialist Labour)	1,504	4.5
Slater, B. (UKIP)	336	1.0
Murphy, M. (Independent)	351	1.1
Braid, D. (Independent)	80	0.2
Labour majority	8,985	26.6
Labour hold		
Turnout		51.9
Swing, Labour to Liberal Democrats		14.3

3

The Conservatives: running on the spot

Philip Cowley and Stuart Quayle

Introduction

William Hague became the youngest Conservative leader since Pitt the Younger just a month and a half after the party had suffered its catastrophic general election defeat in 1997. In an article he wrote for the *Spectator* at the time, Hague argued that the Conservative Party had not just been defeated – 'it was humiliated'.[1] Less than four years later, having led it to yet another humiliating general election defeat, Hague announced his intention to step down from the leadership of the party, admitting that:

> we have not been able to persuade a majority, or anything approaching a majority, that we are yet the alternative government that they need. Nor have I been able to persuade sufficient numbers that I am their alternative prime minister.[2]

This was an understatement of the first order. After four years of energetic campaigning the party had increased its share of the vote by a mere one percentage point, making a net gain of just one seat, up from 165 to 166.[3] At that rate of progress – assuming an election every four years – the Conservatives were on course to re-enter government somewhere around the year 2657. The days when the party was the all-conquering dominant force in British politics – a common view just eight years before – appeared long gone.[4] William Hague became only the second-ever Conservative leader not also to become Prime Minister.[5]

Yet despite the scale of the defeat, Hague claimed that the party had made progress since 1997:

> the Conservative party during the last parliament ... made significant advances.... We will start from a stronger base in this parliament than in the last. The forces of Conservatism are stronger and at least better organised than they were four years ago.[6]

This chapter examines the changes to the Conservative Party between 1997 and 2001. To what extent did the party make 'significant advances'? To what extent did the Conservatives in 2001 'start from a stronger base'? And was the Conservative Party 'stronger and ... better organised' after four years of Hague's leadership? But we begin with an important prior question: why was it William Hague who led the party to its second catastrophic election defeat?

The 1997 leadership election

When he was a *Hansard*-reading teenager William Hague cannot have anticipated taking over a party in the state the Conservatives were in by 1997. Yet without a defeat on the scale of 1997, Hague would probably not have become leader when he did. Almost any defeat other than a landslide win for Labour would have meant that Michael Portillo would not have lost his seat in Enfield Southgate; and had Portillo thus been able to run for the leadership in 1997, it is probable that he would have won. In such circumstances, it is unlikely that Hague would have run.[7]

As well as the absence of other potential candidates, such as Portillo and Michael Heseltine (whose attack of angina ruled him out of the race), two other main factors enabled Hague to take the leadership.

First, the right of the party – especially the Eurosceptic right – shot themselves in the foot. Table 3.1 shows the type of support that each of the five candidates for the leadership received from the voters in the contest, the Conservative Parliamentary Party.[8] Ken Clarke's support came mainly from the pro-European MPs. Hague's support came mainly from MPs in the centre of the party. But three candidates – John Redwood, Peter Lilley and Michael Howard – drew their support predominantly from the Eurosceptic right of the party, splitting the sceptic vote into three, and ensuring that they came third, fourth, and fifth, respectively. But between them they amassed over seventy votes, enough to have put one of them in first place, at least in the

Table 3.1. First-round voting in the 1997 Conservative leadership contest

	Pro-Euro (%)	Centre (%)	Sceptic (%)	No. of votes
Clarke	56	37	7	49
Hague	14	56	31	41
Redwood	0	0	100	27
Lilley	5	32	64	24
Howard	0	40	60	23

Table 3.2. Changes in support between rounds in the 1997 Conservative leadership contest

	Round 1	Round 2	Change	Round 3	Change
Hague	41	62	(+21)	92	(+30)
Clarke	49	64	(+15)	70	(+6)
Redwood	27	38	(+11)	–	–

first round of the contest. Had there been just one candidate from the right, therefore, it is entirely plausible that Hague would have ended up in third place in the first round of the contest and been forced to withdraw.

The second main cause of Hague's success was that he was the least unpopular of the candidates. Given the number of candidates standing for election, there were almost bound to be multiple rounds of voting in the contest – in the event there were three – and as a result it was crucial for candidates to be able to attract support from MPs whose first choice had dropped out of the race: the winner needed the parliamentary equivalent of sloppy seconds. As Table 3.2 shows, this was exactly what Hague was able to do. After the first round, his vote went up by twenty-one, compared with an increase of fifteen for Clarke and eleven for Redwood. After the second, his vote went up by thirty, compared with just six for Clarke. At each stage, then, Hague's support went up by the largest amount.

Hague's inoffensiveness was confirmed by a survey, conducted before the 1997 election, of Conservative MPs and prospective candidates.[9] It asked two key questions. Who would they like to see as party leader? And to whom would they object as party leader? Hague was the only candidate with a respectable level of support who attracted no hostility. Indeed, only one respondent objected to Hague – and that was only because he said that he did not know what Hague stood for.

This enabled William Hague to take the leadership, but it also presented him with a problem, because it meant that he enjoyed little enthusiastic support. His initial support – those who backed him in the first round of the contest – was limited to a small group of MPs in the centre of the party. Just a quarter of his parliamentary party voted for him as first choice. Indeed, many of that 25 per cent would have preferred Michael Portillo, had he been available. Much of Hague's later support, and even some of his initial support, came to him *faute de mieux*, because there was no one better. As a result, Hague's support was broad – being able to take in large parts of the parliamentary party – but it was not deep. There was little or no ideological core to his support. There were few people in the party who wanted William Hague because of what he could deliver.

Reforming the party

The first stage of Hague's leadership was characterised both by attempts to consolidate his position as leader and by widespread reforms to the party structure (many of which also had the effect of strengthening his position).

In the months following Hague's election, the Conservative Party conducted the most comprehensive internal consultation exercise in its history, culminating in the publication and adoption of a new constitution in February 1998. The reforms – outlined in Box 3.1 – constitute the largest changes to any British political party since the advent of mass politics in the nineteenth century.[10] The Labour Party underwent more dramatic changes between the mid-1980s and the mid-1990s, but Labour's changes occurred piecemeal over a decade or more. The changes to the Conservative Party, by contrast, occurred in under a year. In itself this was a remarkable achievement, although it is highly debatable whether the reforms were successful in achieving their aims.

The first main aim was to revive the party's membership, which had been in decline for decades.[11] *Blueprint for Change* (1997) established the ambitious (and ultimately unrealistic) target of recruiting 'a million members for the millennium', with Hague pledged to double membership within two years. Yet membership continued to decline. Just under 400,000 ballot papers were

---

Box 3.1. Conservative reforms under Hague: new features of the party

- *A single party*, where before there had been three separate units (the parliamentary party, the professional party and the voluntary party).
- A *Board* decides all matters of organisation and management.
- *The National Conservative Convention* (NCC) – which meets twice a year – is a focus for the views of members, and acts as a link between leader and members.
- *The Conservative Policy Forum* (CPF) is the party's 'think-tank' and organises discussions through which party members can seek to influence policy.
- A centrally administered *national membership list*. This helps keep Central Office in touch with party members and enables ballots of the party membership.
- An *Ethics and Integrity Committee* can investigate cases referred to it by the Board or by the leader. It was the Ethics and Integrity Committee – in what is to date its one and only investigation – that expelled Lord Archer from the party for five years.
- A *reformed leadership election*. The leadership election process was entirely reformed, with the involvement of the grass roots for the first time via a ballot in the final round of the process.

Table 3.3. Conservative Party membership ballots, 1997–2000

Ballot	Date	Total votes	Yes (%)	No (%)
Endorsement of both reform principles and Hague's leadership	October 1997	176,314	81	19
Endorsement of *Fresh Future* proposals	February 1998	114,590	96	4
Ballot on British membership of the euro	October 1998	207,050	85	15
Endorsement of *Believing in Britain*	October 2000	50,499	99	1

distributed for the first membership ballot in 1997 (see below), but by March 2001 membership was reported to have fallen by almost a quarter, to just over 300,000 (with three-quarters of those living south of the geographical line from Bristol to the Wash).[12]

The second broad aim was to increase membership involvement in the party. Hague pledged to involve party members more in policy making and procedural matters than any of his predecessors had. Members were given an enhanced role in the selection of candidates for some elections. The most striking innovation, though, was the widespread use of membership ballots. During the course of the parliament Hague balloted the membership on four separate occasions (see Table 3.3), and members were given a constitutional role in electing future leaders.

Although ostensibly democratic, the ballot mechanism can also be seen as a tool for leadership manipulation, on the grounds both that it gives a vote to 'ordinary' members – who tend to be more deferential to the leadership and therefore less troublesome than the activists – and also that, in reality, ballots do not offer a genuine choice.[13] It was, for example, through the use of just such a ballot that Hague first consolidated his position as leader: the first ballot (in October 1997) asked party members both to endorse the principles of party reform outlined in *Blueprint for Change* and to endorse him as leader. Members could not choose one or the other. Nor could they propose any amendments or improvements to the reform package. They had to take it or leave it. Such drawbacks might account for the dramatic decline in turnout: only 16 per cent of members participated in the final ballot, on the pre-manifesto document *Believing in Britain* (September 2000), which led many in the party to question the utility of further ballots.

Similar criticisms have also been levelled at the revised procedure for electing the leader. Although giving a formal role to the extra-parliamentary party was a radical development – previously, the parliamentary party alone had chosen the leader – the new rules involve the membership in the country only after the incumbent leader has resigned, at which point they are merely offered a choice between the two candidates most favoured by the parliamentary party. Indeed, there is no compulsion on the parliamentary party to put two candidates forward to the members at the final stage.[14]

Less widely noted – but probably more effective in encouraging participation – was the development of informal consultation methods. The Conservative Policy Forum (CPF) (a successor to the Conservative Political Centre) was established to try to revitalise the involvement of members. But despite more members becoming involved in CPF discussion groups, it is hard to identify examples where the CPF had a direct and measurable impact on policy.[15] However, during June and July 2000 the CPF also held eleven regional meetings attended by shadow cabinet members to discuss policies before the publication of *Believing in Britain*. This, the first time that such an exercise was undertaken, went some way to fulfilling the kind of CPF that Hague had talked about during the reform process. In addition, between the publication of the pre-manifesto document and the close of the ballot, local CPF groups were encouraged to hold meetings to discuss the proposals. In total, over 250 associations did so, giving over 10,000 members the opportunity to discuss the document.

The reforms to the Conservative Party, therefore, were dramatic. But their impact should not be exaggerated. For one thing, they were largely a case of the party playing 'catch-up', bringing its own structures up to date with those in other parties. They also did not greatly alter the balance of power within the party. The new bodies – such as the CPF and the National Conservative Convention – are advisory. Formally at least, power largely remains where it had always been: with the leader. In spite of repeated claims to the contrary, the Conservatives remain structurally the most top-down political party in British politics. Moreover, although important organisationally, the Conservative reforms lacked the symbolic impact of some of Labour's changes, such as the abolition of Clause 4.[16] These were largely internal reforms – of Conservatives, by Conservatives, for Conservatives – lacking resonance with the general public. But perhaps most importantly of all, the overarching motivation for the party's reforms was 'reviving the greatest political party of this century'.[17] As the general election result showed – and as discussed below – in this they were far from successful.

Policy

Most accounts of Conservative Party policy between 1997 and 2001 tell a similar story: Hague begins his leadership aiming to broaden the base of Conservatism and then, when this new inclusive style fails to have a positive impact on the opinion polls, he reverts to a more traditional, moral authoritarian form of Conservatism in an attempt to bolster his core support. This latter stage is characterised by widespread criticism that the party was moving to the right and that its leader was pursuing short-term extremist policies and jumping on populist bandwagons (earning him the nickname 'Billy Bandwagon' from one commentator).[18] As one unnamed shadow cabinet member argued:

> We seem to have reversed the normal electoral cycle. Instead of starting by re-securing our core support and then broadening the appeal to the centre, we began with a wide appeal and spent the last two years narrowing it.[19]

It is certainly true that the beginning of Hague's leadership was marked by his attempts to embrace a more tolerant and inclusive form of Conservatism. Within weeks of his election as leader, Hague made a much-publicised visit to the Notting Hill Carnival, and many of his speeches at the time were characterised by references to tolerance and inclusion of groups in society, such as homosexuals and ethnic minorities, who had not always viewed the Conservative Party as their natural home.[20] In part, this was in tune with his social liberal instincts – Hague was, for example, one of just a handful of Conservative MPs who had voted in 1994 for the homosexual age of consent to be lowered to sixteen years – but it also reflected a desire on the part of Hague's advisers to broaden his popular appeal and recognition.[21]

It is also true that the later period of his leadership saw the Conservatives play to a more populist agenda, beginning with the publication of the *Common Sense Revolution* in 1999.[22] For example, during 1999 and 2000 Hague variously led the party in a protracted opposition to the abolition of Section 28 (which prohibited local authorities from 'promoting' homosexuality), reasserted the party's commitment to the institution of marriage and led the charge against the increasing number of asylum seekers and the problems that he believed they contributed to. He also toughened the party's stance on law and order and backed populist causes such as advocating tougher sentences for paedophiles and giving rhetorical support to a Norfolk farmer imprisoned for shooting a burglar.[23]

This populist tone intensified in the run-up to the election, especially when the party was discussing Europe, where dramatic rhetoric was regularly employed. At the launch of *Believing in Britain*, Hague stated starkly: 'say whatever you like about a Conservative Britain, but at least a Conservative Britain will still be Britain'.[24] And in his speech at the 2001 Conservative spring conference in Harrogate he talked of Britain becoming a 'foreign land' if Labour won a second term in office.[25]

Yet the full picture of Conservative policy under Hague is slightly more complicated than this simple dichotomy between Nice Hague and Nasty Hague (or Nasty Hague and Nice Hague, depending on your point of view). There are three possible problems with this conventional account: the chronology; the description; and the ideological direction of the critique.

The chronological problem is that there was not the simple division between the two periods presented in this conventional account. For example, at exactly the same time as he was promoting social inclusiveness, Hague tackled the divisive issue of Europe head on. In October 1997, the party's position became that of ruling out membership of the single currency for the remainder of the parliament and the whole of the next one. The basic thrust of the party's European policy ('Keep the Pound') was therefore established right from the beginning of Hague's leadership. In doing so, Hague aligned himself with the majority opinion in the Conservative parliamentary party, which was overwhelmingly Eurosceptic.[26] But he also went out of his way to alienate those on the 'pro-European' wing of the party, saying that he would 'rather people resigned so that we have a united team'.[27] The policy provoked fierce attacks from three former Conservative cabinet ministers, led to two members of the frontbench team resigning and provoked one Conservative MP (Peter Temple-Morris) to defect to Labour and a Conservative MEP (James Moorhouse) to the Liberal Democrats.[28] There was precious little inclusiveness here from the beginning.

Similarly, right in the middle of the supposed social authoritarian phase, there was a deliberate attempt to broaden the appeal of the party to reach beyond the core vote by returning to some of the earlier rhetoric.[29] *Believing in Britain* (2000) was deliberately presented as representing a 'bold social agenda'.[30] The 2000 conference was preceded by the announcement of a policy to reinvigorate inner cities and saw the launch of a team to 'renew' the 'one nation' policies of the party.[31] It was during this conference that Michael Portillo called for a more inclusive party – 'We are for people whatever their sexual orientation' – and John Major – effectively excluded from the conference in 1999 – was brought in from the cold to symbolise the 'one nation' status of the policies.[32]

The second problem is that of description. Many of the criticisms equate Hague's policies with 'extremism'. This tag appears to have derived largely from his strident position on a small number of (admittedly) high-profile policies on the euro, Section 28 and asylum seekers. Yet Hague firmly rejected the charge, arguing that Conservative policy in these areas was frequently more in line with the views of the majority of the population than was the government. At the party's spring conference in 2000 he painted the Labour Party as the extreme party and spoke of Conservative policies appealing to the 'mainstream majority' – a phrase that he repeated eleven times during the speech. Most polls showed that the public did not support the repeal of Section 28, for example.[33] On Europe, polls consistently demonstrated that the views of the public were moving in the Conservatives' direction, with opposition to the single currency growing.[34] And, as we show below, one of the few issues that people thought the Conservatives would handle better than Labour was that of asylum seekers. As the leaked memos from Tony Blair's pollster Philip Gould in the summer of 2000 indicated, the government was aware of – and worried about – the popularity of these policies in 'middle England'.[35]

The third problem with the conventional account is its ideological direction: it is a predominantly left-of-centre critique, contending that Hague took the party too far to the right. But there is also a critique from the right: that he did not take it far enough to the right. The charge is most clear over the euro. Although Eurosceptics within the party were happier with the party's new position than Europhiles, there were plenty of sceptics who would have liked Hague to have gone further and rule out membership of the euro forever. There were also criticisms about the extent to which the Conservatives accepted many of Labour's policies, such as devolution, the London mayoralty, abolition of the right of (most of) the hereditary peers to sit in the House of Lords, and, under Portillo's shadow Chancellorship, the independence of the Bank of England and the minimum wage.

Moreover, there were complaints that the Conservatives were involved in little fundamental rethinking about the role of the state. What reforms the party did advance – such as in pension provision (proposals which in any case were subsequently scaled down) and the policy of 'free schools' – were viewed by some as little more than tinkering at the edges.[36] As the *Independent* argued in relation to proposals to reform the NHS:

> The Tories have spent months lurching towards any bandwagon that passed them on the right. But when it comes to the public sector, they have shown awful timidity and swerved the party firmly back to the middle of the road.... The Tories should abandon this centrist consensus seeking. They should do themselves – and the country – a favour by taking a bold approach ... [and] offering radical solutions.[37]

Similar calls were made in the popular press. The *Sun* argued that 'What is actually needed is a root-and-branch examination of our state-funded society. We need big ideas from the Tories. Vision. Perhaps that is a challenge for the Conservatives after the election'.[38]

Although much was made in the election of how the Conservatives would 'cut' public expenditure if elected, they were in fact merely proposing a reduction in its rate of growth: Labour were proposing a rise in expenditure by £68 billion, compared with the Tories' plan of £60 billion. And the Tories pledged to match Labour spending on health and education, as well as law and order, transport and defence, during the lifetime of the parliament.[39]

So the orthodox account suffers from some clear drawbacks. There was not the neat dividing line between the inclusive Hague and the authoritarian Hague – there was far more variation in policy (and rhetoric) than this implies.[40] Hague's policies may have been misguided or wrong, but they were extreme only insofar as the majority of the British public are extreme. And Conservative policy under Hague was far from the stuff of right-wing wet dreams. Yet the orthodox account still contains a basic truth. For most of the parliament, the Conservatives did predominantly speak to their 'core vote', and at times they did so in a way that might be considered populist. This tendency became more exaggerated as the parliament went on, and as the party appeared to be making little progress in the opinion polls. The trouble with this populism, however, was that there was little evidence that it made them popular.

The electorate and the Conservative Party

Between the two catastrophic general elections of May 1997 and June 2001 the Conservatives enjoyed sporadic electoral success. Against expectations, the party doubled its number of MEPs (to thirty-six) in the 1999 European elections, outperforming Labour in terms of the percentage of the vote (36 per cent compared with 28 per cent). It also (slightly) outpolled Labour in the elections to the London Assembly in May 2000. It did respectably well in local elections, outpolling Labour by 8 per cent in 1999, and even the local elections held on the same day as the general election in 2001 saw the Conservatives gain control of an additional five county councils in England. Conservatives also did well in local council by-elections, and won the first by-election to a devolved body when they won in Ayr in May 2000.

Conservative politicians frequently made much of these results and argued that they showed the party's electoral position was improving. Yet the story from other 'real' elections was much less positive. The party won seats in the devolved legislatures in Scotland and Wales, but this was largely as a result of proportional representation: in both, the Conservative share of the vote fell from that achieved in the general election, and they won just one first-past-the-post seat in Wales and none in Scotland. It also failed to take a single Westminster by-election from the government – its share of the vote rising on average by less than one percentage point – and even managed to lose the constituency of Romsey to the Liberal Democrats in May 2000.[41] Moreover, many of their more impressive results – such as in the European elections – were achieved on very low turnouts. For example, although hailed (by Conservatives) as a great Conservative triumph, fewer people voted Conservative in the European election than in any nationwide contest since women gained the right to vote in 1918.[42]

The story from the opinion polls was even worse. In four years, the Conservatives led Labour in the polls for just ten days. Between 14 and 23 September 2000 – at the height of the fuel protests – the Conservatives were equal with, or ahead of, Labour in every published opinion poll. One poll – an NOP poll for Channel 4 – put them eight points ahead. Yet that blip aside, the Conservatives ran behind in the polls for the entire parliament. The percentage of people who said that they intended to vote Conservative – the so-called 'headline' figure – improved very gradually throughout the parliament. The post-election period of 1997 saw the Conservatives poll an average of 25 per cent. The pre-election period of 2001 saw an average of 31 per cent. But this was merely identical to its share of the vote gained in the 1997 election. Conservatives routinely dismissed the opinion polls – as most politicians do when the polls look negative – but they were accurately reflecting the party's lack of progress.

The problem for the Conservatives becomes even starker when we look at the wider images of the party held by the public. For example, a key Conservative strength in the 1970s and 1980s was that it was perceived to be the party of economic competence. Even when the Labour Party was popular – indeed, even when Labour was winning elections – the Conservatives at least used to be viewed by the public as the more competent party. The Conservatives lost that reputation in September 1992, on Black Wednesday, and they have still not got it back. With one exception – again, September 2000, at the height of the fuel protests – Labour maintained its lead throughout the parliament as the party seen by the public as best to manage the economy.[43]

Similarly, Conservative divisions during the 1992 parliament – largely, although not exclusively, over European integration – had meant that they had fought the 1997 election being widely perceived as divided.[44] Under Hague there was a slight improvement in the public's view of the party, but for the entire parliament Gallup still found that a majority of the population saw the Conservatives as divided.

Other impressions were just as damaging. A MORI poll in May 2001 found that just 13 per cent of people thought the Conservatives had the best team of leaders to deal with the country's problems (compared with 47 per cent for Labour); just 17 per cent thought that the Conservatives had the best policies (compared with 42 per cent for Labour); and a staggeringly low 9 per cent thought that the Conservatives were the 'most clear and united about what its policies should be' (a figure that was even lower than that for the Liberal Democrats, who scored 16 per cent). Just three months before the election, Gallup found that only 20 per cent of all voters – and fewer than half even of prospective Conservative voters – thought that the Conservatives were ready for power or looked like a government in waiting.[45]

There was also little comfort for the Conservatives from the public's views of the Conservatives on specific issues. Table 3.4 shows the issues that the public claimed were most important to them in determining their vote (ranked in descending order of importance), along with the lead enjoyed by Labour on that issue among voters who said the issue was important. Labour led on all but four of the seventeen issues, often by large margins. This was a slight improvement on the position two years before, when Labour led on every single issue, but unfortunately for the Conservatives Labour still led on nearly all of the issues that people said were most important to them.

Although the Conservatives were criticised after the election for not talking more about health and education – the public's two main concerns – it is

Table 3.4. Party strengths on important issues, 2001

	Percentage saying the issue was important	Percentage Labour lead among those saying it was important
Health care	61	+35
Education	53	+34
Law and order	44	+2
Pensions	35	+30
Taxation	35	−3
Managing the economy	29	+34
Unemployment	25	+53
Asylum/immigration	24	−22
Public transport	23	+21
Protecting the natural environment	20	+7
Europe	18	−16
Housing	18	+29
Animal welfare	13	+6
Defence	9	−20
Constitution/devolution	5	+2
Northern Ireland	5	+15
Trade unions	3	+42

Source: MORI/*Economist*.

pretty clear why they did not: because on both issues, as the table shows, the public trusted Labour far more than they did the Conservatives. The Conservatives therefore tried to push those issues on which they had a lead (or where Labour's lead was very small), such as law and order, taxation, asylum and immigration, and (especially) Europe. As two of the MPs responsible for the Conservative campaign noted wryly: 'there were not many other policies we had which were supported by over 70 per cent of the public'.[46] The trouble for the Conservatives was that for the most part these were issues that came fairly low down on the public's list of priorities. On issues that the public thought important, they trusted Labour. On issues that the public thought unimportant, they trusted the Conservatives. It is hard to play to your strengths when you do not have many.

The electorate and William Hague

Nor could the Conservatives rely on their leader to be an electoral asset. Two features were noticeable about the public's view of William Hague. The first was its direction: once the public became aware of William Hague, they

Table 3.5. The public's view of William Hague, 1997–2001

1997		2001	
Phrase	*%*	*Phrase*	*%*
Rather inexperienced	52	Rather inexperienced	33
Out of touch with ordinary people	29	Out of touch with ordinary people	28
Tends to talk down to people	21	Rather narrow minded	24
Patriotic	18	Tends to talk down to people	23
Rather narrow minded	16	Patriotic	21
Understands the problems facing Britain	10	Understands the problems facing Britain	17
Too inflexible	9	Too inflexible	13
A capable leader	9	A capable leader	12
More honest than other politicians	9	Down to earth	12
Down to earth	8	More honest than other politicians	11
Understands world problems	6	Understands world problems	10
Has sound judgement	5	Good in a crisis	6
Has got a lot of personality	5	Has sound judgement	5
Good in a crisis	3	Has got a lot of personality	5

Source: MORI/*The Times*.

decided that they did not rate him. The second was its consistency: having so decided, they did not waver in that belief.

For example, the left-hand side of Table 3.5 shows the phrases that voters attributed to Hague in October 1997, just after he had become leader. The right-hand side shows the responses given three and a half years later, just before the start of the general election campaign. The similarity between the two – in terms of both the ordering and the scores themselves – is striking. In 1997, Hague was most likely to be described as 'rather inexperienced', which was also the most commonly chosen label in 2001. The next most popular description in 1997 was 'out of touch with ordinary people', also the second most common in 2001. In fact, the top six characteristics in each poll were exactly the same, and in pretty much the same order; and of those six, only one – being seen as patriotic – could be classed as positive. Conversely, the phrases *least* likely to be ascribed to Hague in 1997 were all positive: being good in a crisis (3 per cent), having sound judgement (5 per cent) and having a lot of personality (5 per cent). Again, these were exactly the same phrases that were the least likely to be ascribed to Hague in 2001.[47]

Figure 3.1 shows Hague's net satisfaction rating with the public: that is, the percentage of people who thought Hague was doing a good job minus the percentage of people who thought he was doing a bad job. As the figure

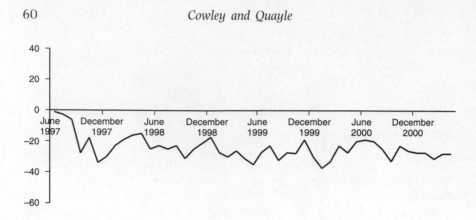

Figure 3.1. Net satisfaction with William Hague as leader of the opposition. *Source*: MORI/*The Times*.

shows, Hague's satisfaction rating was persistently and strongly negative. For his entire leadership more people thought he was doing a bad job as leader of the opposition than thought he was doing a good job, and – as the figure shows – the gap between the two groups was not small. On average, for every person who thought Mr Hague was doing a good job, there were two who thought he was doing a bad job. For large parts of his leadership, he was even scoring a negative rating among Conservative supporters.

Hague's ratings tended to be worse than those of this party. In all but two of the forty-seven monthly tracking polls in which MORI asked about both voting intention and satisfaction with Hague, the percentage saying that they were satisfied with Hague was lower than the percentage saying that they were going to vote Conservative – by an average of five percentage points.

His standing as a potential Prime Minister was even worse. Gallup regularly asks voters who they think will make the best Prime Minister. Hague was regularly bettered by Blair 'on a scale quite without historical precedent'.[48] The last Gallup poll before the election put Blair on 52 per cent and Hague on just 20.[49] Even many Conservative voters – sometimes even *most* Conservative voters – did not think Hague would make the best Prime Minister. The percentage of voters who said that they would be voting Conservative was always greater than the percentage who said that they thought Hague would make the best Prime Minister. Similarly, in May 2000, MORI found 32 per cent of people saying they were inclined to support the Conservatives, but just 18 per cent who thought Hague was 'ready to be Prime Minister'.

The direct effect of this on the Conservatives' fortunes is almost certain to be less than is commonly thought: when the public was asked directly why they were not voting Conservative, William Hague was not the most common explanation.[50] But we can be fairly sure of one thing: Hague was not an electoral asset to his party. People voted Conservative despite William Hague, not because of him.

Conclusion

William Hague inherited a Conservative Party that was in a catastrophic state. It had suffered its worst election defeat in terms of votes since 1832 and won fewer seats than at any time since 1906. Its extra-parliamentary party had been in decline for years. It was widely perceived to be incompetent and divided.

Four years later, the visible evidence of improvement was scarce. The party's reforms did not yield the increase in members that was planned and the prospect of further reform has not been ruled out. It is currently better financed, although this is largely as a result of two very large donations – one of £10 million, another of £5 million – rather than as a result of any revival at the grass-roots level. And it has slowly – very slowly – begun to rebuild its electoral base outside Westminster, although (with the exception of the European elections) the gains have largely been recapturing ground lost before Hague's leadership. The public's image of the party has improved slightly but it remains overwhelmingly negative.

Beneath the surface, though, lie other achievements. The reforms to the party's machinery were long overdue and have made for a leaner and more efficient party, if not one that is necessarily any more democratic. Hague's policy on Europe was easy to criticise – the internal logic of a policy to keep the pound at all costs, but only for eight years, was not immediately obvious to many – but it was at least a policy behind which the vast majority of the party could unite, and it enabled the 2001 election campaign to be fought without the scale of infighting that characterised the election four years previously. Similarly, while it is easy to criticise the party's concentration on mobilising its core vote – elections cannot be won simply by getting a party's most committed supporters to vote – it was both an understandable tactic (as we have shown, on those issues in which the majority of the public were interested they did not trust the Conservatives) and one that appears to have worked: the core vote did turn out. Both during the election and before, there was considerable speculation about the Conservatives suffering a fall – quite possibly a dramatic fall – in their number of MPs. In the event, the Conservatives managed largely to neutralise the threat from both the UK Independence Party (UKIP) (which could have taken votes from the Conservatives, indirectly costing them seats) and the Liberal Democrats (who could have taken seats directly). For all the Liberal Democrat talk of becoming the 'effective opposition', the Conservatives clearly remain the official opposition: for every Liberal Democrat MP there are three Conservatives. The Conservatives may have made little progress towards becoming the first party of British politics, but they did at least not slip to being the third.

For four years, then, the Conservatives effectively ran on the spot. They are (very) slightly healthier as a result. They did at least not go backwards. But they have yet to move forwards – and there is as yet no consensus on the exact direction that this movement will take.

Acknowledgements

Research into the 1997 contest for the Conservative leadership was funded by the Nuffield Foundation. We are also grateful to MORI for granting us permission to use their data and to those who offered assistance in the writing of this chapter, including Matthew Bailey, Edward Clark and Mark Stuart.

Notes

1 W. Hague, 'Energy, enthusiasm, beliefs – these I offer', *Spectator*, 10 May 1997.
2 Speech at Conservative Central Office, 8 June 2001.
3 Given that one of the Conservative gains was Tatton – a seat held by the independent MP Martin Bell since 1997, but in which Bell was not standing in 2001 – the net gain from other political parties was effectively nil.
4 See, for example, A. King, 'The implications of one party government', in A. King *et al.*, *Britain at the Polls 1992* (Chatham, NJ: Chatham House, 1993).
5 The other being Austen Chamberlain, Conservative leader between March 1921 and October 1922.
6 Central Office, 8 June.
7 Private information.
8 See P. Cowley, 'Just William? A supplementary analysis of the 1997 Conservative leadership contest', *Talking Politics*, 10 (1997), pp. 91–5, for full details of the analysis.
9 *Ibid.*, pp. 91–2.
10 The reforms are discussed more fully in J. Lees-Marshment and S. Quayle, 'Empowering the members or marketing the party? The Conservative reforms of 1998', *Political Quarterly*, 72 (2001), pp. 204–12; and R. Kelly, 'Democratising the Tory Party. The Hague agenda', *Talking Politics*, 11 (1998), pp. 28–33.
11 See P. Whiteley, P. Seyd and J. Richardson, *True Blues* (Oxford: Clarendon Press, 1994).
12 J. Landale, 'Conservative troops desert on the eve of battle', *The Times*, 13 March 2001.
13 P. Mair, 'Party organisations: from civil society to the state', in P. Mair and R. Katz, *How Parties Organize* (London: Sage, 1994).
14 For more details on the changes in the method of selecting the leader see K. Alderman, 'Revision of leadership election procedures in the Conservative Party', *Parliamentary Affairs*, 52 (1999), pp. 260–74.
15 The one notable exception appears to be its influence on the policy change to direct married couples tax relief, giving it only to couples with young children rather than universally.
16 See, for example, T. Bale, '"The death of the past": symbolic politics and the changing of Clause IV', in D. M. Farrell, *et al.* (eds), *British Elections and Parties Yearbook 1996* (London: Frank Cass, 1996).
17 Lord Parkinson, letter to Conservative Constituency Association chairs, 16 February 1998.
18 P. Routledge, *Daily Mirror*, 5 March 2001.
19 P. Wintour, *Guardian*, 21 April 2001.
20 '"New" Tories are caring says Hague', *Daily Telegraph*, 10 October 1997.
21 J.-A. Nadler, *William Hague* (London: Politico's, 2000), pp. 211–12.
22 The title was borrowed from the Conservative Party of Ontario, where it had been electorally popular.

23 See P. Riddell, 'Over-the-top Hague is taking party further to the fringe', *The Times*, 28 January 2001.

24 Launch of *Believing in Britain*, 5 September 2000.

25 Speech at the 2001 Conservative spring conference, 4 March 2001.

26 See D. Baker, A. Gamble, D. Seawright with K. Bull, 'MPs and Europe: enthusiasm, circumspection and outright scepticism', in J. Fisher, P. Cowley, D. Denver and A. Russell (eds), *British Elections and Parties Review Volume 9* (London: Frank Cass, 1999); and P. Cowley, 'British Parliamentarians and European integration', *Party Politics*, 6 (2000), pp. 463–72.

27 P. Riddell, 'Tories could learn from Labour's mistakes', *The Times*, 4 November 1997.

28 Temple-Morris via an interim spell as an independent Conservative.

29 A. Grice, 'Hague puts social policy at the heart of agenda', *The Times*, 6 September 2000.

30 'Hague's "caring" campaign to soften stance on hardline issues', *Independent*, 5 October 2000.

31 See *Growing Up in Britain. The Prospectus of the Conservative Party's Renewing One Nation Team* (London: Conservative Central Office, October 2000).

32 Speech at the Conservative Party conference, 3 October 2000. See also 'Hague invites Major in from cold to back "one nation" policy switch', *Guardian*, 4 September 2000; and D. Smith, 'Hague's new best friends could play hard to get', *Sunday Times*, 8 September 2000.

33 For example, a MORI poll in February 2000 found that 54 per cent wanted Section 28 to remain; the equivalent figure in Scotland – where the issue had a higher profile – was 60 per cent.

34 See, for example, 'Britain's support for euro at new low', *The Times*, 25 July 2000.

35 Nadler, *William Hague*, pp. 283–4.

36 P. Riddell, 'Who do you think you are kidding Mr Hague?', *The Times*, 9 February 2001.

37 'The Tories are too timid about reform of the NHS', *Independent*, 21 February 2001.

38 'Hague's error', *Sun*, 6 March 2001.

39 'Fight to death over a thousand cuts', *The Times*, 24 January 2001. See also 'Spending: Hague ups the stakes', *Guardian*, 23 January 2001.

40 As Hague himself realised at one point, 'his own views, although fiercely held, could sometimes seem to contradict each other.... Hague was aware that his gut instincts and intellect sometimes led him in opposite directions' (Nadler, *William Hague*, pp. 233–4).

41 I. Crewe, 'Elections and public opinion', in A. Seldon (ed.), *The Blair Effect* (London: Little Brown, 2001), p. 81.

42 R. Mortimore and S. Atkinson, 'Hague's progress', unpublished paper presented to EPOP conference, Northampton, September 1999.

43 According to Gallup data, reported in A. King (ed.), *British Political Opinion 1937–2000* (London: Politico's, 2001), pp. 116–19, and updated by the authors, the gap between the two parties did narrow somewhat over the course of the parliament. But according to MORI – which asks the question in a slightly different way – Labour's lead on economic competence was even greater than in the previous parliament. Either way, for the Conservatives – the party of business and the City – it was a remarkable state of affairs.

44 P. Cowley, 'The Conservatives: decline and fall', in A. Geddes and J. Tonge (eds), *Labour's Landslide. The British General Election 1997* (Manchester: Manchester University Press, 1997), pp. 40–3.

45 *Daily Telegraph*, 16 March 2001.

46 A. Lansley and T. Collins, 'Don't panic, we now have a foundation for the future', *Daily Telegraph*, 14 June 2001. They also noted that when the Conservatives tried to push issues of public services, 'Labour's lead in the polls never dipped below double figures'.

47 An undergraduate essay marked by one of the authors argued that while Blair appeared 'strong and dynamic', Hague appeared 'bald and useless'. This may not be the most sophisticated of judgements – and one that is extremely unfair (he may be bald, but he is quite clearly far from useless) – but it is one that, broadly speaking, was widely shared by the public.

48 Crewe, 'Elections and public opinion', p. 75.

49 Poll for the *Daily Telegraph*, 6 June 2001.

50 In 1999 Gallup found that the most common reason given for not voting Conservative was 'The Conservatives did not do a good job when they were in power'. 'William Hague would not make a good Prime Minister' ranked fourth. By September 2000, Hague had climbed to third, but was still cited by only 22 per cent of voters.

Dorset West

If things were not difficult enough for sitting Tory MP Oliver Letwin in Dorset West, he compounded his vulnerability to tactical voting with a reference in a *Financial Times* interview to a possible £20 billion worth of tax cuts under a future Conservative government. This far exceeded the official Conservative plans for £8 billion in cuts and so opened his party to attack and rendered more vulnerable Letwin's 1,800 majority over the Liberal Democrats. Dorset West was eighth on the list of Liberal Democrat targets.

Tactical voting had famously been a key feature of the 1997 election, with the *Observer* helpfully providing a list of Conservatives susceptible to a tactical vote, including Michael Portillo in Enfield Southgate. The musician Billy Bragg was a key figure behind the web-based 'votedorset' scheme. To paraphrase one of Bragg's most famous songs: 'I don't want to change the world, I'm not looking for a new Dorset'. The scheme was designed to pair up Liberal Democrat and Labour supporters in the neighbouring seats of Dorset West and Dorset South who wanted to vote tactically to oppose Conservative candidates. The campaign urged Labour supporters in Dorset West to vote Liberal Democrat, while Liberal Democrat supporters in Dorset South could vote Labour. The scheme offered an on-line voter matching service. In the longer term, the campaign sought to highlight what was seen as the iniquity of the existing system and thus press for electoral reform.

After Letwin's claim concerning tax cuts he went to ground, prompting Labour to launch a film-style poster dubbing the shadow Chief Secretary to the Treasury 'The Fugitive'. At a Labour press conference Gordon Brown called for the release of 'the Dorset One'. Labour intensified the attack by publishing an eight-page dossier claiming that it had been Letwin who, in the 1980s, had come up with the idea of the poll tax. The Conservative leadership was forced into a damage-limitation exercise in which they distanced themselves from Letwin's remarks.

Letwin's victory was an indication both of the lack of drama on election night and of the failure of tactical voting to have an impact in this particular constituency. True, the 4.1 per cent decline in the Labour vote matched the 4.1 per cent increase in the Liberal Democrat vote, but Letwin also managed to increase his share of the vote by 3.5 per cent. The relatively high turnout of 67 per cent also indicated that this contest had more capacity to enthuse local voters than many others that were fought in 2001. In Dorset South, too, the Conservatives held on with a precarious majority of 153, although that was up from seventy-seven in 1997.

Dorset West

Result

Dorset West		
	No. of votes	% of vote
Letwin, O. (Conservative)	22,126	44.6
Green, S. (Liberal Democrat)	20,712	41.8
Hyde, R. (Labour)	6,733	13.6
Majority	1,414	
Conservative hold		
Turnout		67.0
Swing, Conservatives to Liberal Democrats		0.29

4

The Liberal Democrats

Justin Fisher

Introduction

After the 1997 general election, when the Liberal Democrats doubled their seat total to forty-six, it was reasonable to assert that the party was now a parliamentary force. Events following the 1997 election suggested that this was not a wild overestimation. The party became involved in the Joint Cabinet Committee at Westminster and also participated in coalition governments in Scotland and Wales. The power and influence of the Liberal Democrats appeared to be growing. Yet their enhanced status was potentially fragile and would have been damaged greatly by a poor performance in 2001. Much rested on this election. Yet, once again, the Liberal Democrats performed well. They increased their vote share by 1.7 per cent in the seats they contested, and their parliamentary representation increased by six seats compared with 1997. Not only that, but their marginal seats became safer. Charles Kennedy, fighting his first general election as party leader, answered his critics who had speculated that he was, metaphorically speaking, too lightweight for the contest. He fought a very good campaign, which saw both his and his party's popularity rise. With the Conservatives poised to become embroiled in a divisive leadership contest, Kennedy's assertion that the Liberal Democrats would become the 'effective opposition' did not seem as far-fetched as David Steel's proclamation to 'go back to your constituencies and prepare for government' had appeared twenty years previously. If this was a third-party revival, it was one built upon much more solid foundations than previous false dawns.

Campaign background

The strong Liberal Democrat performance was not immediately apparent from the party's electoral and opinion poll performance following the 1997 general election. A number of indicators suggested a mixed picture. In each round of local government elections, the Liberal Democrats made net losses in terms of seats. By 2000, the total number of Liberal Democrat councillors was 4,450 – 628 fewer than they had had at the same stage in 1996, although still considerably higher than the 3,728 they had had in 1992. These losses also meant that the party controlled fewer councils. Nevertheless, the party's vote share in local elections continued to be impressive – around 24 per cent in 1998, 1999 and 2000,[1] which projected a national equivalent vote share of 25 per cent, 25 per cent and 27 per cent, respectively.[2] By way of contrast, the party's vote share of 12.7 per cent in the 1999 European elections was poor – lower than the 16.7 per cent gained in 1994. Nevertheless, with these elections being newly held under a regional party list system, the Liberal Democrats gained ten of the eighty-four British seats, up from two seats won in 1994 under first past the post.

In the Scottish Parliament and Welsh Assembly elections held in 1999 under the additional member system (AMS), the party made small gains in terms of vote share. Compared with the 1997 general election, the Liberal Democrats moved from 13 per cent to 14.2 per cent in Scotland and from 12.3 per cent to 13.5 per cent in Wales. This meant that the party held all of the constituencies it had won in 1997, added one seat that had been split (Orkney and Shetland) for the Scottish Parliament elections, and added a further five seats in Scotland and three seats in Wales under the AMS. This meant that the Liberal Democrats had seventeen seats in the 129-seat Scottish Parliament and six seats in the sixty-seat Welsh Assembly.

In Scotland, the impact was immediately apparent. Labour failed to gain a majority, while the Liberal Democrats had sufficient seats to hold the balance of power. With the Liberal Democrats being the most logical partners, a coalition government was formed. The impact was profound. The Liberal Democrats were in government beyond local government for the first time. In Wales, Labour also failed to gain a majority but initially tried to govern as a minority administration. However, after nearly eighteen months, Labour and the Liberal Democrats formed a 'partnership government'. This had obvious attractions for the latter. Again, it meant that they had a real taste of power, which would enhance their political credibility. On the other hand, it could suggest that the Liberal Democrats were less independent as a political party. Overall, however, the gains far outweighed the costs.

In the mayoral and London Assembly elections in May 2000, Liberal Democrat performance was reasonably solid. In the mayoral election, a previously little-known candidate, Susan Kramer, performed credibly. In an election dominated by Ken Livingstone standing as an independent candidate, she secured 11.9 per cent of first preference votes and 28.5 per cent of second preferences (the election was held under the supplementary vote system). She secured more than twice the number of second preferences of any other candidate and, combining first and second preferences, won 156,288 more votes than Labour's official candidate. In the Assembly elections, held under the AMS, the Liberal Democrats secured 18.9 per cent of the constituency vote, compared with 14.6 per cent in the general election. This gained them no seats in the fourteen constituencies derived from the seventy-four parliamentary seats in London, but the electoral system provided them with four additional Assembly members. Since no party secured a majority, the Liberal Democrats again acquired influence.

Parliamentary by-elections during the 1997 parliament provided few clues as to the Liberal Democrats' standing. Despite the fact that there were sixteen by-elections in Britain, few were ones where the Liberal Democrats were likely to make spectacular progress. Granted, in the rerun of the Winchester election – which took place after the Liberal Democrat victory by two votes was challenged – the party won handsomely, gaining a majority of 21,556. However, excluding Winchester (and the seat vacated by the Speaker, where no realistic comparison can be made), the Liberal Democrats increased their vote share on average by 3.5 per cent from that in the 1997 election. Between 1992 and 1997, the average gain was 5.3 per cent. Nevertheless, the party did make one significant gain in Romsey, overturning a Conservative majority of over 8,500. This was also notable for the collapse of the Labour vote, by nearly 15 per cent (resulting in a lost deposit), which suggested that tactical voting had played some part.

For all that, the national opinion polls showed little sign of cheer for the Liberal Democrats. From the 1997 election up to the start of the 2001 campaign their polling figures fluctuated between 14 and 15 per cent – at least 2 per cent below their 1997 vote share. That said, the party's poll ratings before the 1997 campaign were similarly disappointing. Then, as in 2001, the exposure that the party received during the campaign appeared to be electorally beneficial.

As far as leadership ratings were concerned, the picture was again potentially discouraging. By the time Paddy Ashdown stood down as leader in 1999, the percentage nominating him as best person to be Prime Minister in the Gallup monthly data was 19 per cent. Charles Kennedy reached that rating only once before the campaign (during the collective madness of the fuel protests) and generally his ratings were around 12–13 per cent. Nevertheless, Ashdown's ratings immediately prior to the 1997 election were very similar. In terms of leader satisfaction ratings, however, MORI's data showed Ashdown on a net score of +39 upon retirement. Charles Kennedy's ratings fluctuated around the mid-teens throughout (with the exception again of the fuel crisis) and he recorded a positive score of +14, +16, +18 and +15 in the four months before the campaign. By way of contrast, Ashdown's rating in the same period prior to the 1997 election were +19, +20, +38 and +41, and +29, +36 and +35 in the three months preceding his first election as leader, in 1992. Significantly, just before the campaign, 45 per cent of those asked to express a rating for Kennedy had no opinion. Only 30 per cent had no opinion about Ashdown in 1997. Again, it would appear as though the campaign was going to be vital to Liberal Democrat success.

The manifesto

The manifesto, entitled *Freedom, Justice, Honesty*, was divided into thirteen policy sections (see Table 4.1). On the basis of word counts, education was the dominant theme. This was different from the 1997 manifesto, where health and welfare were most prevalent, although education was still significant.[3] Nevertheless, word counts tell only a partial story. For example, the party also sought to emphasise its libertarian and environmental credentials. In each section of the manifesto, there were two prominent text boxes – one entitled 'Setting You Free', the other 'Green Action' – which contained the pertinent libertarian and environmental policy pledges. Further evidence of the party's desire to promote an environmental agenda was demonstrated by the occurrences of particular words and phrases in the manifesto. Those concerned with the environment appeared most often.[4]

Table 4.1. Liberal Democrat 2001 manifesto coverage

Manifesto section	*Percentage of manifesto word count*
Education and employment	12.9
Law and order	10.4
Rural, urban and suburban life (including agriculture and the environment)	9.5
Health	9.2
Transport	8.7
Defence and international relations	7.8
Business, commerce and innovation	7.7
Pensions, wages	7.1
Constitution and politics	6.7
Economy	5.5
Civil liberties	5.4
European Union	5.2
Culture, arts and sport	3.9

In terms of policy pledges, there was continuity with the 1997 pledges and few surprises. There was an overall pledge to increase public spending by £11 billion, to be funded in the first instance by a series of tax changes. The basic rate of income tax was to increase by one percentage point. This was projected to raise £3 billion in the first year, rising to £3.5 billion by 2005/6, and was ring-fenced for education. Other areas of income generation were increases in the top rate of tax to 50 per cent on earnings over £100,000, designed to generate £3.7 billion in the first year, rising to £4.6 billion; and changes in capital gains tax, raising £1.7 billion by 2005/6. Like the Conservatives, the Liberal Democrats also planned to fund public service expansion by efficiency savings – particularly in the case of housing benefit fraud. Such initiatives were projected to save £500 million in the first instance, rising to £1.5 billion. Despite the projected tax increases, there were also some suggestions of targeted tax cuts. If resources allowed, the party planned to reduce the lowest rate (10 per cent) to zero, thus relieving 1.4 million of the lowest paid from income tax. Overall, the projection for these tax proposals, unlike for those of the other main parties, was to produce gains for the lowest paid and losses for the highest.

The projections for the 1 per cent basic rate tax increase were plausible – according broadly with Treasury estimates. However, analysis by the IFS suggested that the increase in the upper rate of tax and particularly changes to capital gains tax could produce lower yields, largely because these changes could lead to different behaviour by tax payers, or increased 'tax planning'.[5]

Specific policy pledges included those to recruit 12,500 new primary teachers and 5,000 new secondary teachers – the aim being to cut primary class sizes to twenty-five and restore secondary class sizes to 1997 levels. Importantly, as in Scotland, the Liberal Democrats promised to abolish university tuition fees. This had been a conspicuous success of the Labour/ Liberal Democrat coalition in Scotland. All education pledges were costed at £3 billion per annum. In health, the party pledged to increase the numbers of doctors, nurses and hospital beds. Nurses' pay was also to increase, by £1,000 on average, and the party also promised to restore free NHS dental and eye checks for all adults. Altogether, an additional £1.6 billion, rising to £2.8 billion, was pledged in these areas. The third principal area targeted for spending increases was pensions. The party promised to increase the single pensioner's basic pension by £5, by £10 for those aged over seventy-five and by £15 for the over-eighties. This was costed at £2.8 billion. Other notable spending pledges were in the areas of law and order – where police numbers were to increase by 6,000 a year – and in transport – where car tax was to be abolished for 'more environmentally friendly cars' as well as motorcycles, and public transport fares were to be reduced for students aged under nineteen and pensioners.

The overall impression of the Liberal Democrat manifesto was one of 'tax and spend' – the party was committing itself to raising taxation and public spending. This led some commentators to suggest that the Liberal Democrats were occupying territory traditionally held by Labour. Yet, for all that, the Liberal Democrat spending plans were fairly modest. While it pledged to spend a little more than Labour, the differences were not huge. Unlike Labour, however, it did promise to increase tax.

Two other manifesto domains are worthy of note. The Liberal Democrats have long been advocates of widespread constitutional reform. This used to make the party distinctive. However, after 1997 many of these policies were enacted, although not always as wholeheartedly as most Liberal Democrats would have liked. One area where the Liberal Democrats have not seen their aims implemented is in the field of proportional representation for elections to Westminster.

Labour commissioned an enquiry into electoral reform, which published its findings in 1998. It recommended a system called 'AV plus'. This is a hybrid electoral system comprised of the alternative vote (AV) for constituencies and the AMS for regional 'top up' seats (plus). This system would ensure that all constituency MPs would receive a majority of the vote (by using AV) and that the distribution of all seats would have a proportional corrective (plus). Labour has apparently shelved these recommendations. The Liberal Democrats, however, pledged to introduce the system in their manifesto, with a view to moving ultimately to the single transferable vote (STV). STV would be implemented immediately for local and European elections. In addition to these proposals, the Liberal Democrats also pledged to introduce voting for sixteen-year-olds. The problem, though, for the Liberal Democrats was that they had to perform successfully under first past the post in order for electoral reform for Westminster to be considered seriously.

A second area of note is Europe. The Liberal Democrats inherited – from both the Liberals and the Social Democratic Party (SDP) – a long tradition of enthusiastic support for European integration. At the 2001 election, the party supported enlargement of the EU and, as in 1997, holding a referendum on joining the single European currency. However, they appeared to strike a less Europhile tone by calling for a constitution to define and limit the powers of the EU as well as calling for the EU to be made more democratically accountable by shifting more power to the European Parliament. That said, some see calls for a European constitution to be an explicitly pro-European stance – a move towards closer political integration.

Neither Europe nor constitutional reform was a prominent issue, however, either in the manifesto or in the party's campaign. As Charles Kennedy joked, they were tucked away at the back of the manifesto – 'in the sports pages'.[6] This was deliberate. The party did not want to be pinned down on these policies, choosing instead to pursue an agenda based on more mainstream issues and, critically, ones that the electorate considered to be most important.

The campaign

The Liberal Democrats ran two campaigns – an 'air' campaign (national) and a 'land' campaign (local). Given the party's relatively poor financial endowment, the 'air' campaign was fairly limited. The party spent around £2.5 million over the period leading up to the election – less than had been spent in 1997, when around £3.5 million was spent in the long and short campaigns. As a consequence, there were no national newspaper advertisements and no fixed poster sites. Instead, the party used a series of poster vans, which visited key seats. Most expenditure on the 'air' campaign was devoted to Charles Kennedy's tour. The strategy was realistic. The party wanted to build on the success of 1997, by increasing both its vote share and the number of seats. By doing this it would be more able to keep its issues on the political agenda. But, as Kennedy admitted early on, breaking one of the taboos of election campaigning, the Liberal Democrats were unlikely to form a majority government.

Kennedy's exhausting tour schedule, which covered 15,000 miles, was based upon three criteria. First, he visited target seats. In the 1997 election, the Liberal Democrats demonstrated the clear virtue of targeted local campaigns. They focused on around fifty seats and won forty-six. They pursued the same strategy in 2001, reportedly targeting around seventy seats.[7] The party claimed that there was no fixed list as such – more a 'Premier League', with seats being promoted and relegated as the chances of success became clearer. Nevertheless, all seats that the Liberal Democrats won were targets and Charles Kennedy made an appearance in all the seats that the party gained.

The second criterion was media visibility. Election campaigns generally are probably more significant for the Liberal Democrats than other parties because of their limited visibility between elections. Kennedy also therefore visited locations where there were likely photo opportunities. This included one with the actress Honor Blackman, who reportedly described Charles Kennedy as 'sexier than Sean Connery'. Through such opportunities the party sought to gain local and regional newspaper and television coverage. These were seen as giving better and less dispassionate coverage than the national media.

Third, the party sought to have a broad regional spread in its campaign. This was sensible because, after 1997, the Liberal Democrats held seats in every region bar two – East Anglia and the East Midlands. After the 2001 election, they held at least one seat in every region.

In addition to his tour, Charles Kennedy also held five rallies during the campaign – in Bristol, Edinburgh, Southport, Cardiff and London. Unlike the other two main parties, these were open to the public. This more open policy, however, led to the appearance of a streaker on the stage with Charles Kennedy in London. The prominence of Kennedy's tour in the party's campaign strategy was reflected in his appearances in the media. Kennedy was the only Liberal Democrat to appear in the top-ten ranking of politicians' media appearances. He was ranked third in each of the campaign weeks bar the last (week ending 1 June), when Gordon Brown beat him into fourth place. On average, over the first four weeks of the campaign Kennedy appeared in 12.6 per cent of election coverage. This compared with 27.3 per cent for Hague and 36.8 per cent for Blair.[8]

In policy terms, the structure of the campaign is shown in Table 4.2. Based upon the party's press releases issued during the campaign, we can see that it concentrated on most of the key areas identified in the manifesto and, significantly, those issues that were seen as being core to voters' concerns. Agriculture had perhaps a higher than expected profile, but this may be explained by the fact that the Liberal Democrats were targeting many rural seats, where foot-and-mouth disease was prevalent.

A number of pledges made during the campaign are worthy of note. First, the party made particular efforts to gain support from elderly voters. In addition to pension increases, the Liberal Democrats campaigned on the promise of extending the policy of free medical and long-term personal care for the elderly– a policy the party had already established in Scotland. Second, the party reaffirmed its environmental credentials by issuing a five-point pledge for 'greener government': to make cuts in carbon dioxide emissions; to increase the use of renewable energy; to introduce a national recycling programme to bring doorstep recycling to every household; to support a home insulation programme; and to promote public transport.

What was also significant about the Liberal Democrat campaign was the amount of negative campaigning. The party sought to portray itself as one which campaigned honestly and did not use such tactics lightly. Nevertheless, as Table 4.2 shows, negative tactics formed a considerable part of the party's campaign. Nearly 38 per cent of the party's press releases were negative

Table 4.2. Liberal Democrat press releases during the campaign period

Topic	Number	%
Negative towards the Conservatives	31	17.8
Negative towards Labour	29	16.7
Negative towards both Labour and Conservatives	6	3.4
Campaign/party	22	12.6
Agriculture	10	5.7
Education	9	5.1
Health	8	4.6
Transport	8	4.6
Elderly	6	3.4
Regions and rural issues	6	3.4
Foreign affairs	6	3.4
Law and order	5	2.9
Economy and tax	5	2.9
General public services	4	2.3
Environment	3	1.7
Euro	2	1.1
Other	14	8.0
Total	174	100

towards Labour, Conservative or both. In addition, a further 13 per cent were concerned only with how the party was campaigning. Thus, only around 50 per cent of the party's campaign was based on policies and issues.

Tactical voting also appeared as part of the campaign. Buoyed by the apparent success of tactical voting in the 1997 general election, a number of websites were independently set up to encourage this practice – usually to defeat Conservative candidates. This included the idea of 'vote swapping', where Liberal Democrat and Labour supporters in different constituencies could pledge to vote for the other's party if it stood a better chance of defeating the Conservatives. Similarly, both the *Guardian* and *Observer* identified seats that were ripe for tactical voting, just as the *Observer* had in 1997. In fact, the success of these initiatives was very limited. In the thirteen seats identified by the *Guardian* and *Observer* as potential tactical targets for the Liberal Democrats, the party won only four. Just as in 1997, the media's influence on tactical voting was overstated.[9] Nevertheless, the Liberal Democrats did for the first time officially endorse tactical voting. This was a qualified endorsement, however, since the party endorsed tactical voting only for Liberal Democrats. The exception was in Wyre Forest, where the party withdrew its candidate in favour of the Kidderminster Hospital and Health Concern candidate, who went on to win the seat. This was clearly tactical since the Liberal Democrats fielded candidates against the Kidderminster group in the county council elections held on the same day.

The results

The Liberal Democrat campaign was a success, overall. As Table 4.3 shows, the party's position improved throughout the campaign, especially in the last ten days. They began the campaign with a mean poll rating of 13.1 per cent and ended it on 18.3 per cent. Moreover, voters' images of the party were generally positive. The Liberal Democrats were seen as understanding the country's problems and having sensible policies (on the latter they were regarded as well as Labour). Moreover, unlike Labour and the Conservatives, few saw the Liberal Democrats as being a party prepared to promise anything to win votes.[10] Charles Kennedy's profile also improved. The proportion rating him as best person to be Prime Minister grew and again the biggest improvement was in the latter part of the campaign (see Table 4.3).

Further indications of Kennedy's success are shown in Table 4.4. Using the BES rolling campaign survey, we can see that he made clear gains. At the outset of the campaign, Kennedy had a mean like/dislike figure of 4.9. He ended with a score of 5.4 and, as Table 4.4 demonstrates, the upward trend was fairly uniform. Blair, too, improved his score, although slightly less so than Kennedy. By way of contrast, Hague 'flatlined' – always some distance behind.

Table 4.3. Mean poll ratings during the campaign – voting intention and Kennedy as best person to be Prime Minister

Publication period	Voting intention (%)	Kennedy as Prime Minister (%)
8–13 May	13.1	10.3
14–20 May	13.8	11.3
21–27 May	14.3	10.7
28 May–3 June	16.6	12.0
4–7 June	18.3	14.0

Sources: Pippa Norris campaign polls file (www.pippanorris.com), MORI, Gallup.

Table 4.4. Party leader mean like/dislike scores during the 2001 election campaign

Date	Kennedy	Hague	Blair
14 May	4.9	3.9	5.6
15	4.9	3.8	5.6
16	5.0	3.9	5.8
17	5.0	3.8	5.7
18	5.0	3.8	5.7
19	5.1	3.8	5.7
20	5.1	3.9	5.7
21	5.1	3.9	5.7
22	5.0	3.9	5.7
23	5.1	3.9	5.7
24	5.1	3.9	5.8
25	5.1	3.9	5.7
26	5.1	3.9	5.7
27	5.2	3.9	5.7
28	5.2	3.9	5.7
29	5.2	3.9	5.7
30	5.1	3.9	5.7
31	5.1	4.0	5.7
1 June	5.2	4.0	5.7
2	5.2	3.9	5.8
3	5.3	4.0	5.8
4	5.3	3.9	5.9
5	5.4	3.9	5.9
6	5.4	3.9	5.9

Source: British Election Study.
Note: Scores run from 0–10, where 0 equals 'Strongly dislike' and 10 equals 'Strongly like'.

Further evidence of the Liberal Democrats' success is shown in Table 4.5. The party improved its vote share in every region bar its strongest (the South West), where there was a modest decline. Of particular note was the party's performance in Scotland. Retaining its position as Scotland's second party in terms of seats, it now overtook the Conservatives in terms of votes – the

Table 4.5. Vote shares in 639 seats contested by the Liberal Democrats

	Share of vote (%)	Change in vote share, 1997–2001 (%)
All contested seats	18.9	+1.7
By region		
South East	21.6	+0.2
East Anglia	19.0	+1.1
Greater London	17.5	+2.9
South West	31.2	−0.1
West Midlands	15.0	+1.2
East Midlands	15.4	+1.8
Yorkshire and Humberside	17.1	+1.1
North West	16.5	+2.2
North	17.1	+3.8
Wales	13.8	+2.0
Scotland	16.5	+3.4

	Mean vote share (%)	Change in mean vote share, 1997–2001 (%)
By incumbency		
All Liberal Democrats winning seats	46.7	+3.8
Liberal Democrat gains (n = 8)	44.0	+8.6
All Liberal Democrat incumbents (n = 40)	48.1	+4.3
Liberal Democrat winning incumbents (n = 38)	48.6	+4.7
Liberal Democrat incumbents in 1997 gains (n = 26)	47.5	+4.3
Liberal Democrat winning incumbents in 1997 gains (n = 24)	48.3	+5.0
Liberal Democrat seats with new candidate (n = 7)	44.1	−4.9
Liberal Democrat defeats	38.3	−4.4

Source: British Parliamentary Constituency Database 1992–2001.
Note: The Liberal Democrats did not field candidates in Glasgow Springburn (Speaker's seat) or Wyre Forest (Kidderminster Hospital and Health Concern candidate). The calculations for national and regional vote shares above do not therefore include these seats.

Liberal Democrats are now Scotland's third party on the basis of that criterion. Wales continued to provide the least impressive Liberal Democrat vote share (where it remains the fourth party), although once again the party won two seats, while the second-placed Conservatives (in terms of vote share) won none. In both Scotland and Wales, the improved vote share suggested that the Liberal Democrats' closeness to Labour in devolved government had done the party no electoral harm.

It is also worth comparing Liberal Democrat performance in the seats that they won. Table 4.5 also shows that, on average, the party gained 46.7 per cent of the vote – an improvement of 3.8 per cent – in these seats. The biggest increase in vote share was, predictably enough, in the eight seats that the party gained – the vote share rising on average by 8.6 per cent. However, what is also worth noting is that incumbent Liberal Democrats performed well. Vote share for all Liberal Democrat incumbents (winners and losers) was on average 48.1 per cent, an increase of 4.3 percentage points on 1997. For those winning their seat, the figures were 48.6 per cent and 4.7 per cent respectively. For those MPs who gained seats in 1997 and stood again, vote share on average was 47.5 per cent, a gain of an additional 4.3 per cent of the vote. Among those who won again in 2001, those figures rose to 48.3 per cent and 5.0 per cent. By way of contrast, where new candidates were standing in existing Liberal Democrat seats, the mean vote share was 44.1 per cent, declining on average by 4.9 percentage points. This pattern is common with the 'slump' that occurs following an MP's retirement. In the first post-retirement election, the incumbent party's vote share tends to decline, in part because inheritors 'lack the status, political credibility, and public recognition which the office bestows on MPs'.[11] On the face of it, there would appear to be an incumbency advantage, which was to benefit the Liberal Democrats especially in 2001, since they had so many more incumbents.

Yet for all that, there were some downsides to the Liberal Democrats' performance. Despite the Conservatives' disarray, the Liberal Democrats won only three of the thirteen most marginal seats (where the successful candidate won by less than 5.0 per cent) in which it was placed second in 1997. In one of these (Conwy – held by Labour) the party actually slipped to third place behind the Conservatives. In addition, they won only two of the eleven next most marginal seats (5–9.9 per cent), slipping to third again in two of these (Southend West, and Worthing East and Shoreham). Overall, while the party consolidated its existing seats and made a few impressive gains, it is entirely possible that more ground could have been made.

Second, of the twenty most marginal seats, the Liberal Democrats hold seven. Indeed, they hold the most marginal seat in Britain (Cheadle, won by only thirty-three votes). That said, the party held the three most marginal seats in 1997: Winchester (two votes), Torbay (twelve votes) and Kingston and Surbiton (fifty-six votes). The majorities in those constituencies, all of which were held by the Liberal Democrats, are now 9,634, 6,708 and

15,676, respectively. Finally, of course, the party lost two seats (Taunton and the Isle of Wight), both gained by the Conservatives and where the Liberal Democrat vote share fell 4.4 per cent on average. Nevertheless, for all those setbacks, the Liberal Democrats' targeting strategy was generally a success.

Evidence for this can be found in Table 4.6. In 'battleground' seats with the Conservatives, Liberal Democrat vote shares increased most in the most marginal seats. On average, their vote share went up 4.5 percentage points. In seats that the Liberal Democrats won, the effect was even more dramatic. Liberal Democrat vote shares went up on average 7.8 percentage points in the most marginal battleground seats with the Conservatives and 4.6 percentage points in the next most marginal group. In battleground seats with Labour, the Liberal Democrat vote share actually fell slightly in the most marginal seats. However, in the seven of these seats that the Liberal Democrats won, vote share improvements were impressive.

Table 4.6 also suggests that tactical voting helped the Liberal Democrats. Labour's vote share fell in all but the least marginal of Liberal Democrat and Conservative battleground seats and fell most in the most marginal ones. Indeed, in the seats that the Liberal Democrats won, Labour's vote share fell by nearly 5 percentage points in the most marginal seats and by over 2 percentage points overall. In Labour battleground seats, there is also limited evidence of anti-Labour tactical voting. Conservative vote share fell in all but the least marginal seats and by 0.4 per cent overall. In these contests which

Table 4.6. Voting in Liberal Democrat battleground seats

1997 majority	<5%	5–9.9%	10–14.9%	15–19.9%	>20%	All seats
Conservative/Liberal Democrat seats (n = 110)						
Liberal Democrats	+4.5	+0.6	−0.5	+0.5	+0.2	+1.1
Labour	−3.2	0.6	−0.3	−0.1	+0.1	−0.9
Liberal Democrats winning seats (n = 44)						
Liberal Democrats	+7.8	+4.6	+0.5	+3.5	−0.9	+3.8
Labour	−4.8	−1.1	−1.4	−1.5	+0.8	−2.2
Labour/Liberal Democrat seats (n = 38)						
Liberal Democrats	−0.3	+0.3	+9.7	+8.9	+1.6	+2.3
Conservatives	−3.2	−0.4	−2.6	−0.1	+0.1	−0.4
Liberal Democrats winning seats (n = 7)						
Liberal Democrats	+11.0	+4.6	+11.8	+5.9	−10.6	+5.6
Conservatives	−6.7	+2.0	−1.6	+4.0	+6.4	+0.7

Source: British Parliamentary Constituency Database 1992–2001.

the Liberal Democrats won, Conservative vote share also fell in two of the most marginal groups. However, caution should be expressed here as to any indication of a trend. The Liberal Democrats only won seven of the battleground seats with Labour, and only one was marginal at a level below 5 per cent and two between 10 and 15 per cent. Nevertheless, in Tweeddale, Ettrick and Lauderdale, at least (which was the most marginal Liberal Democrat/Labour battleground), it does appear as though significant anti-Labour tactical voting occurred. For all that, however, the failure of the Liberal Democrats to capture more seats suggests that tactical voting was more limited than some had predicted.

Conclusion

Like 1997, 2001 was a good election for the Liberal Democrats. They succeeded in consolidating their position and made gains in terms of both vote share and seats. The great leap forward of 1997 was clearly not a freak result. While they could have made more gains, it is perhaps a measure of the party's standing that, despite making more gains than any other party, its performance could be viewed as in any way disappointing. While tactical voting did help the party to a degree, the fact that it was not as extensive as had been predicted is also good news for the party, since it suggests that its electoral support may be stronger. Moreover, as memories of Conservative governments fade, so tactical voting is likely to diminish. Charles Kennedy also had a good election. He performed better than most had expected and the electoral improvements mean that he has greatly enhanced his leadership.

So what now? Charles Kennedy has identified five key tasks for the Liberal Democrats in this parliament: holding the government to account on public services and the environment; remaining united as a party; putting forward practical and costed alternatives to government policy; offering 'vision' based around the core value of freedom; and, finally, speaking on issues often seen as marginal, such as global poverty and the environment.[12] With his party as well established as it is, Kennedy's hopes to implement these tasks as the 'effective opposition' are not necessarily unrealistic.

Notes

1 J. Fisher, P. Cowley, D. Denver and A. Russell (eds), *British Elections and Parties Review Volume 9* (London: Frank Cass, 1999); P. Cowley, D. Denver, A. Russell and L. Harrison (eds), *British Elections and Parties Review Volume 10* (London: Frank Cass, 2000); J. Tonge, L. Bennie, D. Denver and L. Harrison (eds), *British Elections and Parties Review Volume 11* (London: Frank Cass, 2001).
2 C. Rallings and M. Thrasher (eds), *British Electoral Facts 1832–1999* (Aldershot: Ashgate, 2000).

3 J. Fisher, 'Third and minor party breakthrough?', in A. Geddes and J. Tonge (eds), *Labour's Landslide. The British General Election 1997* (Manchester: Manchester University Press, 1997), p. 54.

4 news.bbc.co.uk/vote2001/hi/english/newsid_1333000/1333462.stm#top, 16 May 2001

5 news.bbc.co.uk/vote2001/hi/english/newsid_1331000/1331609.stm#top, 16 May 2001

6 *Guardian*, 22 May 2001.

7 *Guardian*, 9 May 2001.

8 *Guardian*, 14, 21, 28 May, 4 June 2001.

9 P. Cowley, '*The Observer*: Good at observing, less good at influencing?', *Political Studies*, 50 (2002, forthcoming).

10 www.mori.com/election2001/ec0525.shtml.

11 P. Norris and J. Lovenduski, *Political Recruitment* (Cambridge: Cambridge University Press, 1995), pp. 230–1.

12 *Observer*, 10 June 2001.

Southport

The inability of the Conservatives to regain Southport was indicative of their sad plight in the 2001 election, while confirming the ability of the Liberal Democrats to hold seats in England beyond their West Country heartland. The required 6.2 per cent swing was viewed as attainable by Conservative optimists and William Hague visited the constituency, as did the Liberal Democrat leader, Charles Kennedy. Though Southport ought to represent a reasonably safe Conservative seat, it had changed hands in the previous two elections. The Conservative defeat in 1997 was symbolic of the national collapse of their vote, but their 'victory' in the town in the 1999 European election gave some hope that Liberal Democrat dominance at local council level might not transfer to the general election. The Conservatives hoped that Southport's large elderly population would help return the seat, although, before the campaign, a MORI poll placed Labour 24 percentage points ahead on pensions among those regarding the issue as important (*The Times*, 22 February 2001). The Liberal Democrats offered free personal and medical care to the elderly.

A major concern for the Liberal Democrats before the campaign was the replacement for retiring veteran MP Ronnie Fearn, a popular local figure. The short-list included prominent figures such as the former ITN political correspondent David Walter, but, aware of the importance of fielding a local person, the party selected Sefton council leader and private school teacher John Pugh. In the 1997 election concerted national press campaigns identified Southport as a key seat for tactical voting for the Liberal Democrats. This time, Labour increased its vote share by 4.5 percentage points, while the Liberal Democrats' vote share fell by a similar amount. Although the Conservatives halved the Liberal Democrats' majority, this appeared due to abstentions and a rise in the Labour vote. The Conservatives' vote share was virtually static, emphasising the party's failure to win back voters and confounding the myth that the Conservatives are inevitable beneficiaries of large reductions in turnout (the low poll was a surprise in a constituency normally recording high figures). The Conservative candidate, Laurence Jones, indeed blamed the low poll, having expected it to be in the high sixties. Now three times an election loser, the defeated candidate told the Southport *Visiter* (13 June 2001) that the Conservative Party's leader was 'not popular with the electorate' and the party itself was 'in meltdown'.

Result

Southport		
	No. of votes	% of vote
Pugh, J. (Liberal Democrat)	18,011	43.8
Jones, L. (Conservative)	15,004	36.5
Brant, P. (Labour)	6,816	16.5
Green, D. (Liberal)	767	1.9
Kelley, G. (UKIP)	555	1.3
Liberal Democrat majority	3,007	7.3
Liberal Democrat hold		
Turnout		58.1
Swing, Liberal Democrats to Conservatives		2.4

5

The 'Tony' press: media coverage of the election campaign

Dominic Wring

Introduction

Compared with previous campaigns, the 2001 election made for a less compelling journalistic story.[1] The competitive race of 1992 had been followed by an extraordinary Labour victory in 1997. Though several commentators had labelled both campaigns boring, there was a consensus that the 2001 election was tedious. Perhaps not unrelated to this were the unprecedented levels of voter abstention. After the election, media contributors joined defeated politicians to reflect on shortcomings in their performances.

When discussing the democratic process scholars disagree over the precise nature, if any, of media effects.[2] During the 2001 campaign this debate was minimal because the size and consistency of the Labour lead in public opinion polls diminished interest in this particular topic. Nonetheless, politicians did appear to believe that the media mattered because they spent considerable time and sums of money on using the two complementary promotional techniques of public relations and advertising.[3]

Public relations strategists, the so-called 'spin-doctors', coordinated contact with the 'free' media of journalism. Getting favourable coverage through news reporting would, it was hoped, help politicians reach the electorate. Conservative leader William Hague had former Mirror Group Newspapers executive Amanda Platell oversee and direct the public relations machine at the party's Central Office headquarters. This pitted Platell against Labour's Alastair Campbell, one of her former journalistic colleagues. Campbell, an experienced tabloid reporter turned Prime Ministerial Press Secretary, worked closely with the party headquarters at Millbank Tower to help Labour stay 'on message'.

In addition to developing their public relations strategies parties also retained the services of advertising agencies. These so-called 'image makers' helped conceive and execute 'controlled' media campaigns. Though regarded as less influential than 'free' coverage, advertising plays an important role because it allows politicians to communicate directly with the electorate. Labour hired leading agency TBWA. In a convenient piece of self-publicity, the firm's initials featured in its last election poster, 'Tony Blair Wins Again'. Agency work was overseen by the high-profile, Labour-supporting executive Trevor Beattie. For the first general election in over twenty years the Conservatives were without the services of the Saatchi brothers' agency. Their account went to the relatively unknown firm Yellow M. The Liberal Democrats could not afford to spend anything like their main opponents on advertising but did hire the Banc agency.

This chapter discusses the role of the media and party communication strategies during the election. Topics to be considered include the various ways broadcast as well as the more obviously partisan print media covered the campaign. To use *Mail on Sunday* journalist Peter Hitchens' term, much of the former so-called 'Tory press' had arguably become the 'Tony press'.[4] These newspapers' expressed admiration for Blair was tempered by their more conditional support for his party. The sycophantic cheerleading for Thatcher in the 1980s had gone and in its place a sometimes more complex and nuanced pattern of press coverage was being established.

Television

Television is widely regarded as the most important medium of political communication.[5] Thus every day at the main parties' morning press conferences broadcast journalists were privileged with an opportunity to cross-examine the relevant spokesperson on the platform. This was because spin-doctors calculated that they were more likely to gain favourable exposure for their party's message if they prioritised the requirements of those reporters contributing to the major television channels' news programmes. These and other journalists did, however, regularly ignore the conferences' chosen theme for the day in favour of their own questions. Answers to these queries were not always forthcoming and included 'sound-bites' consisting of short, pre-prepared and oft-repeated phrases. Journalists criticised the messengers as well as the messages. Many complained that women on the platforms rarely spoke for their parties. The issue arose at a Labour conference when Gordon Brown was laughed at for attempting to answer a question on the subject intended for his colleague Estelle Morris.

Press conferences provide an important public forum for politicians and journalists. Their continuing existence reflects a growing concern within the media over the rise of so-called 'spin'. Understood to be the slant put on stories by frequently unnamed party spokespeople often talking privately and 'off the record', spin has been criticised for undermining healthy democratic debate.[6] Growing public awareness of this activity provides a partial antidote to its impact. Yet in the competitive realm of political journalism even the more reluctant reporters may be pressured to cultivate spin-doctors in order to guarantee their future access to important new stories and leads from a particular party source.

The Blair government's perceived dependence on spin to manage the news agenda was a major topic of debate during its first term and continued to be discussed during the campaign. It formed a recurrent theme in media reporting of the election process (see Table 5.1).[7] Predictably this alleged 'control freakery' was a feature of Conservative attacks. Labour's determined approach to news management was underlined from the outset of the campaign when Tony Blair chose to stage his announcement of the election at a high-achieving school. In doing so the Prime Minister replaced the traditional statement to parliament with a photo opportunity designed to emphasise his commitment to education. Many of the journalists present criticised his decision to give such a political speech to a bemused-looking group of children. After the election, BBC political editor Andrew Marr called the event a 'hideous, cringe-making example of soft propaganda'.[8] The speech itself appeared to give ammunition to popular satirical attacks on Blair's allegedly sermonising, preachy style.

The tension between public relations and public opinion was demonstrated on three separate occasions in a single day early in the campaign. Visiting a new hospital development in Birmingham, Tony Blair was challenged by Sharon Storrer, the partner of a seriously ill cancer patient. In a memorable attack on the government's stewardship of the NHS, an irate Ms Storrer confronted an uncomfortable-looking Blair. Her comments about the poor state of hospitals electrified the early evening news bulletins. Earlier in the day Home Secretary Jack Straw had faced highly newsworthy barracking

Table 5.1. Top ten issues in the news (percentages of selected media coverage)

2001		1997	
Election process	39.4	Conduct of the campaign	31.6
Europe	8.7	Europe	15.3
Health	5.8	Sleaze	9.5
Politicians' conduct	5.6	Education	6.6
Taxation	5.5	Taxation	6.2
Crime	4.3	Constitution	5.0
Education	4.3	Economy	3.8
Public services	3.5	Health	2.5
Social security	3.2	Social security	2.2
Economy	2.9	Northern Ireland	2.1
Other	16.8	Other	15.2

Source: Loughborough University Communications Research Centre.[9]

during his speech to delegates at the Police Federation. But this and the Blair incident, together with the party's manifesto launch that day, were over-shadowed by an extraordinary altercation in north Wales between the Deputy Prime Minister and an agricultural worker, Craig Evans. Evans, a Countryside Alliance supporter, was filmed throwing an egg from point-blank range at John Prescott. In an instinctive reaction Prescott punched his assailant and a mêlée ensued. The incident attracted more coverage across all media than the likely next government's manifesto plans.[10]

Worried by the security implications of the Prescott incident some in the Labour hierarchy began to question whether journalists might be encouraging aggrieved voters to vent their disaffection by confronting politicians during campaign visits. This debate intensified following the widespread publication of a private memorandum on the matter from Margaret McDonagh, the party's General Secretary, to the main broadcasters. McDonagh's comments were widely derided as an ill-judged attempt to intimidate journalists. Interest-ingly none of Labour's elected spokespeople appeared keen to defend or explain their beleaguered official's request.

The major terrestrial and satellite/cable/digital news programmes featured large amounts of election coverage both before and during the campaign. There was, however, a noticeable attempt not automatically to relegate other important stories. The forced delay of the election due to the crisis over foot-and-mouth disease had led to a 'phoney' war in which the main parties debated key issues and gave a good foretaste of what was to come. During the campaign proper, BBC1 did not extend its main evening news programme as it had done in 1997. Its newly established slot of 10 p.m. placed it in direct competition with the rival ITV bulletin. Both these and the stations' other main news services were supplemented by regional reports and pro-grammes. Party spin-doctors appeared keen to cultivate local journalists in the belief that they were less cynical than national reporters. They were also seen as a means of communicating with voters in the key marginal seats that would determine the outcome of the election.

Both regional and national news reports devoted considerable time to leading politicians' constituency visits. The main party leaders were trans-ported to these in their so-called 'battle buses'. The visits were designed to support the local candidate and took the form of a walkabout, photo opportunity, formal address, voter question session or supposedly impromptu speech 'on the stump'. The leaders' partners regularly attended these events and this contributed to the highly presidential nature of the campaign. Blair and Hague alone accounted for 62 per cent of the coverage given to all politicians.[11] The presence of minders and assorted media personnel ensured that few members of the public met the politicians during these carefully choreographed events. There was, however, some compensation for keen election watchers, in that the BBC News 24, BBC Parliament and Sky News cable channels provided live, comprehensive, round-the-clock coverage.

The politicians' desire to gain favourable publicity led to stage-managed visits and meetings with known sympathisers. Tony Blair highlighted the type of voters he was interested in when he was filmed taking tea with an attractive, professional-looking couple in the marginal 'middle England' seat of Warwick and Leamington. The pair turned out to be party supporters specially recruited for the purpose. Such events encouraged a media backlash against the parties' desire to manipulate or 'spin' news stories. One obvious manifestation of this was 'the man in the white suit', Channel 5 News' self-styled journalistic champion of the people. Many of his reports showed how difficult it was to gain access to the party leaders, who were continuously protected by a close circle of aides. The journalist also attacked the high cost of a place on the parties' battle buses by spending the equivalent sum on champagne and the hiring of a stretch limousine. Given the chance, reporters on board might have done the same because many complained of feeling neglected and excluded from the campaign. This mood was particularly strong among those travelling with Tony Blair; in the final week of the election exasperated photo-journalists temporarily went on strike in protest at their treatment by the party's publicity machine. Earlier in the campaign its robust approach had been demonstrated by the decision to ban satirist Rory Bremner from Labour's battle bus.

If the politicians desired managed contact with the electorate, broadcasters felt obliged to facilitate more meaningful and genuine public dialogue. Both major television broadcasters organised prime-time studio-based sessions featuring a single party leader taking questions from an invited audience. BBC *Question Time*'s 'Leader special' was presented by David Dimbleby while over on ITV his brother Jonathan hosted *Ask the Leader*. William Hague appeared at ease with the format. This may have been because of his noted ability to cope with Prime Minister's Question Time. Indeed, Hague regularly appeared to better Blair in House of Commons debates. Yet this did not boost his personal public opinion ratings and they remained well below those of the Prime Minister. Compared with Hague, Blair looked more uncomfortable during his appearances on both public debate programmes. But, by peak-time viewing standards, relatively few people noticed. Barely 2.5 million saw Blair's BBC1 debate. Over on ITV at the same time 11 million viewers watched the British Soap Awards. Rather conveniently the person making the main tribute speech turned out to be Cherie Booth, the Prime Minister's wife. It was another indication of Labour's preoccupation with the large numbers of voters consciously avoiding the campaign coverage. Blair, for instance, appeared on the largely party-politics-free GMTV breakfast programme and talked about one of his children, thereby reinforcing his family image to viewers.

The BBC and ITV Sunday lunchtime political programmes continued during the campaign. ITV maintained its usual audience participation format, whereby Jonathan Dimbleby invited politicians to debate foreign and domestic policy issues. The BBC's *On the Record* with John Humphrys did much the same. Unfortunately for the broadcasters Blair had refused to debate with rival leaders, so other spokespeople fielded the questions. When his deputy Andrew Smith stood in for Chancellor Gordon Brown it had the effect of downgrading the programmes and the stature of Brown's shadow, Michael Portillo. Throughout the week BBC2's *Campaign Live* also used panels to structure live discussions between politicians and voters on a variety of topics.

The BBC once again broadcast the now established *Election Call* programmes. Moderated by Peter Sissons, the programmes enabled people to phone in or e-mail their questions to a politician live on air. Most guests coped well and there was nothing to match the most famous exchange of this kind in which Diana Gould embarrassed Margaret Thatcher during the 1983 campaign over her government's sinking of an Argentine warship during the Falklands War. This time some politicians even went on the offensive, notably Margaret Beckett, who sternly rebutted the claims of an anxious patient over Labour's record on health. It is perhaps significant that *Election Call* was relegated from its usual BBC1 slot to BBC2. It was placed in direct competition with *Kilroy*, another programme with an audience participation format. Though presented by a former MP, this discussion-based programme avoided election-related topics in favour of its usual diet of personal testimonies and moral debates.

Public access was a major feature of Channel 5's election coverage. The channel had actually only just started broadcasting during the early stages of the 1997 election but played little role in that campaign. This time the main evening news bulletins were supplemented by *Live Talk*, a studio, telephone and e-mail participation programme. Fronted by married couple Lucy and James O'Brien, the consumer affairs style of format enabled the presenters and members of the public to discuss issues and express their opinions. Even senior politicians such as Peter Lilley were expected to telephone in order to make a point.

Broadcasters recognised that only certain types of motivated people were likely to participate in public-access programming. Consequently the opinions of key voters were actively sought out. BBC *Breakfast Time* issued selected undecided viewers with video equipment to enable them to record comments that were broadcast during the election. Like the politicians, *Channel 4 News* employed a battle bus to enable Krishnan Guru-Murthy to visit marginal constituencies and gauge the opinions of undecided voters. BBC *Newsnight* also had a vehicle. Jeremy Vine's 1970s vintage 'Dormobile' took in John o'Groat's and Land's End during a nationwide tour. Several memorable interviews included an uncomfortable encounter with Peter Mandelson and, following an enforced stop due to a breakdown, a political discussion with the mechanic mending the van.

Broadcasters' attempts to engage with and understand the public mood were augmented by specially commissioned research findings. In some cases these went beyond the standard survey format. *Channel 4 News'* Mark Easton reported on his programme's Message Poll, a method designed to assess voter concerns on a given issue. The feature strove to offer an insight into the data and not just selected results. Frank Luntz, the prominent American campaign consultant, helped devise the studies and also took part in expert panel discussions of the findings. Other channels reported public opinion results but these were given less prominence compared with previous campaigns. Sky News' evening bulletins, for instance, ran the latest results in a continuously rotating by-line. The failure of most surveys to predict the Conservatives' 1992 victory has dented journalistic faith in the method. It was one reason why some media outlets began to commission their own focus group studies.

Similar in format to *Channel 4 News*, BBC2's *Newsnight* offered extended, analytical coverage of the campaign. Features on all aspects of the election included Jeremy Paxman's unsettling interviews with leading spokespeople. His discussion with William Hague was a particularly bruising encounter. Following his resignation as leader, Hague reportedly admitted that he had found Paxman's questioning particularly unsettling because it had accurately reflected what disloyal Conservative colleagues had been privately saying about his leadership. This interview, it was claimed, contributed to his eventual decision to step down. On the Labour side Robin Cook's perceived inability to deal with Paxman's cross-examination of the party's stance on the euro raised doubts about him remaining as Foreign Secretary. Journalist Jackie Ashley suggested Blair's surprise demotion of Cook in the post-election cabinet reshuffle could be partly explained by his poor performance in this set-piece interview.

As in 1997, a Saturday edition of *Newsnight* was broadcast throughout the campaign. The programmes attempted to go beyond the relatively narrow agenda of the election and took a longer-term view of key trends and issues. In a programme on class and education, comedian Mark Thomas offered a critique of the government's promotion of meritocracy. His report formed the backdrop to an expert-led discussion free from party sound-bites. The BBC's other main investigative input was provided by John Ware for the *Panorama* programme during the final week of the campaign. Ware's controversial report revisited findings of a previous edition to question again the validity of government spending claims on health, education and transport. There was a predictably swift rebuke from Labour's Millbank headquarters.

In contrast to other broadcasters' and its own previous coverage, Channel 4 partly abandoned conventional election reporting in favour of a series entitled *Politics Isn't Working*. Various programmes explored the apparent deepening public disaffection with the democratic process. Reporters criticised corporate-sponsored globalisation, social inequality, racial intolerance and the perceived triviality of the election. Reflecting the growing trend in reality-style 'fly on the wall' television, a documentary called 'Party crashers' in the series had undercover reporters working for each of the main parties. This was the nearest the series got to a Westminster slant on the election. In many ways *Politics Isn't Working* was an attempt to re-engage with Channel 4's original mission to offer an alternative perspective to mainstream broadcasting.

For the younger viewer BBC's *Newsround* co-sponsored school-based elections. In a hung parliament, the Conservatives came out as the largest party. 'Other' candidates did very well in what was perhaps another indicator of youth disaffection with traditional politics. Reflecting this the presenters of Channel 4's *Big Breakfast* morning programme ridiculed the election as a 'yawn'. It was a common theme of many journalistic stories. Perhaps aware that viewers were avoiding the election coverage, both ITV and Channel 4 took the opportunity to launch major 'reality' television series during the campaign. Both received considerable media attention. Several journalists contrasted the apparent public apathy about taking part in a free general election with the willingness of viewers of *Big Brother 2*, the Channel 4 programme, to pay to vote out by telephone their least favourite character in the series. People, it appeared, were still keen to participate in certain kinds of poll.

Radio

Despite the dominating presence of television, radio played an important role during the election. While commercially owned organisations relegated the campaign to brief mentions on their news bulletins, the BBC's public service ethos meant it devoted considerable time to following developments. A network of regional and local radio stations offered election features, discussion and debate. The relaxation of legal restrictions meant broadcasters found it much easier to invite individual candidates on to their programmes. Reflecting their audiences, the national stations' coverage differed. Radio 5 Live provided round-the-clock news from the campaign. The mid-morning phone-in programme allowed voters to call in with their frank views. Presenter Nicky Campbell combined a popular touch with detailed political knowledge. The programme included daily updates from Fi Glover and Mark Mardell on the parties' campaigns.

Radio 5 Live's less reverential approach contrasted with that of Radio 4. It aired *Election Call* simultaneously with BBC2 in direct competition with Campbell's largely politician-free show. Radio 4's breakfast morning programme, *Today*, continued to be the key agenda-setting medium for party elites. Here leaders and their lieutenants were scrutinised by John Humphrys and colleagues. Blair, in particular, faced close interrogation over his endorsement of Minister for Europe Keith Vaz and former Paymaster General Geoffrey Robinson as Labour candidates. Both faced ongoing investigations into their personal conduct in office. Radio 4's other coverage included an election series of the debating programme *Any Questions* and a nightly *Campaign Update* bulletin.

Reflecting its core interests, Radio 3 did its main election feature on the arts. The other two stations targeted their audiences by age. For the older listener, Radio 2's *Jimmy Young Show* had panels of politicians discussing a policy area. Young also interviewed leaders. In a telling exchange with Tony Blair, the veteran presenter invited the Prime Minister back on to the programme in the not too distant future and inadvertently revealed what he and most voters assumed would be another Labour election victory. Publicly most journalists felt obliged to keep up the pretence that the campaign might have a surprising outcome.

Youth-oriented Radio 1 tended to avoid politicians and focused its coverage on issues of potential interest to their audience. Polly Billington, a reporter with the *Newsbeat* programme, selected interviewees and subjects in an attempt to make the election appear relevant. The main leaders were cross-examined by a studio audience of young people. 'Minute manifestos' were also broadcast at midday. While two of the younger SNP and PC candidates presented their pitches, the Conservatives fielded Steve Norris to make his party's case in sixty seconds.

Newspapers

British law requires broadcasters to provide unbiased election coverage, though relaxation of the code (under the Representation of the People Act 2000) gave broadcasters more discretion over what to report during the 2001 campaign. No such restrictions apply to the print media. Most national newspapers support a party. Most endorsed the winning party in 2001. This reflects a trend dating back to Margaret Thatcher's 1979 victory. Thatcher's electoral success cemented a relationship between her party and the so-called 'Tory press'. These papers remorselessly attacked Labour and its leadership. Conservative victories in 1987 and 1992 led some to conclude that the press might have a certain degree of influence over voter attitudes.[12] Like the outcome, the pattern of press realignment during the 1997 election was dramatic. Papers once Tory now supported the seemingly invincible Tony Blair. At the very least, this removed a public impediment to Labour. During the 2001 election press support for the party actually increased (Tables 5.2 and 5.3).

Rupert Murdoch's News International Corporation owns the largest-selling collection of newspapers in Britain. Their influence derives from huge readerships together with the proprietor's cultivation of politicians. Murdoch has been keen to foster relationships with governments that could threaten his media interests with new regulations. Tony Blair is one such acquaintance. That said, Murdoch's best-selling daily tabloid, the *Sun*, has not been uncritical of the Labour leader, despite having endorsed him in 1997. During the last parliament it even called Blair the 'Most Dangerous Man in Britain' because of his perceived pro-euro stance.

Table 5.2. Newspapers' political allegiances and circulations[13]

| | 2001 | | 1997 | |
	Allegiance	*Circulation (millions)*	*Allegiance*	*Circulation (millions)*
Dailies				
Sun	Labour	3.45	Labour	3.84
Mirror/Record	Labour	2.79	Labour	3.08
Star	Labour	0.60	Labour	0.73
Mail	Anti-Labour	2.40	Conservative	2.15
Express	Labour	0.96	Conservative	1.22
Telegraph	Conservative	1.02	Conservative	1.13
Guardian	Labour	0.40	Labour	0.40
The Times	Labour	0.71	Eurosceptic	0.72
Independent	Anti-Conservative	0.23	Labour	0.25
Financial Times	Labour	0.49	Labour	0.31
Sundays				
News of the World	Labour	3.90	Conservative	4.37
Sunday Mirror	Labour	1.87	Labour	2.24
People	Labour	1.37	Labour	1.98
Mail on Sunday	Conservative	2.33	Conservative	2.11
Sunday Express	Labour	0.90	Conservative	1.16
Sunday Times	Labour	1.37	Conservative	1.31
Sunday Telegraph	Conservative	0.79	Conservative	0.91
Observer	Labour	0.45	Labour	0.45
Independent on Sunday	Various	0.25	None	0.28

Source: Audit Bureau of Circulation.

Table 5.3. Daily circulation by partisanship (figures in millions)

	2001	1997
Total	13.05	13.83
Supporting Conservatives	1.02 (7.8%)	4.5 (32.5%)
Supporting Labour	9.4 (72.0%)	8.61 (62.2%)
Supporting Liberal Democrats	0	0
Anti-Labour	2.4 (18.4%)	0
Anti-Conservative	0.23 (1.8%)	0
Eurosceptic	0	0.72 (5.2%)
Non-aligned	0	0

Source: Calculations based on figures in Table 5.2.[14]

During the run-up to the campaign the *Sun* published exclusives on the likely date of the election and composition of the next cabinet. This suggested the paper enjoyed privileged access to Number 10 Downing Street. Though it endorsed Labour, successive editorials were respectful to William Hague and sympathetic to his anti-euro platform. Hague's treatment was very different to the crude mockery meted out to past opponents such as the Labour leaders Michael Foot and Neil Kinnock. Not that populist, cliché-ridden journalism was absent from the modern *Sun*. Right-wing columnist Richard Littlejohn savaged the three main leaders and gratuitously insulted Cherie Booth.

The decision by the *Sun* to declare for Blair at the beginning of the election did not have the same impact as it did in 1997. Reflecting a deepening of the relationship between Murdoch and Blair, the other News International titles moved towards the party. Having encouraged readers to vote for named Eurosceptic candidates in 1997, *The Times* had already broken with its long-standing tradition of supporting the Conservatives. In 2001 there was a modest endorsement of Labour. More surprising was the once arch-Thatcherite *Sunday Times*' support for Blair. Arguably these editorial changes had more to do with company than wider politics and may explain the relative lack of interest in these papers' declarations. The biggest-selling Sunday tabloid, the *News of the World*, was noticeably more sincere in its embrace of Blair this time. This stance was aided by the presence of soon to be Labour MP Sion Simon as a political columnist.

Like the *News of the World*, the *Daily Star* had been less than resounding in its endorsement of Labour in 1997. The switch then was probably wise given its readership's overwhelming support for the party. This time the paper's stance was more wholehearted in its embrace of Tony Blair. Under former editors the *Star* had been trenchantly right wing. Political populism in the modern paper now came from left-leaning columnists like Dominik Diamond, who, lamenting New Labour's centrism, declared his intention to abstain. That said, the paper's election coverage was insubstantial. The most animated reporting featured the campaign by a favourite glamour model to become an independent MP in Manchester. The candidate, Jordan, had regularly featured in adult publications owned by Richard Desmond, the paper's new proprietor.

While acquisition of the *Star* complemented his existing media interests, Desmond's purchase of the other Express Group titles has led to difficulty. Once dominant titles in circulation terms, the previously staunchly Conservative *Express* and *Sunday Express* papers are in decline, partly because their ageing readerships are literally dying out. Though they stayed loyal to the Tories in 1997, dramatic editorial changes have repositioned the titles and they now support Labour. Nonetheless, Desmond's tenure has downgraded the papers' news content in favour of celebrity features.

Unlike the Express papers, the *Daily Mail* and *Mail on Sunday* continue to be firmly right wing in outlook. Labour was attacked throughout an election campaign in which the *Daily Mail* also criticised the Liberal Democrats' close proximity to Blair. The least predictable thing the *Mail* did was not formally to endorse the Conservatives. The paper's sympathies were nonetheless obvious and differed little from those of its declared Tory-supporting sister, the *Mail on Sunday*.

Unlike the *Mail*, the *Mirror* has traditionally supported Labour. Yet this relationship has been strained in recent years. Blair's cultivation of the *Sun* has upset Mirror Group executives. The paper retaliated by backing Conservative candidate Steve Norris in the London mayoral elections. The relationship was, however, renewed in time for a 2001 campaign in which the *Mirror* ran a polemical campaign against William Hague. A satirical feature entitled 'Vote Tory' depicted what the paper believed Britain would be like under Hague. The tone of this ridicule was in marked contrast to that adopted during the previous election. Then the *Mirror* had issued a supplement warning of the dire consequences of re-electing the Conservatives and Michael Portillo becoming Prime Minister. Other Mirror Group tabloids gave loyal support to Labour. The *Sunday People* provided the most enthusiastic endorsement of the government. Sister Scottish paper the *Daily Record* continued to support the party despite disagreements between it and the new Labour-led Scottish executive.

Mirror Group broadsheets the *Independent* and *Independent on Sunday* were critical of the Hague leadership. In an editorial the daily urged people to vote against the Conservatives. The paper was probably keen not to alienate its large number of Liberal Democrat readers by coming out for Labour. In a scattergun declaration the *Independent on Sunday* supported the need for more Greens, Liberal Democrats and even moderate Tories. Like the *Independent*, the *Financial Times* opposed the Conservatives' anti-euro stance and again endorsed Labour. Predictably the *Guardian* and its Sunday sister paper, the *Observer*, also fell in behind Blair. In offering support both reiterated liberal left concerns over certain policies. The papers' ideological rivals, the *Daily* and *Sunday Telegraph*, were fulsome in their support for the Conservatives.

The striking point to note about the partisanship of different newspaper readerships is that, unlike in previous elections, there was no clear pattern to it (see Table 5.4). There were modest swings to Labour within the readerships of four of the government-supporting dailies. Of the other sympathetic papers, only the *Express* registered a greater shift towards the party. In marked contrast there was a notable swing towards the Conservatives among *Star* readers. But the most dramatic change involved *Guardian* and *Independent* voters. Here the Liberal Democrats benefited from major defections from Labour. Predictably the readerships of the two anti-government titles, the *Mail* and *Telegraph*, hardened in their already strong support for the Conservatives.

When considering the figures on the partisanship of readers a number of factors need to be taken into account. While editorial content may influence readers it should be noted that the press has been noticeably less strident of late. It is possible that the 'Tory' press did have influence during the 1980s precisely because of the intensity and repetitiveness of its attacks on the then

Table 5.4. Voting intentions of newspaper readers, 2001 (figures in percentages; 1997 equivalents in parentheses)

	Conservatives		Labour		Liberal Democrats		Swing: Labour to Conservatives (Liberal Democrats)
Election result	33	(31)	42	(44)	19	(17)	2
Sun	29	(30)	52	(52)	11	(12)	−0.5
Mirror	11	(14)	71	(72)	13	(11)	−1
Star	21	(17)	56	(66)	17	(12)	7
Mail	55	(49)	24	(29)	17	(14)	5.5
Express	43	(49)	33	(29)	19	(16)	−5
Telegraph	65	(57)	16	(20)	14	(17)	6
Guardian	6	(8)	52	(67)	34	(22)	(13.5)
Independent	12	(16)	38	(47)	44	(30)	(11.5)
The Times	40	(42)	28	(28)	26	(25)	−1
Financial Times	48	(48)	30	(29)	21	(19)	−0.5

Source: MORI.[15]

Labour leadership. This is now not the case. The effect may have been to neutralise the electoral importance of the print media. Furthermore, while the newspapers themselves have changed, so have their readers. Fewer papers are being sold and read. Bucking the trend is the *Mail* and this may offer an explanation for its readers' swing to the Conservatives. Its ability to attract right-wing voters may be directly linked to the declining circulation of the *Express* and in turn that paper's more pro-Labour audience.

The most interesting changes of allegiance occurred among readers of the *Guardian* and *Independent*. These papers' criticisms of Blair's perceived shift to the right might have had some impact. Alternatively the voters may have been predisposed to supporting the Liberal Democrats. Whatever the case, it will undoubtedly encourage the editors to continue with their criticism of the government. Most puzzling was the swing away from Labour among those taking the *Star*. The paper hardly talked about politics and when it did it was generally supportive of the government. This change could, as with the *Express*, be explained by declining market share. A further and perhaps more important factor is that, alone among the dailies, a majority of *Star* readers did not vote in the general election.

Advertising and other media

For the first time in an election politicians were required to obey new limits on the amount they could spend on national campaigning.[16] The rule changes did not, however, prevent parties from producing expensive advertising. Rather the key problem for strategists turned out to be the delay of the general election. Having already booked their sites, the Conservatives displayed posters in the month before the formal launch of the campaign. The main slogan read 'You paid the tax: so where are the teachers?' with alternative versions substituting 'trains', 'hospitals' or 'police' for 'teachers'.

During the actual campaign the Conservatives' agency produced some memorable advertisements, including one featuring a pregnant Blair captioned 'Four years of Labour and he still hasn't delivered'. If the copy rekindled memories of the famous Saatchi and Saatchi agency's work for Thatcher this was not surprising, as the image had originally been used by the firm in a 1970s birth control campaign. Blair was also a target of an eve-of-poll advertisement that called on voters to 'Burst his bubble' and deny a smug looking Prime Minister a second term. Unlike his predecessor John Major, William Hague was largely absent from the party's advertising campaign, which was overwhelmingly negative. It was a telling omission and one that suggested Conservative strategists knew Hague to be an electoral liability.

The TBWA agency's campaign for Labour also used negative or 'knocking' copy. The most memorable images again featured the rival leader. 'Just William' used a picture of a teenage Hague from the time he made his first Conservative conference speech. The image suggested a precocious schoolboy debater in the mould of comedian Harry Enfield's reviled 'Tory Boy' character. Labour strategists were keen to suggest Hague was a clone of Margaret Thatcher. A striking poster featuring Thatcher's hairstyle superimposed on the balding leader's head amplified this attack. The image was recycled in media debates over its appropriateness. Negativity also featured in classic Hollywood film-style posters replete with anti-Tory slogans like 'Economic Disaster II' and 'The Repossessed'.

The negative election advertising marked a change from the pre-campaign strategy of stressing achievements through 'The work goes on' theme. This in turn had followed 'Thank you' advertisements featuring perceived bene-ficiaries expressing their gratitude to Labour's 1997 voters for policies such as the New Deal programme.

For positive campaigning neither major party could outdo the Liberal Democrats. Their modest advertising budget was spent on commissioning a few designs from the Banc agency. These highlighted the party's potential to make an electoral breakthrough and the qualities of leader Charles Kennedy and his policies. Lacking the resources to display posters, the Liberal Democrats relied on television news coverage of launches. Of the minor parties, only the UKIP invested sizeable sums on newspaper advertising, courtesy of helpful donations from Eurosceptic businessman Paul Sykes.

Fewer organisations were granted party election broadcasts (PEBs) than the record numbers that qualified in 1997. Revised rules made it more difficult for smaller parties to get slots. Most PEBs ran for three minutes. This condensed formula encouraged the type of higher-quality production made by advertising agencies and specialist filmmakers. Labour successfully promoted a PEB on government achievements by revealing the guest appearance of pop singer Geri Halliwell. Conveniently for Halliwell this exposure coincided with the release of her new record. More embarrassing was the allegation that the singer was not actually registered to vote (on security grounds). Similar reports followed the final PEB featuring celebrities from youth soap opera Hollyoaks. This unsophisticated film targeted young voters by showing the actors being thanked by various people for taking the trouble to support Labour. The message was undermined when a front-page *Sun* story suggested that one of the celebrities was unable to vote because she was too busy. Other PEBs featured Blair, a cinema-style commercial attacking the Conservatives, and personal testimonies from assorted beneficiaries of Labour's first term.

The Conservatives' PEBs were about as negative as the Liberal Democrats' were positive (see below). Successive broadcasts attacked Labour's record on crime, tax and possible membership of the European single currency. The alleged victims of these policies were represented on screen. William Hague was limited to an appearance in the final PEB. The inability of the most emotive PEBs to provoke debate underlined the Conservatives' problems. One film was criticised for portraying school-aged teenagers as louts. Another, an attack on a government parole scheme, reworked a successful television advertisement that had helped the US Republicans win the presidency in 1988.[17] This attempt to use the same potentially explosive device failed in spite of accusations that Labour's 'soft on crime' policy had led to the premature release of serious repeat criminals, including rapists.

The Liberal Democrats' PEBs set out their main policy objectives and reinforced the party's progressive image. The exception to the series was a broadcast that focused on Charles Kennedy and featured his family in their Highlands community. Kennedy's SNP rivals included similar imagery in quirky films featuring men in kilts and assorted voters crying 'jump!'. The SNP's Welsh counterpart, PC, also received PEBs. Following some uncertainty over the rules, a handful of minor parties qualified for a single PEB apiece. The Greens used children in their film to warn voters of the need to guarantee the environmental welfare of future generations. Acclaimed director Ken Loach made the recently formed Socialist Alliance's first ever PEB. It featured assorted spokespeople putting the Alliance case. Loach's former colleague Ricky Tomlinson appeared alongside Arthur Scargill in their film for the rival left-wing SLP. Famous for his portrayal of Jim in the BBC's *Royle Family* comedy, the actor said his stance had led to the withdrawal of an invitation to make a keynote vote of thanks to his former producer Phil Redmond at the British Soap Awards. Not that politics appeared to be the problem: Tomlinson's replacement turned out to be fellow Liverpudlian Cherie Booth.

Despite some hype and comment this was not really the first 'e-election'.[18] Parties did have websites of varying quality but an Industrial Society survey suggested that as few as 2 per cent of Internet users went on-line for campaign-related information.[19] Several million visits or 'hits' were, however, registered on election-related sites set up by entrepreneurial web designers. Visitors were able to play games such as 'Election invaders' and 'Splat the MP'. Radio 1's site even enabled you to get the noted beer connoisseur William Hague drunk. The other BBC sites were among the most visited during the campaign. These did particularly well on election results night.

After a sustained traditional media advertising campaign the Guardian Unlimited site received over a million visits. Similarly, the less successful Tacticalvoter.net site relied on press and television exposure to mobilise its potential constituency of strategic defectors. Newer technologies such as mobile phones were also used in attempts to cultivate younger voters. Labour, for instance, text-messaged potential supporters with slogans such as 'R U up 4 it?' These voters' parents were the targets of other tactics, including voter videos featuring actor Tony Robinson and a women's magazine, *Your Family*, which used assorted celebrities to promote government achievements. The major parties also did a considerable amount of telephone canvassing in an attempt to mobilise their core and potential supporters.

Conclusion

Like the result, the media's role in the 2001 general election was broadly similar to that in 1997. Many journalists and voters once again complained of boredom with the campaign. The most surprising thing, besides the Deputy Prime Minister punching someone, was the low turnout. This trend was reflected in the apparent audience desertion of election coverage across all media. The public service broadcasters will, in particular, be keen to reassess their approach to the apparent growth in public disaffection with the democratic process. Commercially owned newspapers may opt to downgrade their coverage further, to suit their marketing strategy.

The continuity with the 1997 general election is perhaps most striking in relation to the generally neutral or supportive newspaper treatment of Labour. Nevertheless, it should be noted that while many of these newspapers were highly conditional in supporting the party they did appear more enthusiastic about Tony Blair. There were even some new members of the so-called 'Tony' press. Once staunchly Conservative, the *Express* titles' decision to support Labour in 2001 was symbolic of the changed mediated political culture. Here a party that had been in office for four years received less criticism than in previous campaigns when it had been the official opposition for some time. The majority of newspapers appeared to want to back the winner. This of course may be to do with following their readerships but, as proprietors like Rupert Murdoch show, it is also about organisational rather than wider political concerns. When politicians change their opinion journalists often interpret this as a sign of weakness; when newspapers do the same it is supposedly an indication of their virtue.

Notes

1 I am grateful to David Deacon and other colleagues in the Loughborough University Communications Centre for their thoughts on this and other issues discussed in this chapter.
2 P. Norris *et al.*, *On Message: Communicating the Campaign* (London: Sage, 1999); K. Newton and M. Brynin, 'The national press and party voting in the UK', *Political Studies*, 49 (2001), pp. 265–85.
3 B. McNair, *An Introduction to Political Communication* (London: Routledge, 1999).
4 Comment made on BBC Radio 4's *Broadcasting House*, 13 May 2001.
5 W. Miller, *Media and Voters* (Oxford: Clarendon, 1991).
6 B. Franklin, *Packaging Politics* (London: Edward Arnold, 1994); N. Jones, *Soundbites and Spin Doctors* (London: Cassell, 1995).
7 B. Franklin, *Tough on Soundbites, Tough on the Causes of Soundbites: New Labour and News Management* (London: Catalyst Trust, 1998); N. Jones, *Sultans of Spin* (London: Victor Gollancz, 1999); S. Barnett and I. Gaber, *Westminster Tales – The 21st Century Crisis in Political Journalism* (London: Continuum, 2001).
8 A. Marr, 'The retreat of the spin doctors', *British Journalism Review*, 12:2 (2001), pp. 6–12.
9 Loughborough University Communications Research Centre analysed over 3,000 items from the newspapers listed in Table 5.4 plus the *Scotsman* and *Daily Record*, *Today* (8–9 a.m.) on BBC Radio 4 and the five terrestrial television stations' main evening news bulletins. See P. Golding and D. Deacon, 'An election that many watched but few enjoyed', *Guardian*, 12 June 2001. Note that, for coding purposes, some of the categories for 1997 and 2001 have changed but there are obvious overlaps between, for instance, 'Election process' and 'Conduct of the campaign'.
10 D. Deacon, P. Golding and M. Billig, 'Press and broadcasting: "real issues" and real coverage in the 2001 campaign', *Parliamentary Affairs*, general election special issue (forthcoming, 2001).
11 Golding and Deacon, 'An election that many watched but few enjoyed'.
12 Miller, *Media and Voters*; M. Linton, 'Was it the *Sun* wot won it?', Seventh Guardian Lecture, Nuffield College, 30 October 1995.
13 Allegiance is determined by the newspapers' editorial declaration for a particular party.
14 It should be remembered that readerships are often two to three times the size of circulations.
15 I am grateful to Ben Marshall of MORI's Social Research Institute for these figures.
16 The new rules on spending are being overseen and enforced by the recently established Electoral Commission.
17 K. Hall Jamieson, *Dirty Politics* (New York: Oxford University Press, 1991).
18 R. Gibson, S. Ward and J. Crookes, 'Was this the first e-election? Yes and no', *Fabian Review* (2001), summer.
19 J. Crabtree, *Whatever Happened to the E-Lection?* (London: Industrial Society, 2001). See http://www.indsoc.co.uk/isociety/resources.htm.

Brentwood and Ongar

One of the most unusual contests of the election was that in the Essex constituency of Brentwood and Ongar. Former BBC war reporter Martin Bell had been victorious in the Cheshire constituency of Tatton in a famous contest in 1997. In defeating Conservative Neil Hamilton on the issue of sleaze (although Hamilton still maintains his innocence) Bell pledged to his constituents that he would serve only one term, a pledge, given his love of parliament, he was soon to regret. The independent, now dubbed 'ethics man', chose to stand in Brentwood and Ongar after allegations of sleaze in respect of the local Conservative Party. It was claimed that the Peniel Pentecostal Church had infiltrated the local organisation, mainly in the Pilgrim's Hatch ward.

To Bell's critics, the charges looked a thin veneer, exaggerated to sate his desire to remain an MP. The incumbent Conservative MP, Eric Pickles, had no connection with the Church. He argued that Bell combined 'evangelical zeal and naivety' (*The Times*, 21 May 2001). Furthermore, as a local Labour supporter told the *Guardian* (23 May 2001) 'there's no suggestion that that church controls him [Pickles] ... I can't understand why Bell got involved'. Bell defended his candidature on the grounds that he had received 200 letters asking him to stand. Declining to attack Pickles, Bell conducted a campaign reminiscent of Tatton. This time, however, he was opposed by the Labour and Liberal Democrat parties, making any prospect of unseating Pickles even more remote, whatever Bell's claim that Pickles' majority of 9,000 was 'nothing' (*The Times*, 21 May 2001). It was a tribute to Bell's personal popularity that he achieved a very respectable vote. While targeting the Conservatives, Bell appeared to draw votes from all parties. The Conservatives' share of the vote fell by 7 per cent, but Labour's fell by 9.5 per cent and the Liberal Democrats suffered most, with an 11 per cent drop. Personality politics and disillusionment with the main parties, rather than major concerns with sleaze in Brentwood and Ongar, almost allowed Bell a second term and enabled him to bow out with dignity intact.

Result

Brentwood and Ongar		
	No. of votes	% of vote
Pickles, E. (Conservative)	16,558	38.0
Bell, M. (Independent)	13,737	31.6
Kendall, D. (Liberal Democrat)	6,772	15.6
Johnson, D. (Labour)	5,505	12.6
Gulleford, K. (UKIP)	611	1.4
Others	359	0.8
Conservative majority	2,821	6.5
Conservative hold		
Turnout		67.3

6

Exorcising ghosts: how Labour dominated the economic argument

Mark Wickham-Jones

Introduction: the ghosts of economic mismanagement

During the long run-in to the May 1997 general election, the Labour Party was haunted by its past failures of economic management.[1] Whether such failures were real or imagined was, in one sense, irrelevant. What mattered was a widespread perception, among commentators, voters and politicians alike, that past Labour governments had not handled the economy successfully. Negative images from previous administrations included the general austerity of the 1945–51 Attlee government's economic approach, especially the devaluation of 1949. This severity was followed by the deflations of the 1964–70 Wilson administration, which failed to prevent another humiliating devaluation in 1967 as financial markets forced policy realignment upon Britain. Most recent were the experiences of the Wilson (1974–76) and Callaghan (1976–79) governments: administrations that had appeared to stagger from crisis to crisis, teetering on the brink of hyperinflation, dabbling with pseudo-monetarism, and seemingly unable to control events. Labour's long record of fiascos included the 1976 International Monetary Fund (IMF) crisis, in which a foreign institution was apparently needed to dictate the terms of necessary but painful economic adjustments, and the 'winter of discontent', in which the fragile strategy of the Callaghan administration was shattered by greedy trade unions.[2] Taken together such episodes demonstrated an innate weakness on the part of the Labour Party: given, among other factors, its commitments to the trade unions and to redistributive policies, Labour could not be trusted with the economic wellbeing of the UK.

In the mid-1990s, for leading figures within New Labour, most obviously Tony Blair, its leader, and Gordon Brown, the shadow Chancellor, exorcising the ghosts of economic mismanagement was a central objective. Before the May 1997 general election, they went to extraordinary lengths to assuage business fears about the modesty of their intentions. Before and after May 1997, they distanced themselves repeatedly from the measures of the past. Of course, they were also critical of Conservative administrations. Brown

103

disparaged the 'crude Keynesian fine tuning of the fifties and sixties and the crude monetarism of the seventies' that had characterised economic policy.[3] In his 1999 Mais Lecture, one of the defining statements of his Chancellorship, Brown condemned 'vested interests cooking up compromises in smoke filled rooms'. The resulting policies 'broke down in a series of divisive conflicts'.[4] In his 2001 Labour Party conference speech, Brown was again dismissive of the past:

> And let me tell conference that our spending plans are affordable precisely because we have not made the mistakes of the last two Labour governments who, by refusing to take early action to maintain stability ended up cutting, not increasing, public spending – and were denied the capacity to fulfil their social goals.[5]

As well as condemning Labour's record in office, Blair and Brown criticised the party's promises made in opposition. Discussing the party's strategy during the 1980s, Blair was blunt: 'What they [voters] were frightened of was the fact that they thought the Labour party wasn't going to run a sensible economic policy and was just itching to get their taxes up whenever we could.'[6]

Once in office, Labour's leaders followed a cautious path in terms of economic policy. One of the administration's guiding principles appeared to be not to repeat past mistakes. Indeed, for the first two years of office they accepted the public spending plans laid out by John Major's Conservative administration. Commentators and academics noted that many of Labour's economic policies were stolen from the Major government: they concluded that a new, effectively right-wing consensus had emerged in British politics.[7] In May 2001, in an interview, Blair said, 'in the first term we were proving why it [his administration] wasn't the old Labour party. How you [his government] could be trusted with the economy, trusted on issues of tax, sensible, mainstream and centre-ground.'[8] Such were the objectives of Blair's first administration.

By 2001, the ghosts of past economic disappointments had been exorcised successfully. During the first term of the Blair administration, two economic storms (the inheritance of an overheating economy in 1997; and the Far East crisis of 1998) were weathered. Inflation remained low, declining to its lowest level since the 1960s, while the numbers of unemployed had fallen impressively, dropping below one million for the first time since 1975. Growth averaged 2.9 per cent (an improvement on the rate achieved under the Conservatives) and public finances shifted into surplus.[9] To be sure, such an outcome did not mean that, at some stage in the future, a Labour administration would not run into economic difficulties of its own making. It was by no means certain where the praise for economic success between 1997 and 2001 should be directed: many commentators concluded it was due partly to the judgement of Chancellor Gordon Brown and partly to his luck.[10]

Labour's economic approach might not have fared so well in more testing economic circumstances. Moreover, such success had been attained, arguably, at a high cost in terms of the extent to which New Labour had abandoned interventionist policies aimed at egalitarian goals, the *raison d'être* for many of the social democratic project. Nevertheless, the completion of a full parliamentary term without the eruption of the kind of economic crisis that had bedevilled previous Labour administrations was, in the eyes of many commentators, a major achievement.

An indication of Labour's success was given by the praise offered to Brown by the IMF and by another international body, the OECD, which had been a stringent critic of previous Labour administrations. In February 2001, the IMF Article IV annual consultation endorsed Labour's economic approach: 'The United Kingdom is experiencing the longest period of sustained non-inflationary output growth in more than 30 years.'[11] The report continued, 'These substantial gains are due in no small measure to strengthened macroeconomic and structural policies underpinned by improved monetary and fiscal policy frameworks.' The OECD noted, 'the credibility of monetary policy has improved considerably over the past few years'.[12] Though guarded, it concluded, 'These changes [in economic policy under Labour] are welcome and in certain ways narrow the scope for opportunistic tinkering.' Public finances had been placed on a 'sound footing'.[13]

Popular support and economic management

There was a wider, electoral dimension to Brown's management of the economy during Labour's first term. Between May 1997 and June 2001 Labour dominated the economic argument between the major political parties in a persistent and transparent fashion. The opinion pollsters Gallup regularly ask respondents which party, Conservatives or Labour, has the better economic policy. In the fort-nine months of the first Blair administration, more respondents, in every poll, bar one (September 2001), favoured Labour over the Conservatives. Several points about Labour's ascendancy over the Conservatives concerning the economy and economic policy can be noted.

First, the extent of Labour's domination is striking. The lead established by Tony Blair's government over William Hague's opposition was neither erratic nor tenuous. Month after month, Labour led by huge margins: in only five months did the lead dip below 10 per cent and in only one month did the Conservatives briefly take the lead, by the slenderest of margins (see Figure 6.1).

Second, Labour's success is all the more remarkable when the previous difficulties, noted above, that the party had encountered in economic management are recalled. On this issue, the party trailed the Conservatives in the run-up to the 1992 general election. An indication of Labour's success in 2001 is given by a comparison of the government's lead with that the party

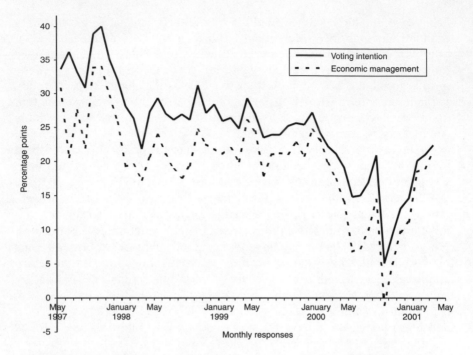

Figure 6.1. Labour's lead in voting intention and in economic management, 1997–2001.
Sources: A. King (ed.), *British Political Opinion 1937–2000. The Gallup Polls* (London: Politico's, 2001), pp. 24–5, 118–19; Gallup Political and Economic Index.

enjoyed in the run-up to 1997 general election. In the months before May 1997 Labour's lead had dipped to around 12 per cent: in 2001, following a brief drop in the preceding autumn, it had surged forward once again, averaging over 20 per cent.[14]

Third, disaggregating the different core economic issues of unemployment, taxation and inflation highlights the extent of Labour's supremacy. In April 1997 Labour led the Conservatives on tackling unemployment by 28 per cent.[15] Four years later, Labour's rating had risen even higher, by a further twenty per cent, over the opposition.[16] On tax, the issue that had done so much damage to Neil Kinnock's hopes at the April 1992 general election, Labour had enjoyed a slender advantage in April 1997, of 6 per cent. By May 2001, the government led by 16 per cent.[17] In April 1997, Labour trailed the Conservatives as the party better able to deal with inflation. Once elected, that deficit was transformed into a Labour lead, an advantage that persisted in the 2001 general election. By May 2001, Labour was preferred on this issue over the Conservatives by 30 per cent of respondents.[18]

Fourth, there appears to be a clear link between Labour's advantage over the Conservatives concerning economic management and the party's lead over William Hague's opposition in terms of voting intention. Figure 6.1 indicates how the two moved closely together, rising after the 1997 general election, dipping during the autumn of 2000, before rising once again in the run-up to June 2001.[19] The figure is based on two questions. First, if there was a general election tomorrow, which party would you vote for? Second, with Britain in economic difficulties, which party do you think could handle the problem best – the Conservative Party or the Labour Party? According to the Gallup figures, Labour's poll lead peaked in October 1997 at 40.0 per cent; the same month saw the party's lead on economic management peak at 33.9 per cent. In September 2000, the opposition secured their best result concerning voting intention: they cut Labour's lead to 5.1 per cent. That month was the only occasion on which Labour lost its lead as the party better able to manage the economy (by 1.0 per cent).[20]

In the remainder of this chapter, I examine Labour's management of the economy and ask how the government was able to dominate economic arguments between the main parties so successfully from May 1997 to June 2001. The chapter proceeds as follows. In the next sections, I discuss, in turn, Labour's approach to monetary and fiscal policy. In each, I focus on the government's commitment to economic stability. In the following section, I address the other, microeconomic aspects of Gordon Brown's economic strategy. It is important to note that the government's economic strategy has encountered some difficulties: a section is devoted to them. The next section discusses briefly the economic policy marshalled by the Conservatives. (I raise some points about Conservative economic policy at other relevant places.) For reasons of space, tinged with political realism, I do not address the economic strategies of the Liberal Democrats, the SNP or Plaid Cymru. It is important to note, however, that devolution in Northern Ireland, Scotland and Wales raises significant questions for the future regarding the economic management of the UK and the coherence of any strategy implemented at Westminster. The economic tensions of devolution played no part in the 2001 general election and I do not attend to them.

The new monetary policy agenda: economics without politics?

In speeches and in interviews, Gordon Brown committed the Labour government to the goals of full employment and economic growth.[21] The former was defined as 'employment opportunity for all'.[22] To secure these objectives, he outlined a number of conditions that must be met. The conditions varied: compare his Mais Lecture with his speeches to the IFS and to the Royal Economic Society.[23] Broadly, however, they revolved around similar themes, including stability, employability and productivity. I discuss these conditions below, starting with stability, which can be attained via two main routes, that of monetary policy and that of fiscal policy. One point should be observed.

Understandably, commentators and scholars have focused on the Chancellor's pursuit of economic stability. It remained the central, defining pillar of his strategy ('The foundation of all we do').[24] We should not, however, lose sight of the other conditions that have formed part of Brown's approach to economic matters. One of his constant refrains has been that 'prudence is for a purpose': economic stability is a means to other objectives, including full employment and the creation of a fairer society.[25]

On 6 May 1997, Brown met the Governor of the Bank of England for a routine meeting to discuss interest rates, under the arrangements established by the Conservatives in the aftermath of 'Black Wednesday', 16 September 1992, the occasion on which the United Kingdom was ejected from membership of the European Exchange Rate Mechanism (ERM). As expected, Brown elected to increase interest rates by 0.25 per cent. The decision was to be his first and last in setting interest rates. He announced that he was handing over operational responsibility for the conduct of monetary policy to the Bank of England. A new Monetary Policy Committee (MPC), made up of nine members (five Bank officials and four outsiders), would make future decisions concerning interest rates. The Chancellor would set the inflation target to which the MPC would work and would appoint the four outsiders (as well as the Governor and two Deputy Governors who would sit on the committee). A Treasury official would be in attendance at the meetings of the MPC. Brown's decision took immediate effect and was subsequently legislated in the 1998 Bank of England Act. A month later, Brown fleshed out the arrangements in his Mansion House speech: if the MPC missed the inflation target by more than 1 per cent the Governor would write an open letter to the Chancellor explaining the circumstances.[26]

Giving independence to the Bank of England was undoubtedly the single most important economic decision taken by Labour during its first term back in office. The new MPC became Brown's key means to attaining economic stability. The decision had been planned in the run-up to the election, following a trip to the United States and discussions with Alan Greenspan at the Federal Reserve. Ed Balls, Brown's influential economic adviser, had long been a proponent of such a reform. Blair was consulted at a relatively late stage and the cabinet was not involved in the decision. Brown's move was widely praised: the stock market FT-SE 100 index hit a record high in its wake. *The Times* described it as 'one of the biggest changes in economic policy-making this century'.[27] The *Financial Times* commented, 'For investors, this looks like unequivocally good news'.[28]

The decision to give operational independence to the Bank of England took many commentators as well as financial markets by surprise. It is easy to see why. Although the move was understandable, given the emphasis placed by Labour while in opposition on establishing credibility, it had been explicitly ruled out by Brown and Blair in policy documents and speeches. Before May 1997, they placed considerable weight upon attaining a trustworthy reputation: in effect they promised a series of measures that were intended to persuade financial markets about the manifest moderation of their intent. Brown and Blair hoped that, because there could be no deviation from the trajectory they had laid out in such detail without a massive and extremely damaging loss in credibility, they would be believed. In office, they opted instead for a simpler rules-based approach in which they handed over the control of monetary policy to non-elected officials.

In later speeches, Brown acknowledged explicitly how much of the monetarist argument that controlling inflation was the single most important responsibility of a government he had accepted.[29] It was also apparent that finding a credible, non-politicised mechanism by which to attain low inflation was central to the Chancellor's approach. In his statement about giving independence to the Bank, Brown commented, 'We must remove the suspicion that short-term party political considerations are influencing the setting of interest rates'.[30] In his 1999 Mais Lecture, Brown endorsed Milton Friedman's 1968 presidential address to the American Economics Association: 'the long term effect of trying to buy less unemployment with more inflation is simply to ratchet up both ... conclusive evidence for this proposition came in the 1980s'.[31] The Chancellor broke with the founding father of modern monetarism over his policy recommendation: 'while Friedman's diagnosis was right his prescription was wrong'. The simplistic notion of a link between the money supply and inflation was misplaced. However, Brown went on, 'The answer is not no rules, but the right rules'. Granting independence to the Bank provided the basis for those rules. Brown's acceptance, albeit qualified, of the monetarist case was an indication of how far Labour had come and just how much the terms of economic discourse had changed. To be sure, in the 1970s his predecessor, Denis Healey, had flirted with the paraphernalia of monetarism. But it had been a reluctant monetarism, one dictated by circumstances. Healey's approach was characterised as 'monetarily constrained Keynesianism' by one economist, a case of monetarism *à mal avis*.[32]

There were several advantages of giving independence to the Bank. Economic theory suggested it was a quick route by which to secure a tough anti-inflationary reputation. The officials setting interest rates could be trusted in their anti-inflation intent: they would work in a uncomplicated fashion towards meeting the inflation target and would not be liable to the kind of temptations that could entice politicians, however honest they might be. Such integrity was imperative to economic wellbeing: 'governments which lack credibility – which are pursuing policies which are not seen to be sustainable – are punished not only more swiftly than in the past but more severely and at a greater cost to their future credibility'.[33] Not only did the government demonstrate its trustworthiness with regard to ensuring low inflation, potentially at any rate, but Bank independence also provided a significant means of blame avoidance. When interest rates went up in future, it would be as a result of the MPC's deliberations and not directly because of the actions of a Labour Chancellor. Moreover, the quick decision, within days of taking office, gave a clear signal to markets about Labour's intent: this decision was not one that had been forced on a reluctant government in the face of external economic pressure.

Politically, the decision wrong-footed the opposition: effectively it outflanked them by taking control of what was the Conservatives' natural territory, a tough anti-inflationary position. More than that, it served as an indictment of their past record. The widespread positive response to Labour's decision was indicative that, under previous administrations, interest rate decisions had been perceived to be politicised, a judgement reinforced by the comments of Nigel Lawson and Norman Lamont, former Conservative Chancellors.

There were drawbacks, potential ones at any rate. For the previous eighteen years, setting the interest rate had been a central component, arguably the pivotal element, of the Conservatives' battery of policy measures. At different times, changes in interest rates had been aligned with the money supply, the rate of inflation and the exchange rate. In a memorable criticism, during a House of Commons debate in March 1989, the former Conservative Prime Minister Edward Heath had described the then Chancellor of the Exchequer, Nigel Lawson, as a 'one-club golfer' because of his reliance upon the interest rate to the apparent exclusion of other policy devices.[34] Yet here was a new government, consisting of a party that had been out of office for nearly twenty years, handing over the golf club to another player while asking to remain in the tournament on the basis of someone else's performance. Control of an important lever of economic policy had been given to officials who might not be sufficiently sensitive to the wider realities of making economic policy. A hawkish Bank might have little regard for any other policy objectives. The existence of two centres of economic policy making, the Treasury and the Bank, might lead to tension between fiscal policy (regarding taxation and public spending) and monetary policy (regarding inflation). It remained to be seen how the new arrangements would work in practice.

During Labour's first term, the work of the MPC can be divided into three phases. The first phase, between June 1997, when the committee first met, and December 1997, marked its foundation. In this period, the MPC was under-strength as its members joined gradually and voted unanimously.[35] In a fairly non-controversial manner, the MPC increased interest rates four times in six months. The second phase, between January 1998 and February 2000, was characterised by frequent disagreements in the MPC and considerable policy activism. Some commentators had been concerned about the impact that split votes (publicised when the minutes of meetings were subsequently published) would have on market confidence. In the twenty-six monthly meetings in this period, however, the MPC split on twenty-two occasions. On two occasions (February and March 1998), Eddie George as Governor made use of his second casting vote to force a result. On three occasions, the committee split three ways: while most members favoured no change in interest rates, one favoured a cut and one an increase. In this phase, twelve alterations were made to interest rates. Having peaked at 7.5 per cent in June 1998, the MPC then cut them down to 5.0 per cent by June 1999, before they crept back up once again. The third phase of the MPC's work lasted from March 2000 to the date of the general election in June 2001. This period was characterised by less policy activism: in sixteen months only three changes were made to interest rates and, though split at times, on five occasions the committee voted unanimously.

Several points can be noted about the work of the MPC. First, the public splits between members of the committee did not appear to damage market confidence in its work. During the second phase, it became clear who were the 'hawks' (those who favoured pre-emptive increases in interest rates to squeeze inflation out of the economy) and who were the 'doves' (those who were concerned by the impact high interest rates might have on the private sector). Eddie George's authority as Governor was an important aspect of the reputation that the MPC quickly attained. During Labour's first term, the committee never voted against his own preference. (That two of the Bank members of the MPC usually voted with him helped in establishing this pattern: David Clementi, Deputy Governor, and Ian Plenderleith voted against George on only three occasions.)

Second, the policy activism of the second phase was probably unnecessary: the MPC moved quickly to get interest rates up and down in response to economic events and statistical data. Arguably, a more cautious approach, such as that in evidence during the third phase, would have worked just as well. The second phase saw more interest rate changes than in many other countries.[36]

Third, it was the academic economists on the MPC who turned out to be the hawks. This outcome is surprising. Economic theory leads us to anticipate that non-elected officials (such as George, Clementi and Plenderleith) would be insensitive to the difficulties that high interest rates might place upon economic actors. Academic economists might be expected to be aware of these pressures. In practice, during two spells, one in 1998 and one in 2000, the academic economists voted on several occasions unsuccessfully for higher rates against the preference of the officials.

Fourth, the MPC's record between 1997 and 2001 does not preclude future conflict with government. Certainly the independence of the MPC means that it serves as a direct check on the government's fiscal policy: the framework of monthly meetings will act as a constant reminder to any administration that the integrity of its policy is under scrutiny. During 1998, as interest rates rose, press reports indicated that some members of the Labour administration were concerned at the apparent determination of the MPC to control inflation regardless of any short-term costs. It is by no means certain that the open letter system devised by Brown is sufficiently flexible, as Ed Balls claimed in his advocacy of 'constrained discretion', to react to exogenous shocks.[37] For example, members of the MPC might choose to pursue the inflation target despite temporary economic difficulties: such a decision to avoid the open letter mechanism could result in greater volatility of output than would otherwise be the case. Equally, adverse market reaction to the open letter, on the basis of its apparent lack of credibility, might lead to falling confidence and thus an exacerbation of the economic situation. Between 1997 and 2001, the open letter process remained untested.

Many commentators, including some erstwhile critics, concluded that the MPC had played an important part in attaining the low rate of inflation that the United Kingdom enjoyed during Labour's term in office between 1997 and 2001. Probably the decision to hand over control to the committee helped simply to adjust inflationary expectations downwards. The IMF concluded that 'The monetary policy framework appears to be working well'.[38] The OECD maintained that 'The monetary policy framework inaugurated in mid-1997 is still relatively new but has performed well thus far, not least in comparison with the previous regimes'.[39] One possible downside to the MPC's success in achieving low inflation was a high value of the pound, the consequence of cautious committee members pushing interest rates higher than was, arguably at an rate, absolutely necessary to meet the inflation target.

The golden rule: fiscal policy

The work of the MPC was not the only means by which economic stability was pursued between 1997 and 2001. Gordon Brown complemented monetary policy with a tight fiscal stance. Following a similar logic to that underlying the decision to give independence to the Bank of England, in opposition he had proposed two rules with which to govern the conduct of fiscal policy: first, the so-called 'golden rule' that the government should borrow only to invest (and not to consume); and second, that the ratio of public debt to national income should be stabilised over the economic cycle. The first rule limited the use to which public borrowing could be put. The second rule limited the extent of that borrowing by placing a ceiling on it over any period of economic expansion and retrenchment. Both rules gave the Chancellor some discretion: most obviously the definition of investment was an unresolved issue. Nevertheless, with the publication and legislation of *The Code of Fiscal Responsibility* in 1998, Brown made plain his commitment to a rules-based approach. He also brought in the National Audit Office to examine fiscal policy and public finances.

In January 1997, Brown promised to adopt the Conservative spending plans for the first two years of a Labour government. It was a move intended to reassure markets and voters about the party's probity. Once again, it wrong-footed the Major administration; and, for a time at any rate after

1997, it placed William Hague's opposition on the defensive. How could they criticise a government that had adopted their own plans? That Labour stuck to the projections when many senior Conservatives felt the plans to have been unrealistically tight added to the opposition's discomfort.

As well as stringent control over public spending, Brown's tough fiscal stance was enhanced by taxation increases during the first Blair administration. In his first budget, in July 1997, the Chancellor introduced a windfall tax on the privatised utilities, the one taxation increase to which the party had committed itself in opposition. This move was accompanied by the unexpected abolition of tax credits on dividends. By June 2001 a series of revenue-raising measures had been implemented: major changes included the reduction followed by the abolition of both mortgage tax relief and married person's tax allowances; increases in stamp duty and the road fuel escalator (the latter was a decision that led to political difficulties); and the raising of the NI ceiling. These tax increases were accompanied by reductions in corporation tax, a 1 per cent cut in the basic rate of income tax (in March 1999) and in value added tax (VAT) on fuel. In all, the net revenue raised was around £38 billion.[40] A further indication of Brown's cautious approach to the public finances is given by the use of the £22 billion raised from the auction of third-generation mobile phone licences to pay off the national debt.

A striking feature of many of Brown's tax increases is that they were 'illusory'. Given that they did not have an immediate effect on pay packets (or for that matter, with some exceptions, on everyday purchases), they had no obviously noticeable direct and instant impact on most people's welfare. They were not politically salient in the way that increases in the rates of income tax would have been. The Conservatives described them as 'stealth taxes'. For example, the removal of tax credits on dividends did not have a transparent direct bearing on incomes, yet by 1999/2000 it was raising £5.4 billion a year. Brown may have learnt from the Conservatives. In the mid-1990s they had paid a high political price for the clear and phased increase of taxation. By the autumn of 2000, however, protests against fuel tax increases suggested that there might be limits to further increases by stealth.[41]

The result of Brown's miserly approach was that public finances improved considerably between 1997 and 2001. From a deficit on entering office, they moved into a surplus of £4.5 billion in 1998/99 and one of £18.0 billion in 1999/2000. Assessing the extent to which Brown's policies were directly responsible for this dramatic improvement is difficult. There were three other reasons that also contributed to the turnaround. First, the tax increases of the Major administration played a part in putting revenue on a sounder footing. Second, a buoyant economy meant tax revenues were increasing (regardless of any change to the structure and rates of taxation) while falling unemployment meant less public spending was required on those out of work. Third, a degree of underspending by departments played a part. Public spending as a percentage of GDP fell from 41.2 per cent in 1996/97 to 37.7 per cent

in 1999/2000. State expenditure fell in real terms between 1996–97 and
1999–2000.

Retaining the Conservatives' public spending plans was politically hazardous
for the Blair administration. It meant that a previously announced cut in
lone-parent benefit had to be enforced by Labour, a decision that generated
considerable back-bench disquiet. The cut was unnecessary but by the stage
at which this became clear the government's credibility was at stake.[42] To
offset unrest, Brown made carefully orchestrated announcements about future
spending at particular points. In July 1997 he raided the contingency reserve
to increase the allocations to health and education. In July 1998 he announced
further increases, though in reality the extent of these proved to be disappointing.

Two years later, the Comprehensive Spending Review (CSR) heralded a
change in direction for the government. The review was published in July
2000. In it, the government laid out new plans for public expenditure for
three years from 2001–2 to 2003–4. In these plans, Brown committed the
administration to significant increases, mainly for capital investment projects,
in most areas of public spending, starting in 2001. Health (£13 billion) and
education (£12 billion) were each allocated around 6 per cent extra over the
rate of inflation. Larry Elliott in the *Guardian* noted the contrast with previous
Labour administrations:

> At this point in Wilson's governments, a chancellor would have been outlining
> spending cuts, not increases. In the 60s and 70s the announcement would
> have been the start of the slippery slope to election defeat. The mood could
> not have been more different yesterday.[43]

After difficult years, Brown had dug deep into his war chest (reserves of
public revenue), though the results of the CSR would also mean a return
to deficit for the public finances. The CSR appeared to signal a notable shift
in governmental priorities. In 1999 Labour had cut income tax: in 2000,
the emphasis was on increases in public spending. It proved extremely popular
with the public. In one poll, 87 per cent of respondents supported it and
only 11 per cent were against it.[44] The poll was an indication that the trade-
off between tax cuts and spending increases might have shifted in favour
of the latter.

The microeconomic Treasury

Stability was not, as noted above, the only condition for which Brown worked.
His economic strategy included a number of other objectives. These included
full employment, economic growth and the reduction of poverty. The main
measure by which Labour sought to increase employment was the New Deal,
a package put together by Brown in November 1995. Under the scheme,

young people out of work between the ages of eighteen and twenty-four were offered on one of four choices: a subsidised job in the private sector, voluntary work, a place on an environmental taskforce or a return to education. The New Deal was significant because of its conditionality: those who refused to participate lost part of their benefit. In office, the programme was run from the Department for Education and Employment. However, both Blair and Brown took a great deal of interest in its operation.

Several features of the New Deal in practice were significant. First, the process by which the unemployed were prepared for an option (called the Gateway) was much more important than had been anticipated. Many, around 60 per cent of participants, left it directly to go into work and other activities. Second, the private sector subsidised option was much less relevant than had been planned: only around 40,000 (out of 540,000 entrants) were found such work. New Labour continued to emphasise the importance of private sector support for the scheme. Third, having begun as a temporary programme, such was the New Deal's success that Labour decided to entrench and expand it. It became a permanent feature of the government's labour market policy and a Green Paper in March 2001 indicated that it would be extended to a variety of groups in society.[45] Fourth, having been projected as expensive, it proved to be relatively cheap. By 2001 only £1 billion of the £5.2 billion earmarked from the windfall tax had gone on the New Deal (because of the success of the Gateway). The New Deal had been one of the government's five key pledges at the 1997 general election: in November 2000, the target of getting 250,000 young unemployed people into work was met, though not all had permanent jobs and not all the work was unsubsidised.

Critics of the New Deal questioned the quality of the options and noted the impermanence of many of the jobs into which participants went. Many ended up back on benefit. On over 30,000 occasions sanctions were applied while some participants were given mandatory placements on an option not of their choosing. The cost of the scheme per job created was condemned. A further question concerned how many of the beneficiaries would have found jobs in any case: the fall in the number of young unemployed people did not greatly outstrip the general decline in joblessness. A similar fall in unemployment had occurred in the last years of John Major's administration. Some commentators argued that the fall was much more a result of the prevailing benevolent economic circumstances than of the arrangements of the New Deal. Defenders of the government retorted that the economic circumstances reflected the success of Brown's search for stability.

Attempts by the Labour administration to increase productivity and growth were, on the whole, less successful and attracted less attention. In opposition Brown had attracted ridicule for his endorsement of 'post-endogenous neo-classical growth theory'. In government, little progress was made in implementing measures, though some tax changes were made to improve incentives for investment. In November 2000, following the IMF's draft report, Brown stated, 'I agree with the IMF that we need to focus on the need to improve our productivity performance, what they describe as the "Achilles' heal of an otherwise strong economy"'.[46] Part of the Chancellor's claim was that, in time, the benefits of economic stability would filter through to generate productivity gains.

Labour made better progress, arguably at any rate, in tackling poverty and in creating a fairer society. The government chose employment as its main route: the poor would become better off by taking jobs. In a series of measures, Brown sought to integrate the tax and benefits systems to remove traps whereby people were better off on benefit than in employment. The most important measure, announced in the 1998 budget, was the working families tax credit (WFTC). The credit operated by offering an automatic top-up to those in work on low incomes. For some families it meant a huge increase in income: one million households received it.[47] The WFTC was complemented by the minimum wage and, from 2001, a children's tax credit.

Brown's approach involved more targeting of benefits on those who were identified as being most in need. On occasion, this targeting backfired. As universal benefits were downgraded in importance, in 2000 the government increased the old-age pension by 75p per week, an addition that seemed mean-spirited and calculated to generate resentment. Blair admitted later that it was a mistake. The miniscule raise was offset by other, often targeted benefits for pensioners, including the introduction of a minimum pension guarantee. As errors go, this one was expensive: Brown improved on the 75p increase with a £5.00 per week rise in April 2001.

Overall, between 1997 and 2001, the impact of Brown's budgets was redistributive: benefits were channelled so that the worst off gained while the best off paid more, though not that much more, in tax. In 1999, one study concluded that:

> the three Labour budgets [thus far] contain changes which together significantly redistribute resources towards low-income households. The lower the income on average, the higher the proportional increase in income.[48]

In 2000, the proposals in Brown's last pre-budget report were acclaimed as especially generous. Andrew Dilnot of the IFS argued:

> These are very, very substantial changes. It really is a dramatic change.... I can't think of any economic measure giving such a large group of the population gains on this scale in 20 years of tax and benefits policy.[49]

Figures from the IFS indicated an income gain of 10 per cent for those in the poorest tenth of the population (higher for particular categories within that group) while for the top tenth the gain was just 1 per cent.[50]

For some the scale of Labour's redistribution was inadequate. Many commentators accused New Labour of being a neoliberal government, one that was in effect Thatcherite. This judgement may reflect an overemphasis on the Chancellor's commitment to economic stability. (By the mid-1990s many economists accepted that stability was fundamental to economic wellbeing.) Other aspects of Brown's strategy, most notably the use of tax credits as well as Labour's New Deal, are indicative of a rather different approach. Indeed, an important though little-noticed shift had taken place in the alignment between the machinery of government and the administration's objectives. Previous governments had used the Treasury primarily as the basis for macroeconomic management: it was responsible for the broad aggregates of supply and demand in the economy, and for the conduct of fiscal and monetary policy. By contrast, Brown was little interested in macroeconomics and passed on responsibility for monetary policy to other actors. Under his Chancellorship, the Treasury was focused on microeconomic matters: under Brown, much of its work has been directed at designing specific measures to reduce poverty and to provide incentives for individuals to take employment.

Whether this strategy was social democratic is open to interpretation. There are three reasons why Brown's economic approach can be considered to be reformist. First, as noted above, there was a redistributive aspect to it. Second, for all his disavowals, there remained an element of tax and spend. Look at the tax changes and at the CSR for confirmation of this point. Third, aspects of the strategy remained interventionist. In 1998, when Fujitsu announced job losses in his Sedgefield constituency, Blair was frank about the free market realities that he perceived to constrain governments:

> It would be totally dishonest to pretend government can prevent such decisions.... Let us not kid ourselves. In certain sectors there will be an impact.... We can't as the government do much about the twists and turns of world markets in an increasingly globalised economy.[51]

But the Prime Minister's outlook was at odds with those of the New Deal and tax credits, which presumed market failure in the allocation of employment to be endemic. Tellingly, when BMW moved to close Longbridge, the government was quick to offer aid. The emphasis placed upon work by the government's interventionism meant that its reformist initiatives were politically more acceptable to the voters of 'middle England' than in the past. For John Hills, Brown's strategy was one of redistribution by stealth to complement taxation by stealth.[52]

Against these modest but potentially social democratic elements, other aspects of the government's strategy were much less reformist. Labour's use of privatisation (for air traffic control and the Defence Research Agency) and the increasing reliance on the Private Finance Initiative (PFI) to fund spending projects led commentators to question the depth of the government's commitment to the traditional goals of the left's project. The CSR did not herald an immediate boost to public investment: many government departments

struggled to spend the new allocations.[53] Public investment remained lower,
on the whole, than under the Conservatives. Interpreting the statistics
regarding the distribution of income and wealth is complex. Though Labour
redistributed, so (for other reasons) the gap between rich and poor widened,
making the United Kingdom a less equal society.[54] In the election campaign,
Jeremy Paxman pushed Tony Blair eleven times as to whether an increased
gap was acceptable. The Prime Minister refused to answer.[55] For some of the
government's measures, the full impact would not be immediately discernible.

Disputes and difficulties

A number of economic issues created difficulties for the Labour administration.
The most persistent problem that the government confronted concerned UK
membership of the euro. In opposition, Labour had been in favour of Economic
and Monetary Union (EMU), though its ardour had cooled in the immediate
run-up to May 1997. In office, different strands of rhetoric had to be aligned
into a coherent policy. It proved to be a difficult task. In October 1997, after
an interview with *The Times* which appeared to rule out UK membership
during the first Blair term, Brown gave a parliamentary statement which laid
out five tests (see Chapter 8 for the details). They concerned the economic
convergence between the euro zone and the UK, the flexibility of the system
to economic change, and the impact of membership on investment, on the
financial services sector and on employment. All bar the convergence criterion
embodied a degree of flexibility.

The government remained divided on the issue. Brown's doubts appeared
to harden during the parliament as the euro struggled in financial markets.
Public opinion shifted slightly against membership (and much of the press
was hostile). However, some members of the government, most notably Peter
Mandelson, were enthusiastic about membership.

Two other difficulties concerned separate aspects of Brown's fiscal stance.
First, in the autumn of 2000, protests against the increase of fuel prices
dented, for the first time since May 1997, the government's lead over the
Conservatives in both voting intention and economic management (see Figure
6.1). The protests were coupled with panic buying; they raised question
marks about the government's capacity to deal with such a challenge. For
a moment, they threatened a return to the conflict-dominated days of the
1970s. In the event, they fizzled out as rapidly as they emerged. Brown made
concessions on the taxation of fuel in the March 2001 budget.

Second, the CSR led some external authorities to doubt the depth of the
Chancellor's commitment to economic stability. Potentially at any rate Brown
was frittering away the hard-won gains of fiscal frugality that had built up
during the first years in office. It was by no means certain that the expansion
of the CSR could be sustained beyond 2004.[56] Brown reacted angrily to

criticisms from the European Commission: 'I am not prepared for the European Commission to give us lectures about what the level of spending should be in this country'.[57] Qualifying earlier praise, the IMF suggested that Brown's relaxation of the fiscal stance (embodied in the CSR) would place too much weight on the monetary route to economic stability. Interest rates would have to be higher than they would otherwise be and in turn sterling would be higher.

Conservative economic strategy: politics without economics?

Unsurprisingly, the Conservative Party found the return to opposition in May 1997 difficult. The general election result was taken by many as a savage indictment of the Major administration's economic record and, in particular, the events of September 1992 when the UK left the ERM. Out of office, the party found it difficult to articulate an economic agenda that was both coherent and markedly different to that of Labour. The Blair government had stolen some of the party's policies while others had been discredited by events. For much of the period between 1997 and 2001, the opposition resorted to a crude right-wing populism. Conservative economic policy was oriented to opposition to specific Blair initiatives, Euroscepticism and a promise of future tax cuts. The Euroscepticism was popular but failed to ignite much interest among the electorate. The promise of tax cuts, coupled with no major cuts in public services, was not perceived to be plausible. In 2000, the *Economist* commented that the opposition 'has proved unable to offer a credible alternative'.[58] For many, the Conservatives had put political rhetoric before economic coherence.

Many leading Conservative MPs lost their parliamentary seats at the 1997 general election. After a lacklustre first year in opposition, William Hague reshuffled his shadow cabinet and replaced Peter Lilley as shadow Chancellor with Francis Maude. One year later, Hague sacked Lilley as a frontbench spokesperson altogether following a speech in which the latter had argued that 'There are distinct limits to applying the free market paradigm in the public services'.[59]

Lilley's stance was at odds with Hague's pro-free-market outlook. At the October conference, the party's leader unveiled a tax guarantee, one that was intended to form the centrepiece of Conservative economic policy at the forthcoming general election. It promised a reduction in tax regardless of circumstances.

In February 2000 Hague reshuffled the shadow cabinet again, bringing in Michael Portillo, who had returned to the Commons in November 1999, as shadow Chancellor. In part it was a defensive move on the leader's part. However, Portillo quickly moved to realign party policy: within days he abandoned Conservative opposition to Bank of England independence and he accepted the minimum wage. In July 2000, after discussions with his shadow Chancellor, Hague was forced to abandon his tax guarantee. Portillo was manifestly uncomfortable with the promise. Hague stated, 'People can be assured that our commitment to reduce taxation does not over-ride prudent economic management or our vital public services'.[60] It was the most humiliating of a number of U-turns carried out by the Conservative leader. He continued to advocate tax cuts but he also endorsed Labour's spending allocations for health, schools, transport, law and order, and defence. Future Conservative tax cuts would be financed from improved efficiency and welfare reform.

Conclusion

Economic debate played little part in the general election campaign of 2001. The Conservatives tried to suggest that Labour's future spending plans implied corresponding increases in taxation. The Blair administration had, after all, increased taxes since 1997. It was a reasonable charge but one that the government was able, for the most part, to sidestep. Relying on the notion that the taxes that matter most are those that are visible and immediate, Blair offered the same guarantee he had given four years earlier: there would be no change to the rates at which income tax was levied. The commitment gave Labour flexibility over other taxes and over tax thresholds.

The Conservatives repeated the policy approach they had developed earlier: they claimed they would reduce taxes without any corresponding cuts in services. Their manifesto offered cuts of £8 billion. It was an approach that ran into trouble on two grounds. First, one member of the shadow cabinet hinted that the £8 billion would pave the way for further tax cuts. The notion of larger reductions did suggest sustained cuts in public services, a notion that Labour ruthlessly exploited. Second, and more important, the public simply did not believe the Conservative claim that tax reductions, even limited ones, would not affect public services. In one poll, 68 per cent doubted the coherence of the Conservatives' plans, including nearly a third of Conservative voters. Moreover, over half of respondents felt it was wrong to focus on petrol tax when cutting duties.[61]

On the face of it the party's domination of the economic argument was an important aspect of New Labour's second election victory. At times, over the four years, Brown had been the most popular Chancellor since Gallup began polling on the issue in 1946. In his first two budgets 70 and 71 per cent of respondents felt he was doing a good job; in his fourth the score was 63 per cent. No previous Chancellor had done better than match the lowest of these figures. Brown's 1997 budget was the fairest ever according to these polls, with a net positive rating of 70 per cent.[62]

Whether Labour's domination was based on an explicit endorsement of the detail of the government's policies or upon a more general level of support

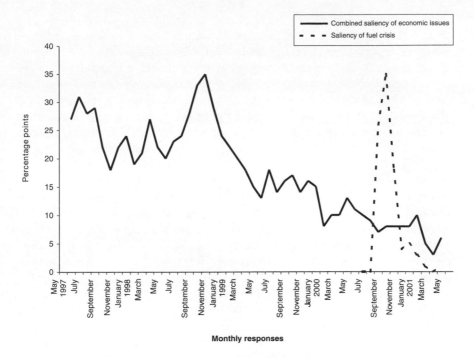

Figure 6.2. The saliency of economic issues, 1997–2001.
Sources: A. King (ed.), *British Political Opinion 1937–2000. The Gallup Polls*
(London: Politico's, 2001), pp. 272–3; Gallup Political and Economic Index.

for the administration, however, is uncertain. Labour's lead over the Conservatives concerning economic management shot up as soon as Blair's administration
took office. But Conservative difficulties in this area dated back to the UK's
ejection from the ERM. Between them, the events of 1992 and the political
upheavals of 1997 marked a new alignment between party popularity and
economic competence in which Labour was able to dominate the Conservatives.
The Conservatives had been unable to win back the electorate's trust, a
confidence that had been lost during 1992–93.

Government policies were broadly endorsed by voters and deserved some
credit for the UK's economic performance between 1997 and 2001. But a
range of factors, in which events before Labour came to office were especially
significant, shaped the popularity of the Blair administration. Figure 6.2
indicates the combined salience of three economic issues (unemployment,
the cost of living, and other economic items) raised by respondents when
asked to note the most urgent problem facing the country. It is striking that
the saliency of economic issues declined between 1997 and 2001. The
saliency of fuel tax rose rapidly during the autumn of 2000, only to collapse

just as quickly. The declining saliency of economic issues can be interpreted in two different ways. It might be taken as an indication that economic issues were less important in shaping popular preferences than in the past. Equally, it might signify that, given a relatively successful performance, voters were able to endorse Labour precisely because of the administration's economic record, while raising a series of non-economic concerns in response to that question. Both explanations indicate the potential for a post-material politics. In each case, declining saliency reflected the relatively buoyant economic circumstances enjoyed by, and partially created by, Labour.

The declining saliency of economic issues is unlikely to be a permanent feature of British politics. The second Blair administration did not inherit a completely trouble-free environment. Issues remain that will need to be resolved during Labour's second term. The government's manifesto commitment to reform of public services antagonised many senior trade unionists, who were not easily reassured by the Prime Minister's rhetorical homilies on the subject. More obviously, of course, the government will have to take a view on UK membership of the euro at some point. The issue will involve attempting to reconcile Brown's Euroscepticism (and that of a potentially hostile electorate) with the much more positive outlook of those members of the government who want to ensure that the UK remains at the centre of the European project. The promised referendum on entry might well place Labour under considerable strain, exacerbating tensions that were sidelined between 1997 and 2001. Two other difficulties should be noted. From the autumn of 2000, economic difficulties in the United States and elsewhere indicated that the external economic environment during the second Blair term would not be so benevolent. Nervous stock markets around the world indicated widespread concerns about future economic events. On top of this context, one consequence of the three-year CSR is that Labour's commitment to increased public investment will run out around a year before the next general election. Sustaining the rate of investment laid out in the CSR will be likely to require tax increases while reducing it might result in further criticisms about the provision of public services. Neither decision will be particularly palatable in the run-up to that election. For all his skills, Gordon Brown may have misaligned the electoral cycle with that of public spending. Whether Labour will be as dominant in economic matters during the second Blair government as it was during the first is by no means certain.

Notes

1 Thanks to Andrew Geddes and Ralph Footring for their comments on and help with this chapter; responsibility, as ever, is mine.
2 This depiction of past Labour administrations is, of course, a caricatured one. However, the caricature was part of British political discourse during the 1980s and 1990s, and one that, in many ways, New Labour accepted.

3 Gordon Brown, speech, Mansion House, 20 June 2001.

4 Gordon Brown, Mais Lecture, 19 October 1999.

5 Gordon Brown, speech, Labour Party conference, Brighton, October 2001.

6 Interview transcript, *Guardian*, 24 September 1999, www.guardian.co.uk.

7 See, for example, C. Hay, *The Political Economy of New Labour* (Manchester: Manchester University Press, 1999).

8 Tony Blair, interview transcript, *Observer*, 13 May 2001, www.observer.co.uk.

9 N. Pain and R. Kneller, 'The UK economy', *National Institute Economic Review*, no. 176 (2001), pp. 9–18, p. 9.

10 See, for example, P. Toynbee and D. Walker, *Did Things Get Better?* (London: Penguin Books, 2001), p. 92.

11 IMF, *United Kingdom: 2000 Article IV Consultation*, IMF country report no. 01/42 (Washington, DC: IMF, 2001), p. 5.

12 OECD, *United Kingdom*, Economic Surveys (Paris: OECD, 2000), p. 11.

13 *Ibid.*, pp. 13 and 14.

14 The 1997 data are from A. King (ed.), *British Political Opinion 1937–2000. The Gallup Polls* (London: Politico's, 2001), p. 118. The 2001 data are from *Daily Telegraph* poll, 21–23 May 2001, www.gallup.com.

15 King, *British Political Opinion*, p. 67. Labour's lead over the Conservatives is calculated by averaging the ratings for each party, in Gallup polls, in April 1997 and then deducting one from the other.

16 *Daily Telegraph* poll, 21–23 May 2001, www.gallup.com. See also I. Crewe, 'Everything is in Blair's favour', *New Statesman*, 26 March 2001, pp. 21–2.

17 King, *British Political Opinion*, p. 71; *Daily Telegraph* poll, 21–23 May 2001, www.gallup.com.

18 King, *British Political Opinion*, pp. 62–3; *Daily Telegraph* poll, 21–23 May 2001, www.gallup.com.

19 I am not making an argument about causality in presenting this figure: it is plausible that support for a party's economic policy might shape an individual's voting preference. Equally, however, voting intention might determine the perception that respondents have of a party's policies. Moreover, both voting and economic management might be shaped by other variables, for example the quality of a party's leadership. My point is simply to note the close relationship between voting intention and perception of economic management.

20 King, *British Political Opinion*, pp. 24–5, 118–19.

21 A useful account of Gordon Brown at the Treasury is given by P. Stephens, 'The Treasury under Labour', in A. Seldon (ed.), *The Blair Effect* (London: Little Brown, 2001). Impressive detail on policy outcomes is marshalled by Toynbee and Walker, *Did Things Get Better?*, especially pp. 92–121, while A. Rawnsley, *Servants of the People* (London: Hamish Hamilton, 2000), provides a good context for an analysis of economic policy making. This chapter draws on all three.

22 See, for example, Gordon Brown, 'Modernising the British economy – the new mission for the Treasury', speech, IFS, 27 May 1999.

23 See, alongside the Mansion House speech and Mais Lecture noted above, Gordon Brown, lecture, Royal Economic Society, 13 July 2000. Each gave four conditions and in each stability was noted first. Each also emphasised employability and productivity (or growth). But the fourth condition varied from 'international engagement' (Royal Economic Society) to responsibility (Mais) to individual potential, tackling child poverty (IFS).

24 Gordon Brown, speech, Mansion House, 20 June 2001.

25 See, for example, as well as the IFS lecture noted above, Gordon Brown, speech, Labour spring conference, Glasgow, 16 February 2000.

26 Gordon Brown, speech, Mansion House, 12 June 1997.

27 *The Times*, 7 May 1997.
28 *Financial Times*, 7 May 1997.
29 He suggested that low inflation and the stability associated with it were a means to secure other goals, such as full employment.
30 Gordon Brown, statement, 6 May 1997.
31 Gordon Brown, Mais Lecture, 19 October 1997; see also Gordon Brown, lecture, Royal Economic Society, 13 July 2000.
32 J. Fforde, 'Setting monetary objectives', *Bank of England Quarterly Bulletin* (June 1983), pp. 200–8, p. 204. My thanks on this to M. Artis.
33 Gordon Brown, Mais Lecture, 19 October 1999.
34 *Hansard*, 20 March 1989, col. 750.
35 Six members took the first decisions (and five that of August 1997). Howard Davies, Deputy Governor, lasted for two meetings before being replaced by David Clementi. Outside members Deanne Julius joined in August 1997 and Alan Budd in December that year. The MPC reached full strength with John Vickers' arrival as a Bank of England member in June 1998.
36 OECD, *United Kingdom*, p. 12.
37 Ed Balls, speech, Oxford, 12 June 2001.
38 IMF, *United Kingdom: 2000 Article IV Consultation*, p. 23.
39 OECD, *United Kingdom*, p. 11.
40 *Ibid.*, p. 73.
41 Stephens, 'The Treasury under Labour', p. 196.
42 Rawnsley, *Servants of the People*, pp. 112–13.
43 *Guardian*, 19 July 2000.
44 *Gallup Political and Economic Index*, no. 480 (August 2000), p. 9.
45 Department for Education and Employment, *Towards Full Employment in a Modern Society*, Cm 5084 (London: Stationary Office, 2001).
46 Press release, Treasury, 22 November 2000.
47 Toynbee and Walker, *Did Things Get Better?*, p. 21.
48 H. Immervoll, L. Mitton, C. O'Donoghue and H. Sutherland, 'Budgeting for fairness? The distributional effect of three Labour budgets', Department of Applied Economics, Cambridge, mimeo, p. 8.
49 *Guardian*, 10 November 2000.
50 J. Hills, 'How Labour is doing good by stealth for the poor', *Independent*, 4 June 2001.
51 *The Times*, 17 September 1998.
52 Hills, 'How Labour is doing good by stealth for the poor'.
53 *Guardian*, 21 March 2001.
54 *Independent*, 14 July 2001.
55 Interview, 4 June 2001, www.bbc.co.uk.
56 European Commission, *Report on the Implementation of the 2000 Broad Economic Policy Guidelines* (Brussels: European Commission, 2001), p. 162.
57 27 April 2001, www.bbc.co.uk.
58 *Economist*, 25 March 2000.
59 Rab Butler Memorial Lecture, 20 April 1999.
60 *Guardian*, 12 July 2000.
61 *Daily Telegraph* poll, 14–15 May 2001, www.gallup.com.
62 King, *British Political Opinion*, pp. 232–7.

Bristol West

Bristol West is one of few seats in England that can be truly considered a three-way marginal. It was high on the list of target seats of both the Conservatives and the Liberal Democrats. Demographically, Bristol West is a heady brew of students, young graduates, older professionals and working-class voters. The Labour MP for the constituency, Valerie Davey, benefited from the national electoral momentum of her party in the 1997 election and the mainly prosperous seat could in no way be considered as safe Labour. Indeed, the constituency has a strong Conservative tradition, although many of the previous local MPs from that party were moderates. The Liberal Democrats were encouraged to believe that they could capture the seat by gains in local elections. Their candidate, Stephen Williams, had experience of fighting an election campaign in Bristol, coming third in the Bristol South constituency in 1997.

The expected closeness of the contest produced a turnout over 6 per cent above the national average. Almost two-thirds of the local electorate went to the polls, a fall of 8 per cent from the 1997 figure compared with the national average 12 per cent drop in turnout. Labour's vote held up well, the party's share increasing slightly. The same could be said for the Liberal Democrats. However, the fall of 4 per cent in the Conservatives' vote, in a seat containing 'natural' territory such as Clifton, was indicative of the electoral problems confronting the party. The Conservatives needed a mere 1.2 per cent swing to take the seat, but never looked like retaking the constituency, being narrowly relegated to third place.

Result

Bristol West		
	No. of votes	% of vote
Davey, V. (Labour)	20,505	36.8
Williams, S. (Liberal Democrat)	16,079	28.9
Chesters, P. (Conservative)	16,040	28.8
Devaney, J. (Green)	1,961	3.5
Kennedy, B (Socialist Labour)	590	1.0
Muir, S. (UKIP)	490	0.9
Labour majority	4,426	7.9
Labour hold		
Turnout		65.6
Swing, Liberal Democrats to Labour		0.37

7

The provision of services: transformation for justice

David P. Dolowitz

Introduction

During the 2001 general election campaign, public service provision and reform became the Labour Party's foremost theme. This debate emerged owing to a perception that Labour had failed to deliver on its 1997 pledges to reform public services. More controversially, and detrimental to the future prospects of the New Labour project, there was an associated perception that what had changed, and what was promised, was leading to a creeping privatisation of the core public services: education, welfare and health care. To dispel the image that little has changed under New Labour and that it has continued the Conservatives' privatisation programme in a different guise, this chapter examines to what extent and in what ways Labour has altered the delivery and function of public services. In particular, it examines what New Labour has done to transform public services along lines suggested by the principles of work, targeting more help on the poor and establishing new delivery mechanisms with the aim of securing some private financing to help the public sector provide better services.

Labour entered office in May 1997 arguing that the Conservatives had systematically starved the public services of vital resources and that this had contributed to the dramatic rise in poverty, particularly child poverty, and social decline between 1979 and 1997. To attack these problems Labour promised an innovative approach to the provision of public services: rights would be matched with responsibilities, but within a framework in which Labour's traditional values of equality and social justice would dominate. Thus, leading to criticism from the left, New Labour's approach to justice and equality did not depend on returning to the policies of nationalisation and macroeconomic redistribution. Rather, New Labour sought to combine economic stability with a new kind of public service in a long-term attempt to attack the physical and emotional poverty that had developed during the Thatcher and Major era.

The underlying view of the incoming Labour government was that poverty was not caused by lack of will or laziness on the part of individuals nor was it limited to a chronic lack of income. Instead, poverty was a culmination of poor education, a lack of opportunity as a child, the lack of a job as an adult, and a steady decline in the value and structure of public services since 1979. To address these issues Labour's CSR (see Chapter 6) resulted in the redirection of resources into public services. Labour believed that public service renewal, centred on helping individuals re-establish their connections with the labour market, was crucial to solving Britain's growing unemployment problem. This situation emerged as a result of the Conservatives' continued underinvestment in education, training and welfare, which had left most unemployed individuals lacking the skills necessary to enter or re-enter the labour market. Thus tens of thousands of adults and young adults had become stranded in a no-pay–low-pay cycle, having left school without the basic skills required in a modern, knowledge-based economy. Compounding these problems, the Conservatives had systematically reduced the real value of unemployment and income-support benefits, and had actually frozen child benefit in 1994. As a result of these policy decisions, between 1979 and 1997 the number of children in poverty had tripled, from one in ten to one in three, and the number of families with no one in work doubled, to one in five. Thus New Labour entered office committed to a new approach to the delivery of their traditional values through a renewal of the public sector so that, in the long term, social justice and equality would once again flourish at the core of British society.

Education, education, education

New Labour entered office believing that the key to transforming society and ensuring long-term economic growth depended on the development of the country's stock of human capital. This meant that education was given priority on New Labour's agenda. By improving the economy's skills base Britain could ensure global competitiveness and long-term economic growth. The key was to guarantee that individuals left the education system with the skills required by the economy and were able to upgrade these skills throughout their working lives in order to take advantage of technological advancements.

To justify its education agenda, Labour had campaigned in 1997 on the argument that, as a result of Conservative policies and a reduction in education spending by £60 per pupil in real terms: the skills gap between Britain and it major competitors had grown; over 40 per cent of children left primary school with poor numeracy, literacy and writing abilities; and over 480,000 infant school pupils were being taught in classes of over thirty students per teacher. Labour's plans to address these failures were ambitious. It promised to reduce class sizes for five-, six- and seven-year-olds, to provide nursery places for all four-year-olds, and to target help for early-year learners (under five years of age) and students in primary education. These ambitions were extended by a range of programmes designed to target extra help on individuals and families from disadvantaged communities through programmes such as Education Action Zones (EAZ), Excellence in Cities (EiC), New Deal for Schools and Sure Start.

Early-years education reform

In fulfilling its pledge to replace the Conservatives' nursery voucher scheme with guaranteed nursery places for all four-year-olds, the Labour government created over 120,000 free nursery places in its first term. This was doubtless good for the party's public relations, but the provision of nursery places does little by itself to improve education and future opportunities. To begin addressing this, the government launched a series of Early Excellence Centres designed to integrate and improve educational and child-care provision for children under five years of age and set aside £100 million in Lottery money to train 50,000 New Deal child-care workers. To consolidate these reforms, the government established a National Childcare Strategy, which required all local education authorities (LEAs) to provide free education to four-year-olds whose parents wanted it, and committed £170 million in Lottery funds to establish a series of new educationally oriented out-of-school child-care places by 2003. Most importantly, the government announced an expanded emphasis on the role of education in child-care provision. By 1999 all 150 LEAs had to organise 'early-years forums' to develop detailed 'early-years development plans' to improve early-years education and child-care services within their area. There was a requirement that these plans stipulate that all nursery providers cooperate with local primary schools to integrate educational strategies for the children in their care. The government also introduced a new 'Foundation Stage' to the education system, which targeted children between the ages of three and six years with new early-learning goals, which established standards all children were to have achieved so that they could easily manage the transition to Key Stage 1.

Reform of Key Stages 1–4

The Labour government's Education (Schools) Act of 1997 abolished the Assisted-Places Scheme and assigned the savings to the reduction of class sizes to thirty or below for all five-, six- and seven-year-olds. By June 2001 the government had achieved its manifesto commitment to reduce class sizes. To begin to address standards and achievement, the government had also required primary schools to introduce daily literacy hours and mathematics lessons. Since the introduction of these reforms, literacy examination results have improved by 10 per cent and numeracy skills by 13 per cent. More telling is that when Labour came to power only 50 per cent of eleven-year-old students were reaching level 4 examination standards in English and maths, but now these figures have increased to 75 and 72 per cent respectively. Labour has promised to increase this to 85 per cent by 2004.

Aside from pledges to accept 'zero tolerance of underperformance' and a commitment to a 'National Grid for Learning', through which all schools were to be wired to the Internet and teachers were to receive training in information technology, few direct promises were made in relation to secondary schools in Labour's 1997 manifesto. However, efforts were made to target secondary students from disadvantaged backgrounds. An important element of this was the introduction of the EiC initiative, which provides secondary schools in Britain's most deprived neighbourhoods with extra funding and support. Complementing EiC, the government also introduced EAZs to encourage schools and LEAs to experiment with new partnerships and strategies to improve the educational attainment of students from disadvantaged backgrounds. Currently there are seventy-three 'large' EAZs and twenty-six 'small' EAZs (working exclusively with EiC). Each EAZ has the responsibility to act as a 'test-bed' for the innovative delivery of the government's educational standards. Controversially, to qualify for EAZ status, areas had to attract business sponsorship in the funding and management of the schools within the Zone. To maintain their status EAZs must show appreciable improvements in students' results. To maximise flexibility, Zone directors have been authorised to adapt the general curriculum to satisfy the employment and training needs of the local community, school hours, course designs and the pay and conditions of the teaching staff.

These initiatives are beginning to show results, particularly in deprived neighbourhoods. For example, the number of individuals leaving school without any GCSEs has fallen by 2 per cent since 1997. Similarly, the proportion of students attaining five good GCSE results has increased by over 4 per cent since 1997. More importantly, since the introduction of these reforms, more students from disadvantaged areas are beginning to go on to study for A-levels.

For individuals who left formal education lacking the skills to enter the labour market, those needing to retrain or those wishing to enhance their educational qualifications, the government established a new public–private partnership (PPP): the University for Industry (commonly called LearnDirect). Operating much like the Open University, the University for Industry offers lessons though videos, interactive technologies and locally delivered educational lessons. To complement the University for Industry the government also introduced new Individual Learning Accounts to give financial support through a credit system to individuals over nineteen years of age who want to save for education and training opportunities. The intention is to provide new supply-side opportunities to those over sixteen years old to address their education and skills deficits while ensuring economic stability and employment subsidies provide demand-side opportunities for re-engagement and advancement within the labour market.

School finance

In 1997 Labour also promised to invest more in education as 'the cost of unemployment' fell and resources were reallocated. To this end, in 1998 Gordon Brown as Chancellor and David Blunkett as Secretary of State for Education and Employment announced a £19 billion increase in education spending between 1999 and 2001, with £13 billion added to cover 2002–04. The apparent announcing and reannouncing of these spending plans was criticised for giving the impression of more money being spent than was actually the case, and which in turn reinforced perceptions of a government dominated by 'spin' and giving less attention to 'delivery'. It was also a cause of much controversy that, as a percentage of GDP, the Labour government did not increase the amount of money being spent on education beyond that spent between 1992 and 1997 until early 2001. However, these criticisms are slightly misleading because of economic growth between 1997 and 2001. When examined in real terms, per pupil, education spending increased by over £300 (with a further £370 increase per pupil promised by 2004).

In addition to these investments, the government began a massive New Deal for Schools building and renewal programme, using over £3 billion from the one-off 'windfall tax' imposed on the excess profits of privatised utilities and private sector finances.[1] Combined, these measures have allowed the government to begin building and repairing over 17,000 schools, with the goal of completely replacing over 620 schools by 2004.

Welfare services

During the 1997 campaign Labour promised a new kind of welfare state: one dedicated to investing in human capital. The idea was to change the 'direction of welfare policy, away from passive support for jobless claimants towards active efforts to improve their chances of securing employment within a more prudently managed and stable economy'.[2] As with education, Labour's plans for the modernisation of welfare services were closely linked to an economic policy designed to provide the conditions for investment and full employment. A stable economy and a welfare system linked to active labour market policies would allow the government to cut the national debt; this would create a virtuous circle of declining debt and welfare payments, which would allow much more public investment in education, health and welfare.

Immediately upon entering office New Labour set about implementing policies designed to address its manifesto commitments, the first step being the introduction of the New Deal programmes, funded by over £3.6 billion of the windfall tax on privatised utilities. Labour's approach was to use measures focused on the supply side of the economy to move the welfare state away from passive support for jobless individuals and towards active support to help individuals enter the labour market. Thus the key element of all the New Deal programmes was the individually tailored mix of support, counselling, job subsidies, job search, and education and training opportunities.

The first, and most trailed, of the New Deal programmes was targeted at eighteen- to twenty-four-year-olds who had been unemployed for over six months. The aim was to provided the education and training necessary to connect them to the labour market before they entered the long-term low-pay–no-pay cycle and joined over five million working-aged individuals already dependent on the benefit system. Based on the success of the programme, the government introduced a series of New Deals for the long-term unemployed over twenty-five years of age, the partners of long-term unemployed individuals, individuals over fifty years of age, lone parents and people with a disability. In each of these programmes there is a combination of help, choice and the support of a personal adviser to promote the move from welfare to work. The philosophy is that individuals should be asked what they are capable of doing, rather than being told what they cannot do, and then be offered the support and guidance necessary for them to enter the labour market.[3]

Complementing the government's New Deal strategy was the introduction of ONE (formerly the Single Work-Focused Gateway). ONE is a 'joined up' venture between the Benefits Agency and the Employment Service (ES); other participants are drawn from the respective local authority, voluntary and private sector organisations. The purpose of ONE is to develop a single 'work-focused' gateway into the benefit system designed to inform claimants of the measures available to support their reintegration into the labour market. What distinguishes ONE from Conservative efforts to link the work of the Benefits Agency and ES is that ONE offers a single point of entry to both the benefit and employment system through a personal adviser trained to develop a support package tailored to the specific needs of the individual benefit claimant.

At the end of Labour's first term, these programmes did appear to be working. The number of young unemployed individuals had fallen by over 270,000. Similarly, the proportion of children growing up in homes where no one was working had fallen from approximately 18 per cent in 1997 to 15 per cent in 2001. The New Deal for people with a disability, when combined with the disabled person's tax credit, had drawn almost 6,000 individuals back into the labour market. And it has been estimated that, as a direct result of the New Deal for lone parents, more than 70,000 unemployed single parents have entered the labour market. Importantly for the government's new 'joined up' approach to the delivery of services, there are indications that ONE has been well received. Most benefit recipients report an improved attitude towards work by the end of their meeting, and over 80 per cent of claimants report being treated as an individual at their meetings.[4]

Welfare reform targeted at children and communities

The government's emphasis on work as the best route out of poverty has been complemented by a series of new programmes designed to eliminate child poverty and rebuild socially and economically disadvantaged communities. Before justice could develop, the government knew it had to ensure that the children of low-income parents were provided with opportunities to succeed. To support this stance, the government turned to evidence that, as early as twenty-two months after birth, children whose parents were in social classes I and II were over 14 per cent higher in educational achievement than those whose parents were in social classes IV and V. Additionally, children in the latter classes tended to have poorer school attendance, lower birth weights and much higher rates of teenage pregnancy.[5] On the basis of these statistics, the government launched the Sure Start initiative with the aim of improving, in the poorest areas of the country, family access to health and family support services, advice on nurturing, and early-learning opportunities. Over £500 million in direct funding between 1999 and 2001 was earmarked, and another £450 million for 2002–04. To help integrate Sure Start into the wider services available to low-income parents the government also encouraged local health and social services, LEAs and community organisations to help develop and fund area programmes.

Complementing Sure Start, the Cabinet Office's Social Exclusion Unit encouraged the government to develop a national strategy for neighbourhood renewal to tackle the root causes of poverty and social exclusion in the country's most deprived areas. As part of this, government introduced Employment Zones along with the new personal adviser service. The key to this strategy is that every unemployed individual in an Employment Zone works with a dedicated (and specially trained) personal adviser to draw up an action plan of activities, funded by a personal job account worth up to £5,000, geared towards re-entry of the labour market. As with the government's other 'Zone' programmes, early indicators are that in areas covered by Employment Zones unemployed individuals are almost twice as likely to find and retain a job than in deprived areas not so covered.

As a further element of its strategy to target public services at the poorest communities, the government launched the New Deal for communities as its centrepiece programme.[6] This attempts to create local initiatives linking the public and private sector to tackle specific disadvantages. The key is to engage influential actors within the community in the development and harmonisation of the New Deal with other government schemes, such as EAZs, Employment Zones and Sure Start.

Early signs of the success of these reforms are encouraging. During the government's first term over one million people re-entered the labour market and maintained their employment for eighteen months or more, although the broader impact of this development on child poverty was less easy to ascertain. More important for the government's long-term strategy, just before the 2001 general election it was able to publish figures demonstrating that it had cut what it called 'the bills of social failure' – for every additional £1 of public spending, only 17p was being spent on debt interest and social security payments, compared with 42p under the previous Conservative administration.

Making work pay

Complementing the government's active labour market strategies have been changes to the tax system designed to ensure that work paid more than benefits. As a start, the government established the national minimum wage, which stood at £3.60 per hour (rising to £4.10 in October 2001), for those over twenty-five years old and £3.00 per hour (rising to £3.60 in October 2002) for those aged eighteen to twenty-five. It has been estimated that, as a result of the introduction of the minimum wage, over one million individuals (mostly women) have seen an average increase in their wages of over 15 per cent.

Shortly after taking office Labour introduced a 10 per cent starting rate of income tax. However, the government was concerned about distortions to the labour market caused by the low level of income at which workers began paying NI. Based on the recommendations of the former head of Barclays Bank, Martin Taylor, the government altered the point at which individuals began paying NI. It raised the lower earnings limit to bring it in line with an individual's personal allowance. This pulled over one million low-paid workers out of the NI system. Second, to ensure individuals who did not pay NI because of the increase in the lower earnings limit did not lose their entitlement to NI benefits, the government abolished the 'entry fee' for both employers and employees by turning the lower earnings limit into an allowance. While these changes were not radical, there are indications that they have led employers to expand the number of jobs available to individuals with basic skills and have encouraged more individuals to accept lower-paid positions, partly because they are able to keep more of their income without losing benefit entitlement.[7]

As part of its programme to draw people back into the labour market, the government also initiated a number of changes to the tax system to target extra in-work support on low-income families and people with a disability, to ensure they received more income in work than on state benefits without lowering the income provided by state benefits. The key was the introduction of a series of tax credits to provide families a guaranteed minimum income while supplementing the cost of child care. At the heart of this was the WFTC. The WFTC was designed to ensure that all families with at least one person working a minimum of sixteen hours per week were guaranteed an income of no less than £214 per week. Within the WFTC there was also a child-care tax credit, under which scheme families receiving WFTC were offered up to 70 per cent of their child-care costs, up to a limit of £100 per week for the first child (increasing to £135 in June 2001) and £150 for two or more children (increasing to £200 in June 2001). Indications are that these measures have increased the income of at least one million families containing around two million children in total.

All told, New Labour's active labour market strategies, in combination with its policies to make work pay, have not only dramatically increased labour market participation rates among low-income individuals and families but have also helped to reduce spending on benefits for unemployed and economically inactive individuals by over 12 per cent per year since 1997.

Health services

In 1997 Labour declared that there were '24 hours to save the NHS'. For Labour, the Conservatives left a legacy of underinvestment, in both the staffing and the infrastructure of the NHS. This in turn had led to a shortage of doctors and nurses, and had left many hospitals, clinics and surgeries in urgent need of refurbishment or replacement. All this led New Labour to argue that under the Conservatives the structures and working practices of the NHS had become outdated and unfair. The government's NHS modernisation plans were set out in the 1997 White Paper *The New NHS: Modern, Dependable*, which reaffirmed Labour's commitment to ensure that access to the NHS would 'be based on need and need alone – not on your ability to pay or on who your GP happens to be or where you live'.[8] It proposed to abolish the internal market and end the 'postcode lottery' in the provision of services. This did not mean eliminating every element of the existing system, but discarding the elements perceived as leading to a decline in the quality and efficiency of the system. To abolish the internal market Labour established two new national institutions – the National Institute for Clinical Excellence (NICE) and the Commission for Health Improvement – and a series new local institutions, known as primary care groups and primary care trusts. These arrangements were designed to replace competition with partnership. To do this, NICE was given the responsibility of creating National Service Frameworks in all medical specialties. These Frameworks were to lay down, on the basis of cost-effectiveness, the appropriate types and delivery methods of treatments, which the primary care groups and trusts were to deliver via three- to five-year contracts with service providers. The Commission for Health Improvement was given the responsibility for carrying out investigations and passing measures to bring any primary care group or trust or health authority into line with NICE guidelines.

Expanded funding

While these arrangements were designed to meet the government's commitments to ending the internal market and establishing tough quality targets, they did not deal with the manifesto commitment to increase spending on the NHS or to reduce waiting lists. To address these commitments, immediately upon entering office Labour announced an extra £1.5 billion to begin its reforms of the NHS, increased to £2 billion in the 1998 budget, targeted on cutting waiting lists and improving services dedicated to children and treating cancer. Then, based on the outcome of the CSR, Gordon Brown announced an extra £21 billion increase in the NHS budget. While the amount of the increase turned out to be lower, due to some questionable accounting mechanisms, the government did substantially increase the funding devoted to health care and continued to do so in subsequent budgets. The effect was that between 1997 and 2001 the NHS budget grew at almost 6 per cent in real terms: almost double the rate of increase between 1979 and 1997. The re-elected Labour government has committed itself to increasing this to 8 per cent by 2010.

Improved health

The government cut waiting lists by over 150,000 individuals in four years: 50,000 above its 1997 manifesto commitment. During the 2001 election campaign, opposition parties argued that Labour had been able to cut the inpatient waiting list only by increasing the number of individuals placed on the outpatient waiting list. However, at the time of the election outpatient waiting lists were only 36,000 higher than when Labour came to power in 1997, which indicates some increase but not large enough to explain the dramatic fall in the inpatient list. Labour entered its second term committed to shifting the focus from waiting lists to waiting times and promised that by 2005 the resources and staff would be provided to guarantee: that no patient would have to wait on the outpatient list longer than three months (six months for surgery); that by 2004 no patient would have to wait over forty-eight hours to see a general practitioner, no more than twenty-four hours to see another member of a primary care team, and no more than four hours for admission, discharge or transfer after entering an accident and emergency unit.

In 1997 Labour had also promised that extra NHS investment would be targeted at developing new structures to expand access to health services to all people, especially those living in disadvantaged communities. Part of this strategy was an ambitious plan to recruit and train more doctors and nurses, and target them at disadvantaged communities. The government recruited almost 15,000 qualified doctors and nurses and offered them a £5,000 bonus to go into practice in deprived areas. Complementing this recruitment drive and the efforts to expand the capacity of the nation's primary care facilities the government introduced two new structures: primary care walk-in centres and NHS Direct. Walk-in centres are nurse-led establishments, situated in convenient and accessible locations; they have flexible opening hours and require no appointment. NHS Direct was introduced to complement other NHS services; it is a twenty-four-hour nurse-led telephone helpline. To target help directly at disadvantaged communities the government also introduced Health Action Zones. As another of the government's efforts to develop joined up services, these Zones bring together local NHS and social services, community and voluntary organisations, and local business representatives to develop and implement a health strategy to reduce the health inequalities apparent in the country's twenty-six most disadvantaged communities.

Underpinning all the government's efforts to reform the NHS were commitments to improve and modernise the technological basis of the NHS and its 'crumbling' infrastructure. The first part of this programme was an increase in capital investment from an average of 1.8 per cent per year between 1979 and 1997 to 8 per cent per year between 1997 and 2001. With this extra funding Labour pledged that by 2010 almost half the total value of NHS estates would be less than fifteen years old, compared with less than a quarter when it entered office in 1997. Funding has been directed towards updating, renovating and replacing general practice surgeries and ensuring all surgeries and walk-in centres have a computerised system for patient records. Accident and emergency departments also benefited from the investment of over £150 million directed at over 289 different modernisation programmes. The government also set aside over £90 million in Lottery money to replace outdated equipment in the NHS.

More ambitiously, Labour came to office promising to adapt and use the Conservative PFI scheme to help fund the construction of new NHS hospitals. As a result of the PFI, and increases in public expenditure, the money dedicated to rebuilding the NHS's infrastructure has increased by almost 50 per cent in real terms, to £2.4 billion. As of June 2001, the government had entered into contracts to proceed with thirty-one major PFI hospital projects, with the private sector contributing over £10 million in each. More controversially, but linked to the use of private money in the construction of new hospitals, has been the government's 'concordat' with the private sector to use private facilities in the delivery of NHS services. Fearing the public's perception of the concordat, the government put in place a stringent set of guidelines to regulate the quality of services being provided to NHS patients in the private sector. To ensure these rules are followed, the Commission for Health Improvement has the power to monitor the care of NHS patients in private hospitals, and to enforce change where necessary.

The government's efforts to reform the NHS have seen real changes in the provision of health care. The internal market has been eliminated in favour of a system that seeks cooperation, long-term contracts and partnerships. That said, the government wanted to create the new structures in such a way as to ensure the new system retained the internal market's drive for efficiency, quality and accountability. To do this, the government created NICE and the Commission for Health Improvement to develop, monitor and enforce tough new standards in the provision of health care. The new Food Standards Agency has an important role in health promotion. With the government's extra £21 billion investment, the NHS was able to reduce waiting lists by more than the pledged 100,000, to begin addressing the massive backlog of repairs and replacements needed in equipment and infrastructure, and to expand the numbers of training places and of active doctors and nurses by over 15,000. As with education and welfare, the government has also made substantial movement towards its goal of providing equal access to all, regardless of where they live or what their income.

Into the future: New Labour's second term

True to its long-standing values of justice and equality but delivered through a new approach to public services, Labour is committed to continuing with the reforms initiated in 1997:

> Renewal of our public services is at the centre of new Labour's manifesto. A single aim drives our policy programme: to liberate people's potential, by spreading power, wealth and opportunity more widely.[9]

It has promised to increase the number of teachers by 10,000 and improve the quality and standards of secondary schools; to recruit an extra 20,000 nurses and 10,000 more doctors; to improve the NHS; and to continue to reform the welfare system, so as to ensure all individuals are provided with opportunities to fulfil their duties to themselves and society.

Education retained a central place in Labour's 2001 manifesto. In addition to promising a nursery place for all three-year-olds and pledging to increase the number of teachers by 2006, the party committed itself to increase the proportion of national income devoted to education so that by 2004 it would have made an increase of almost £700 per pupil in real terms since 1997. The party also committed itself to increasing its spending on infrastructure renewal by almost £8 billion by 2004 and increasing the number and quality of services available to students from disadvantaged backgrounds, such as the Sure Start and Early Excellence Centres.

While most of these commitments are natural extensions of the 1997–2001 reforms, one significant (though logical) change in the government's education strategy has been a shift in emphasis from primary to secondary. In the 2001 manifesto, Labour promised to expand the EiC programme and to target extra resources at educational provisions for eleven- to fourteen-year-olds. Aspects of this include a promised expansion of specialist and 'beacon' schools; the extension of the literacy and numeracy strategies to secondary schools; and the introduction of a new vocational pathway leading to vocational GCSE and A-level qualifications.

One of the more radical strategies promised was the extension of business, religious and community organisations in the 'sponsorship' of secondary schools. While not fully developed, the intention is to 'introduce fixed term "standard contracts" to enable private, voluntary and faith organisations to support the management of schools, both as a means of tackling failing schools and as a way of supporting successful schools'.[10] Even though this policy is based on the success of business and community involvement in EAZs and specialist schools, it has raised a considerable amount of unease because there has been a perception that any business involvement in the comprehensive education system is a step towards privatisation. While the scheme is clearly not privatisation – as no assets, teachers or properties are being sold – the government's willingness to permit business involvement in the management of comprehensive schools is an important change in the way education will be delivered in England. As this will be the first time businesses have been directly involved in the secondary comprehensive school system there is no clear way to predict the outcome of this venture. However, while teachers' unions fear there is a hidden agenda to sideline them in the provision of education, the early signs are that the involvement of business and community groups in the running of EAZs and specialist schools has not reduced the power or influence of teachers. More importantly, there is evidence that business and community involvement has helped improve the educational standards and achievements of students. Whatever the end product turns out to be, there is no doubt that the overarching goal of these reforms is that by the next general election the number of students leaving the formal education system at sixteen will fall and that those who do leave will have the education and skills available to ensure they do not enter the no-pay–low-pay cycle of the past.

Labour's 2001 manifesto also pledged further reforms to the welfare state, based on the principles of work for those who can, security for those who cannot, rewards for those at the bottom end of the income ladder who work and save, and a reaffirmation of the pledge to eliminate child poverty by 2020. A major component of this reform will be the creation of the Working Age Agency, which will have a high street branch network known as Jobcentre Plus. The Agency will unite the ES with the Benefit Agency to ensure that before people are allowed to sign on for benefit they will have to talk to a personal adviser about what education, training and job opportunities are available. Before this merger, individuals were allowed to sign on for benefit before meeting an adviser about the possibility of returning to work. Further extending Labour's partnership approach to the delivery of public services,

Jobcentre Plus offices will work in partnership with the local community to develop opportunities for unemployed individuals to re-enter the local (or at least nearby) labour market. To target public services better on actively supporting individuals' initial moves into the labour market and keeping them attached to it though their lifetime, within days of the 2001 election result Blair announced the reformation of the Departments of Education and Employment and Social Security into two new departments. The first is the Department for Education and Skills, which is to take responsibility for education, training and lifelong learning. The second, the Department for Work, Family and Pensions, will be responsible for work- and benefit-related services for working-age and older people.

Labour also committed itself to making the New Deal programmes a permanent part of the welfare system and compulsory for anyone aged over twenty-five years and the partners of long-term unemployed individuals (if they are not taking care of a child). Additionally, the government has promised to target extra support on 'hard to employ' individuals. Initially, this will come through a new programme of special coaching in numeracy, literacy, information technology and presentation skills, complemented by a new initiative to train long-term benefit recipients to enter 'targeted' market sectors. The idea is to develop a 'sector-by-sector' training approach to provide individuals with the skills necessary to enter the economy's growth sectors: the financial, information technology, construction, hospitality and retail sectors. To continue its efforts to encourage business to invest in disadvantaged communities the government also announced its intention to launch the Recruit programme as an incentive for small businesses to invest in long-term unemployed individuals living in disadvantaged communities. Recruit does this by providing a business grant of up to £2,300 to small employers willing to hire, train and retain individuals participating in the New Deal who come from, and are living in, one of the country's most disadvantaged communities.

While these plans are little more than modifications to the reforms Labour introduced between 1997 and 2001 to help spread justice and equality by providing unemployed individuals with the skills and rewards necessary to become active members of the community, New Labour has proposed two new reforms aimed directly at bringing about the goal of creating a just society with opportunities for all. The first big idea in the 2001 manifesto was an extension of the WFTC to incorporate all people employed over sixteen hours per week, regardless of whether they have children. When the new Employment Tax Credit comes into effect in 2003, it will be the first time any UK government has guaranteed all individuals, regardless of their marital or parenthood status, a minimum income (as long as they are working at least sixteen hours per week). Labour's second radical proposal was the joint announcement of a new Child Trust Fund and Savings Gateway. Both of these initiatives are designed to spread asset ownership to all, but especially children, to ensure all future generations start life with true opportunities, regardless of their family background. The basic idea of the Child Trust Fund is that upon the birth of a child the government would set up an account and deposit a sum of money based on the economic position of the family. From here not only could other family members deposit limited amounts of money, but also the government would deposit a given sum, on a set schedule, until the child's sixteenth birthday. The Savings Gateway is an idea to encourage low-income earners to save by opening an account with a deposit that the government would match, or top up. The account would operate for a fixed period, after which the saver would be given the opportunity to transfer the funds into a traditional savings device: individual savings account, stakeholder pension or Child Trust Fund.[11]

Labour's campaign commitments to the NHS centred on continuing the programmes initiated after 1997. It made pledges to expand the number of nurses, doctors and therapists by 2004; to continue using the PFI to fund the development of hospitals and one-stop primary care centres; to target more resources on cancer and cardiac treatment; and to produce new targets for the care of orthopaedic and ophthalmology patients. In line with earlier reforms, Labour has also committed itself devolve at least 75 per cent of the NHS budget to general practitioners by 2004. This compares with just 15 per cent when Labour came to power in 1997. Controversially, as with the partnerships in education, there is considerable unease with plans to expand the use of the private sector in the delivery of NHS services. While contentious, these plans should be placed in perspective. First, the NHS has always contracted with private organisations to deliver services. More importantly, no assets, employees or infrastructure are being sold to the private sector and the government has passed measures to ensure that all employees will be treated fairly, regardless of whether they are employed within the private or public sector. Finally, while the NHS will be expanding its use of private sector services and facilities, the delivery of these services will continue to be free to the patient. Thus, while it may seem like a major change, leading to the privatisation of the health service, in reality, as with the other public–private initiatives, the average patient would not notice the involvement of the private sector.

One often overlooked possibility of the government's strategy of engaging business and community groups in the provision of public services is the possible long-term indirect benefit. In Britain, businesses have traditionally been the passive beneficiaries of public services. Now that businesses are becoming actively engaged in the development and provision of these services they might begin to exercise social responsibility within the community as well as economic accountability to their shareholders. If this happens, Labour's goal of creating a just society will be much closer and will have been developed without having to resort to the coercive measures used by the party in the past to nationalise the major business sectors and redistribute resources.

'The work goes on'

In his victory speeches Tony Blair went to great lengths to acknowledge that while the government and society had come a long way towards social justice – a society in which rights were matched with responsibilities and people could expect to reap the rewards of their efforts – there was still much to be done, not least of which was to find ways of informing the public of the extent of the change that had occurred since 1997 and how much more the government hoped to do during its second term. The biggest problem the government will face during its second term is not a Tory revival but that society will not accept or appreciate New Labour's approach and change in the public services (partly because of the long-term nature of these reforms). This could result in even greater cynicism than was expressed in the general election of 2001. However, while there is still much to do, given the success and commitment to the reform and modernisation of public services New Labour demonstrated during the 1997–2001 government, there is every hope the pledges for 2001–05/6 will be carried out, and that this will lead to a society where individuals and communities accept their duties to one another and where the government continues to invest and reform public services to enhance and spread economic and social justice for all.

Notes

1 While the New Deal for Schools does use private finances the government retains ownership and control of these facilities.
2 D. Purdy, 'New Labour and welfare', in D. Coates and P. Lawler (eds), *New Labour in Power* (Manchester: Manchester University Press, 2000).
3 The New Deal for lone parents was an important element of the government's welfare reform strategy because lone parents and their children were the group most likely to live in poverty for extended periods of time and the number of single parents had grown to over one million between 1979 and 1997. Of these, the number depending on income support had trebled since 1979.
4 Department of Social Security, press release 2000/377, 30 November 2000.
5 Department of Social Security, *Welfare Reform Focus Files* (London: Department of Social Security, 1997); Social Exclusion Unit, *Teenage Pregnancy*, Cm 4342 (London: Stationery Office, 1999).
6 Social Exclusion Unit, *Bringing Britain Together*, Cm 4045 (London: Stationery Office, 1998); Department of Social Security, *Opportunity for All*, Cm 4445 (London: Stationery Office, 1999).
7 Treasury, *The Modernisation of Britain's Tax and Benefit System (Parts 1–4)* (London: Stationery Office, 1999).
8 Department of Health, *The New NHS: Modern, Dependable* (London, HMSO, 1997), p. 1.
9 Labour Party, *General Election Manifesto* (London: Labour Party, 2001), p. 6.
10 Department for Education and Employment, http://www.dfee.gov.uk.
11 Studies in the United States and Canada have indicated that strategies linking education and welfare reform to policies to encourage employment and to income

supplements have long-term positive effects on the income, living conditions and educational achievements of welfare recipients. Thus Labour's approach to public service reform, if given time, should have a long-term positive impact on people's lives, especially those living on less than half the average income. See D. Bloom and C. Michalopoulos, *How Welfare and Work Policies Affect Employment and Income* (New York: Manpower Demonstration Research Corporation, 2001); P. Morris *et al.*, *How Welfare and Work Policies Affect Children* (New York: Manpower Demonstration Research Corporation, 2001).

Wyre Forest

Dr Richard Taylor, the victorious candidate in the constituency of Wyre Forest, was dubbed the 'man in the white coat'. The retired consultant physician fought the Worcestershire seat as an independent under the Kidderminster Hospital and Health Concern (KHHC) banner and campaigned solely on health issues. The main issue was the closure of Kidderminster Hospital's accident and emergency department in September 2000 along with 192 inpatient beds, as part of a reorganisation of health services in the county. A new hospital was to be built in Worcester and a £14 million one-stop clinic was planned for Kidderminster, where outpatient services would be still provided by the local hospital. The plans were deeply controversial and provided a successful basis for mobilisation by the KHHC, which already had eighteen representatives on Wyre Forest District Council, making it the largest group.

Taylor defeated the sitting Labour MP, David Lock, who had served as a junior minister in the Lord Chancellor's Office in the previous Labour administration. Lock was the only government minister to lose his seat. Taylor took 58 per cent of the vote, which bettered even Bell's tally against the deeply unpopular Neil Hamilton in Tatton in 1997. Taylor said he had an unfair advantage at the polls because he knew so many of his constituents from his time as a doctor. He was also aided by the decision of the Liberal Democrats not to field a candidate. In his victory speech, he said that: 'The message to the Government is you cannot ride roughshod over a local community's feelings without rebellion'.

The 'man in the white suit', the independent Martin Bell (defeated in Brentwood and Ongar) was happy to ease his former schoolmate's transition to his new job, but warned that Taylor could face a frostier reception than he had received. As Bell put it: 'I was in a different position when I arrived in the Commons. I had just ousted an unpopular Tory. I don't know how much hostility Dr Taylor will meet on the Government benches'.

Result

Wyre Forest		
	No. of votes	% of vote
Taylor, R. (KHHC)	28,487	58.1
Lock, D. (Labour)	10,857	22.1
Simpson, M. (Conservative)	9,350	19.1
Millington, J. (UKIP)	368	0.8
Majority	17,630	
Independent gain from Labour		
Turnout		68.0

8

In Europe, not interested in Europe

Andrew Geddes

Introduction

By the time the next general election is called, the pound could have been replaced by the euro, economic policy could be made by the Council of Ministers, while interest rates could be set by the European Central Bank. Yet, despite the Conservative leader William Hague's best efforts to make European integration a key campaign theme and to 'save the pound', Europe failed once again to register as a decisive electoral issue. While it is fair to say that British people appear to be unenthusiastic about the EU and are not eager to replace the pound with the euro, it is also true that they were more influenced at the ballot box by Labour's economic record and concerns about health and education. Of course, this is not to say that the EU is unimportant: its significance is enormous while its actual and potential effects are far reaching.[1] Rather it means that, despite William Hague's best efforts to make Europe a key campaign theme, the 2001 general election was fought on the usual national electoral territory: concerns about the economy and welfare state.

Europe's relative lack of salience as a campaign issue is the focus of the first half of this chapter. I contrast the stances of the three main British parties and explain why the Conservatives' emphasis on their opposition to European integration failed to reap electoral dividends. In the chapter's second half I delve a little deeper. First, I explore Labour's cautious policy on European integration in comparison with the policy positions of other leading EU member states. I then examine British public attitudes to the EU. This allows a better understanding of the challenges facing a re-elected Labour government as the EU 'widens', by admitting new member states, and 'deepens' integration, perhaps even with an EU constitution. Moreover, looking at Europe through the lens provided by British public opinion shows ambivalence about European integration, a lack of any widespread or deep-seated feeling of European identity and a lack of trust in European institutions, all compounded by a lack of knowledge about the EU. While Europe may have failed to register as a salient concern at the 2001 general election, 'yes' campaigners in any future euro referendum will face an uphill battle trying to convince an electorate who are in Europe but who do not appear to be particularly interested in Europe.

Searching for clear blue water

By 2001 the Conservatives had established 'clear blue water' between themselves, Labour and the Liberal Democrats. It has been argued that a clearer Conservative commitment to Euroscepticism could reap electoral dividends for the party.[2] William Hague appeared determined to test this theory. A hardened post-1997 Conservative commitment to Euroscepticism can be linked to four factors: first, the outcome of the post-Maastricht civil war within the party that led to the marginalisation of pro-European voices; second, the lessons drawn by the new leadership from the 1997 general election disaster; third, a still lingering, unresolved bitterness over the removal of Thatcher as party leader; and fourth, the impact on party policy of an increasingly Eurosceptical parliamentary party.[3] The Labour government followed an essentially cautious line on Europe, while the Liberal Democrats preferred not to talk too much about their enthusiasm for a federal Europe. Neither Labour nor the Liberal Democrats sought to make Europe a key campaign issue; the Conservatives did.

The internal divisions within the Conservative Party during the 1990s, caused to a large extent by the ERM debacle, the Maastricht Treaty and its tortuous ratification process, had helped fatally to undermine the Conservatives' 1997 campaign. Former leader John Major had been criticised for failing to open clear blue water on Europe.[4] On the single currency, for instance, both the Conservatives and Labour maintained a cautious 'wait and see' approach. This stance was far from being the settled will of the Conservative Party. Many candidates and party members were much more hostile, but Major had little alternative because leading Conservatives such as his deputy, Michael Heseltine, and Chancellor, Kenneth Clarke, were pro-European and enthusiasts for Britain joining the single currency.

After 1997, the much-reduced Conservative parliamentary party became distinctly more Eurosceptical. William Hague may initially have toyed with a more inclusive image for the party, but this inclusiveness did not stretch to accommodating Europhiles in the shadow cabinet. Ex-Chancellor Kenneth Clarke decided to spend more time with his company directorships and was not a member of the Conservative frontbench team while others, such as David Curry, soon left the shadow cabinet when the mood of the party leadership became clear. The party's stance on the euro was settled when the policy to reject membership for the lifetime of two parliaments was put to a ballot of party members and overwhelmingly approved (see Chapter 3).

Table 8.1. Visions of Europe: Labour, the Conservatives and the Liberal Democrats compared

	Tony Blair	William Hague	Charles Kennedy
Slogan	A leading player in Europe	In Europe, not run by Europe	Freedom through Europe
Role of the nation state	Europe of nation states with power in the Council representing national governments	A 'network Europe' with different nations coming together for differing purposes and for different effects – in other words, a 'flexible Europe'	A federal Europe based on the principle of subsidiarity with strengthened EU institutions
The euro	In favour, in principle, based on assessment early in the next parliament of the 'five economic tests' and a 'yes' vote in a referendum	Rejected for the lifetime of the next parliament	In favour, with membership dependent upon a 'yes' vote in a referendum
European Parliament/ Commission	Proposes a second chamber made up of representatives from national parliaments. Opposes a directly elected Commission President	Opposed to further transfers of power to EU institutions	More powers for the Commission and European Parliament and increased use of qualified majority voting in the Council of of Ministers
Constitution	Opposes both an EU constitution and a legally enforceable charter of rights	Opposed to EU constitution. Renegotiation of the Nice Treaty. Domestic law to establish 'reserved powers' that will prevent the EU over-riding national laws in certain areas	Support an EU constitution that defines the EU's powers and sets out the role of EU institutions, national governments and the regions

Tax harmonisation	Opposed to tax harmonisation. Prefer tax competition	Opposed to tax harmonisation. Campaign allegations of secret plans for harmonisation of income taxes	Continued ability to apply national vetoes on tax measures
Common foreign policy/ defence	Supports common European defence within NATO. Willing to contribute to a European Rapid Reaction Force	Opposed to any EU cooperation that is not under the NATO umbrella	A fully fledged European common foreign and security policy with a significant defence component, consistent with NATO
Enlargement	Supports early enlargement and reform of the Common Agricultural Policy	Supports rapid enlargement with accession of new member states by 2004	Supports rapid enlargement with accession of new member states

In retrospect, it could be seen as Hague's main achievement that he managed to lead a relatively united party into the 2001 general election when only recently it had been tearing itself apart on Europe. Yet the inherent risk with this Eurosceptical stance was that if Europe became *the* issue that defined William Hague's Conservative Party then the party might fail to broaden its appeal beyond core voters. Euroscepticism might excite the party faithful, but could it connect with the concerns of the electorate?

If Europe was an issue that could benefit the Conservatives then they made very sure that their stance was distinguishable from that of their rivals. The opening of clear blue water on Europe is shown in Table 8.1, which compares the stances of Labour, the Conservatives and the Liberal Democrats.

In contrast, and despite rather vacuous assertions about differences in style and tone, Labour's European policies are broadly consistent with the stance adopted by British governments since UK accession in 1973. The agenda has, of course, moved on and Prime Minister Blair has appeared more at ease with the vocabulary of European integration, although compared with his Conservative predecessors this is not too difficult. In fact, compared with William Hague's Conservative Party of 2001, Margaret Thatcher's governments of the 1980s would have appeared decidedly pro-European. But if we look beneath the style and tone of New Labour and examine its policy on European integration then we could ask, 'What has changed?' In its 2001 manifesto, Labour advocated a Europe of nation states and was suspicious of plans for a federal Europe.[5] This suspicion of federalism was combined with a lack of enthusiasm for grand projects such as a European constitution.[6] Labour's manifesto pledged that Britain would be 'a leading player in the EU' – it could hardly say otherwise – but emphasised a central role for national governments. Labour supported an expanded defence and security role for the EU consistent with NATO, as well as the accession of new member states from central, eastern and southern Europe. Labour would countenance only limited transfers of competence to EU institutions and opposed both an EU constitution and tax harmonisation. Labour expressed support in principle for the euro, but a Labour government's support would be dependent on the satisfaction of 'five economic tests' and a 'yes' vote in a referendum.

The Conservatives were far more radical. They proposed to roll back the EU's influence on Britain. 'In Europe, not run by Europe' was Hague's campaign theme. This was accompanied by a vision of a 'network' Europe within which member states could pick and choose those parts of the EU they liked and opt out of those that they did not, such as the euro in Britain's case. There would also be strict limits placed on further transfers of competence to the EU through the introduction of legislation establishing 'reserved powers' for the UK parliament, upon which the EU could not encroach. If such a policy was implemented and other member states rejected this kind of agenda, as they would be likely to do, it would raise serious questions about the UK's continued EU membership.

The Conservative Party appeared to be developing an alternative political economy that questioned both the necessity and inevitability of ever closer ties with the EU.[7] Three elements of this alternative political economy can be identified. First, Britain would become the 'Hong Kong' of Europe, with a deregulated, low-cost economy compared with allegedly high-cost and over-regulated continental European economies. Second, Britain would revert to a global strategy rather than becoming inextricably linked with the EU. To use a metaphor invoked by Winston Churchill, Britain would resurrect a 'three circles' approach with a policy towards the EU coexisting with cultivation of Commonwealth and Atlantic ties. Third, Britain would strengthen Atlantic ties, possibly with membership of the North American Free Trade Area.

The Liberal Democrats remained the most consistently Eurofederal of the three main British parties. They advocated a European constitution that would define the role of strengthened EU institutions, nation states and the regions in a 'multi-level' Europe. The effect would be that nation states would remain key actors, but would share power with European institutions and sub-national government. The Liberal Democrats advocated membership of the euro, dependent first on a 'yes' vote in a referendum. This enthusiasm for a federal Europe was not a central component of the Liberal Democrats' election strategy. They preferred to emphasise their commitment to public services in the well founded belief that this was a much more important issue for the majority of voters. It was also unlikely that enthusiasm for a federal Europe would go down well in the Liberal Democrats' heartlands, in the south-west of England.

The contrasts between Blair and Hague as the two alternative Prime Ministers can also be seen in the type of language used in keynote speeches delivered in the run-up to the election (see Box 8.1). In Blair's October 2000 speech to the Polish stock exchange, he spoke of missed opportunities, cautious support for the euro and a vision of Europe as a 'superpower', not a 'superstate'. Hague's 'foreign land' speech delivered to the Conservatives' spring forum in March 2001 was very different. The EU was portrayed as a threat to parliament, to national identity and thus to self-government. Hague argued that the renewal of Labour's mandate could turn Britain into a 'foreign land', presumably because of alien influences forced on the country by the EU. Opposition to the EU's creeping competencies would apparently require some kind of popular front comprised of like-minded Eurosceptical voters who would 'lend' Hague their vote to defeat the EU.

Europe as a campaign issue

Why did William Hague's Conservative Party pursue this Eurosceptical strategy? The first explanation is quite simple: for Thatcherite Conservatives like Hague and his followers, deeper European integration was a threat to self-government and national identity that had to be resisted. Opposition to

Box 8.1. Tony Blair's and William Hague's Euro-language contrasted

Extracts from Tony Blair's speech to the Polish stock exchange, Warsaw, 6 October 2000

The blunt truth is that British policy towards the rest of Europe over half a century has been marked by gross misjudgements, mistaking what we wanted to be the case with what was the case; hesitation, alienation, incomprehension, with the occasional burst of enlightened brilliance which only served to underline the frustration of our partners with what was the norm.

I have said the political case for Britain being part of the single currency is strong. I don't say political or constitutional issues aren't important. They are. But to my mind, they aren't an insuperable barrier. What does have to be overcome is the economic issue. It is an economic union. Joining prematurely simply on political grounds, without the economic conditions being right, would be a mistake. Hence our position: in principle in favour; in practice, the economic tests must be met. We cannot and will not take risks with Britain's economic strength. The principle is real, the tests are real.

The European Union is the world's biggest single economic and political partnership of democratic states. That represents a huge opportunity for Europe and the peoples of Europe. And as a Union of democracies, it has the capacity to sustain peace in our continent, to deliver unprecedented prosperity and to be a powerful force for democratic values in the rest of the world.

Extracts from William Hague's 'foreign land' speech to the Conservative Party's spring forum, 4 March 2001

Let me take you on a journey to a foreign land – to Britain after a second term of Tony Blair.

That is why the next election will be different. Because we won't just be voting for the next government. We'll be voting on whether the British Crown in Parliament should remain supreme in Britain. We'll be voting to decide whether our people will remain sovereign their own country [*sic*].

We will renegotiate the Common Fisheries Policy and the Common Agricultural Policy because ... these outdated and failed policies have got to change.

And our Reserved Powers Act will write into the law of our land the powers and rights that we hold today and which we will pass to the next generation, so that no stroke of a pen from Brussels, or retrospective court judgement, can take those rights away.

In defending the sovereignty of our parliament, we defend the sovereignty of our people. We defend our right to live under our own laws.

So I appeal today to all those people who may not have voted Conservative before, but who believe in an independent Britain. At this coming election, lend us your vote. Vote for us this time, so that your vote will mean something next time, and the time after, and the time after that.

further European integration and the euro was thus a principled stance derived from a broadly Thatcherite world view. In addition to this are two other explanations. The first can be called the 'core voters' strategy. For realists in Conservative Central Office, a Conservative win in 2001 was unlikely given Labour's 1997 landslide and the fact that Labour had maintained a commanding opinion poll lead since June 1992.[8] The long haul back to power required that the core Conservative vote be shored up. If this was done, the Conservatives could boost their vote by perhaps 4 or 5 per cent at the 2001 election and thus make sufficient in-roads into Labour's majority to secure Hague's continued leadership of the party. Second, and in support of this core voter strategy, opinion research demonstrated that there were very few issues on which the Conservatives' stance was preferred to Labour's. Three good issues for the Conservatives were asylum, tax and Europe. All were emphasised but, of these three, Europe dominated the Conservative campaign.

The Conservatives' approach to the campaign became evident from day one. While Blair launched Labour's campaign with a stage-managed and much ridiculed speech at a London girls' school, Hague travelled to Watford, mounted his soapbox – now the traditional electoral tool of the underdog – and declared the election to be the last chance to 'save the pound'. Hague was surrounded by supporters holding 'keep the pound' placards. This was a high-risk strategy because the Conservatives could end up being seen as a single-issue party with little to say on other issues such as health and education. Moreover, Blair was overwhelmingly preferred to Hague as a candidate for Prime Minister – and hence as Britain's representative on the European stage.

Hague's concentration on Europe did help push the issue towards the top of the media agenda. Surveys of media coverage by academics at Loughborough University for the *Guardian* showed that, in terms of coverage, Europe was a key campaign issue (see Chapter 5). In the campaign's second week, it was the second most covered issue, ahead of education and health. By the third week, Europe was the subject of 9.5 per cent of stories, second only to the electoral process itself, compared with 6.1 per cent and 4.8 per cent for health and education respectively. These figures indicated the ability of Hague to set the agenda. The rules on media balance for broadcasting organisations meant that Hague had to be included in the coverage. If he was talking about Europe – which usually he was – then this was going to have some agenda-setting effects. Whether people were particularly interested is a different question. This points to the difference between Europe as a campaign issue with the power to fascinate political insiders and Europe as an electoral issue with the capacity either to enthuse or to repel large numbers of voters.

There was some unease about Hague's Eurosceptical strategy, and press stories emerged about criticism from within the Conservative Party that the issues that mattered most to people – public services – were not to the fore in the party's campaign.[9] Opinion polls did suggest that Europe was a good issue for the Conservatives. Forty-four per cent of respondents to a MORI poll preferred Tory policy, compared with 28 per cent who preferred Labour's, but the same poll also showed Labour to have clear and commanding leads on health and education (Table 8.2).

Table 8.2. Perceptions of party stances on key issues, by voting intention

	Conservatives	Labour	Liberal Democrats	Other	None	Don't know
Europe	44	28	6	3	6	13
Health	14	49	6	1	7	23
Education	12	46	9	1	7	25

Question: At this general election which, if any, of these issues do you think will be very important to you in helping you decide which party to vote for?
Source: MORI for the *Economist*, 18–25 May 2001.

Whether or not this lead on Europe could benefit the Conservatives would depend upon whether the issue mattered to a large number of voters. The fatal flaw for Hague's campaign and his incessant references to 'saving the pound' was that there was little evidence to suggest that it had enough appeal to enough voters. The message may have reassured Eurosceptical voters, but they were likely to vote Conservative anyway. The risk was that if people were actually more concerned about educational standards and poor standards of health care then William Hague constantly expressing his undying love – albeit for the lifetime of one parliament – for the national currency could appear a little irrelevant. The same MORI poll referred to above showed that 18 per cent of respondents did indeed think that the main campaign issue should be Europe, but this left it in eighth place, lagging far behind health and education, with 61 per cent and 53 per cent respectively. No other polls conducted during the campaign contradicted this general finding. There was some optimism in Conservative ranks when a MORI poll for the *Sunday Telegraph* on the Sunday before the election put Europe as the fourth most important issue, but even then only 14 per cent of respondents saw it as an important issue. The lesson from the polls was clear: Europe lagged behind concerns about poor standards of public service provision as an election issue. Euroscepticism was not the path to follow if the ground lost in Labour's 1997 landslide was to be recovered.

It is possible to feel a sense of déjà vu when reporting these findings. Didn't the Conservatives become obsessed about Europe in 1997 too? During the 1997 general election campaign the *Daily Express* commented that Europe was the issue that made the parties swoon and the voters yawn. There was little to suggest that this mood had changed in 2001. Europe was an issue that could excite Conservative candidates and party members and attract media attention; but a continued focus on Europe gave the impression of an introspective party talking to itself while failing to engage with the concerns of the electorate. This perception was heightened when Margaret Thatcher intervened in the campaign. In a speech delivered to a gathering of the party faithful in Plymouth, she departed from her prepared text and from party policy to state that she would 'never' join the euro. Thatcher's intervention led a few other Conservatives to stick their heads above the parapet. Alan Duncan was quoted as saying that 'The single currency is a socialist project dressed up in business language' while Tim Loughton contended that the euro 'must be resisted at all costs'. The Conservative Party Chairman, Michael Ancram, appeared sanguine when arguing that statements such as those of Duncan and Loughton 'fall within the spirit of party policy'.[10]

Little changed as the campaign progressed. Hague continued to argue that the election would be the last chance to 'save the pound' even though a re-elected Labour government was pledged to hold a referendum on the issue, if it decided the economic conditions were right to join the euro. False promises, argued Hague: Labour would rig the referendum process and the phrasing of the question to ensure a favourable result for Labour. By this reasoning, the general election was *the* referendum on the euro. Conservative Party press conferences became rather surreal events as the possible question in a possible future referendum was discussed (which of course also assumed that Labour would win, otherwise why else would there be a referendum?). This stance infuriated anti-euro campaign groups, such as Business for Sterling, which were building their resources in anticipation of a referendum. Also, as critics pointed out, if the general election was a referendum on the euro and the Conservatives lost, then surely this was an endorsement of the euro? Not so, responded Tory high command, unconvincingly. The net effect was that Hague was not viewed as a credible leader for any future anti-euro referendum campaign. Worse than this, he was weakened by a campaign strategy that veered precariously towards single-issue politics. Worse still, the chosen issue was not one that appeared likely to reap electoral rewards for the Conservatives.

A leading player in the EU?

Opposition to 'more' Europe did not work for the Conservatives. Labour, in contrast, had little to say about the issue. While the attainment of a historic second term is a cause of great satisfaction for Labour and Tony Blair, many problems lie ahead for the re-elected Labour government. Two issues loom particularly large. The first is the future shape and scope of the EU. The second is Britain's possible future membership of the euro.

Table 8.3. Mapping the EU's road ahead

	Tony Blair	Lionel Jospin	Gerhard Schröder
Federal Europe or nation state?	Europe of nation states	A federation of nation states	A federal Europe with strengthened EU institutions
European Parliament/president	A second chamber of the European Parliament made up of national parliamentarians. No elected president	Commission President appointed from the winning bloc in European Parliament elections, with a 'congress' of national MPs to scrutinise the work of the European Parliament	Bicameral European Parliament with the Council of Ministers as the Upper House
Constitution	Opposed	In favour of an EU constitution as the affirmation of a common project	In favour, with the non-binding Charter of Rights agreed at Nice as its basis
Tax harmonisation	Opposed	In favour for reasons of 'solidarity' and to help protect workers' rights. Wants binding social treaty on workers' rights	In favour
Enlargement	Keen advocate	A 'historical necessity' but worried about institutional paralysis	In favour, but with limits on free movement of workers from new member states

Common foreign/defence policy	Supportive, so long as it is consistent with NATO. Prepared to contribute to a European Rapid Reaction Force	Favours common foreign and defence policies and the building up of a European Rapid Reaction Force	A paper by his Social Democrat Party favours 'permanent political and military decision-making structures'
What nationals typically say about themselves	We are the only country that obeys the rules	We invented the EU and are the only people who understand it	We pay all the bills, we should have more say
What others say about them	Make your mind up or leave; America's stooges	Arrogant	Alarmingly ambitious
Biggest fear	Britain submerged into EU superstate	EU as German-led superpower humiliates France	Popular backlash in Germany against euro or eastern enlargement
Biggest hope	EU becomes giant free trade area	EU as French-led superpower humiliates US	Federal Europe solves 'German problem'

Source: Adapted from the *Guardian*, 30 May 2001, the *Financial Times*, 30 May 2001 and the *Economist*, 16–22 June 2001.

First, let us consider the bigger picture. In 2004 EU leaders will meet to consider treaty reforms necessary for an enlarged EU with perhaps ten new member states. Can a Union of twenty-five countries be an effective decision-making organisation while also allowing for accountability and scrutiny? EU leaders have been keen to make their contribution to this debate. Table 8.3 contrasts the view of three prominent centre-left European politicians. French Prime Minister Lionel Jospin actually caused some disquiet in Labour's campaign headquarters when he made a mid-campaign speech on the future of Europe. Millbank feared that a Euro-row could help the Conservatives, but Jospin failed to see why French political life should be suspended for the convenience of the British Labour Party. Moreover, while Jospin is to the left of Blair – for instance, it is hard to imagine Blair arguing, as Jospin does, for a European charter of rights for workers – Jospin's vision of a Europe of nation states was not too far from Blair's own views. The starkest contrast is with German Chancellor Gerhard Schröder's vision of a federal Europe, with an EU constitution and strengthened EU institutions. What becomes clear from Table 8.3 is the essential caution of Labour's vision of Europe. The policy pursued by the Labour government is not dramatically out of line with that followed by British governments since accession. Labour may appear more pro-European, but this is as much a result of Conservative Euroscepticism as it is a result of some conversion to 'ever closer union'. Thus while the EU's agenda moves on, there has been some continuity in underlying British government preferences.

The second question facing the re-elected Labour government is whether to recommend that the pound be replaced with the euro. This deeply controversial issue possesses the potential to derail Labour's second term. It also goes to the heart of the key power relationship in the Labour government, that of Tony Blair with Gordon Brown. The government's stance on the euro is very clear, allegedly. First, the 'five economic tests' (listed in Box 8.2) need to be satisfied. Second, the government may then recommend to the people in a referendum that the UK joins EMU.

Box 8.2. The five economic tests for joining EMU

- Are business cycles and economic structures compatible so that the UK could coexist comfortably with euro interest rates on a permanent basis?
- If problems emerge is there sufficient flexibility to deal with them?
- Would joining EMU create better conditions for firms making long-term decisions to invest in the UK?
- What impact would entry into EMU have on the competitive position of the UK's financial services industry?
- In summary, will joining EMU promote higher growth, stability and a lasting increase in jobs?

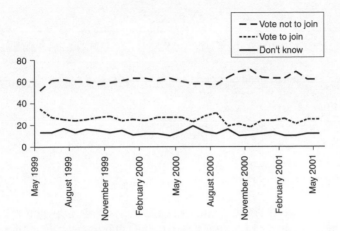

Figure 8.1. Opposition to the UK joining the euro, May 1999 to May 2001.
Source: Commission of the European Community, *Eurobarometer: Public Opinion in the European Union*, report number 54 (Brussels; Commission of the European Community, 2001).

The five economic tests are vague and other equally vague tests have been added, such as reform of the European Central Bank. In fact, the whole point of the tests is that they allow a margin of political flexibility so that any decision about whether joining the euro is right for the country will coincide with the issue of whether it is right for the Labour government too. As a witness to the House of Commons Treasury Select Committee noted: 'The chancellor's tests are so loosely defined that anyone will be able to say that they have either been passed or failed according to the dictates of political expediency'.[11]

Will conditions be right for the Labour government in the near future? Political journalists point to the Blair–Brown relationship as the key variable. A journalist with apparently good Labour government contacts argued that Tony Blair would like to see Britain in the euro.[12] More than this, he sees it as his historical role to lead Britain to a more positive relationship with the EU, which necessarily means engagement with its key features, such as the single currency. Brown, on the other hand, is not so sure. His apparent prevarication is important because the Treasury will conduct the 'tests' and thus possesses veto power. If the main message from the electorate in 2001 was the need to deliver high-quality public services then why jeopardise this with a potentially divisive campaign on the euro? Moreover, why stake the Labour government's reputation on a pro-euro campaign when the public appears to be so hostile? To demonstrate this hostility, Figure 8.1 shows that opposition to the euro has been strong and consistent. In fact, no opinion poll since Labour came to power in 1997 – however worded – has found a majority of respondents in support of membership of the single currency.

Table 8.4. Perceptions of Tony Blair's policy on the euro

	Percentage of respondents
Determined to take us in at the earliest opportunity	24
Wants to take us in, but won't dare unless he is sure of winning a referendum	47
He is prepared for us to stay out indefinitely if the conditions aren't right	19
Don't know	11

Source: NOP for the *Sunday Times*, 3 June 2001.

There are some interesting undercurrents. An opinion poll by NOP for the *Sunday Times* on 3 June 2001 asked people about their perception of Tony Blair's position on the euro. The results are shown in Table 8.4. According to these perceptions, caution is Labour's watchword. Given the anti-euro sentiment shown in Figure 8.1 then the combination of caution and public hostility could mean that a referendum on the euro is delayed. A referendum defeat could badly damage the credibility of the government and have potentially corrosive effects on support at the next general election.

That said, a closer look at the opinion data also suggests an element of fatalism about the single currency. It is clear that British people tend not to like the idea of replacing the pound with the euro but, at the same time, they think that it is going to happen anyway. This is shown by the same NOP opinion poll for the *Sunday Times*, when people were asked 'Regardless of your view, do you think that the UK will join the Euro during the lifetime of the next Parliament, or not?' To which 53 per cent responded that they did, 35 per cent that they did not, while 12 per cent said that they didn't know.[13] These polls suggest that around 65 per cent of people oppose membership, but a majority think that it will happen within the next five years anyway.

How can this be explained? The 'tide of history' is one possible explanation. Euro notes and coins were introduced in twelve member states from 1 January 2002. The single currency will thus become a tangible reality when Britons travelling to the euro-zone exchange their pounds for euros. A second centres on an apparent fatalism that is indicative of a lack of faith in people's ability to shape the political world in which they live. People might not like the euro, they might not want it, but they feel that it will happen anyway. In turn, this points to a basic lack of legitimacy for the EU in the eyes of many British people and implies a gap between political elites pushing for integration and public opinion. European integration has tended to be an elite project built on a permissive consensus whereby national elites forge European policy with a basically compliant public. Europe is thus processed as a foreign policy issue with few serious domestic implications. If this permissive consensus breaks down then people may well feel disengaged from the process of European integration because they may feel that they were not consulted about it. There is evidence from across the EU that, since the problems with ratification of the Maastricht Treaty in the early 1990s, there has been an 'uncorking' of popular opposition to European unification.[14]

This legitimacy gap appears to be more evident in Britain than in other member states. Data from *Eurobarometer* public opinion research conducted at the end of 2000 in all fifteen EU member states show the British to be the most Eurosceptical of member state nationals.[15] When support for the EU was gauged, only 28 per cent of UK respondents thought that membership of the EU had been a good thing for their country, compared with an EU average of 50 per cent. When asked whether they thought that their country had benefited from membership, only 31 per cent of UK respondents agreed, compared with 41 per cent not who thought it had not. Across all fifteen member states, 47 per cent of respondents thought that their country had benefited, compared with 32 per cent who thought that it had not. Only the Swedes ranked lower than the British in this assessment of the relative benefits of EU membership.

By these utilitarian measures, we can see that British people are not great supporters of the EU. In addition to this, European integration also raises important questions about identity and national self-understanding. Figure 8.2 shows that UK respondents felt the least sense of European identity, preferring instead to emphasise their national identities.

These findings were confirmed by an ICM poll taken in January for Radio 4's *Today* programme. People were presented with four options about their sense of identity. Of the respondents, 66 per cent said that they felt British, not European, 27 per cent said that they felt equally British and European, and a mere 3 per cent said that they felt European, not British. The zero-sum 'British not European' option accounted for two-thirds of respondents. Only 30 per cent of respondents chose non-zero sum options that allow the possibility of imagining social and political identities where a feeling of European identity complements rather than detracts from national identity.

This lack of either utilitarian or affective support for the EU is compounded by a lack of knowledge of and trust in European institutions. For instance, when people in the UK were asked whether they trusted the European Parliament, only 28 per cent said that they did, 42 per cent said that they didn't and 31 per cent said that they didn't know. These were the highest figures for 'don't trust' and 'don't know' among respondents in all fifteen member states. The Commission fared even worse, with only 24 per cent of UK respondents saying that they trusted the institution, compared with an EU average of 46 per cent. Respondents to the *Eurobarometer* surveys were also asked to rate their own knowledge of the EU on a ten-point scale. The self-confessed lack of knowledge of British respondents is shown in Figure 8.3.

The small chink of light for pro-euro campaigners is that it was not ever thus. In the late 1980s and early 1990s, when enthusiasm about the single

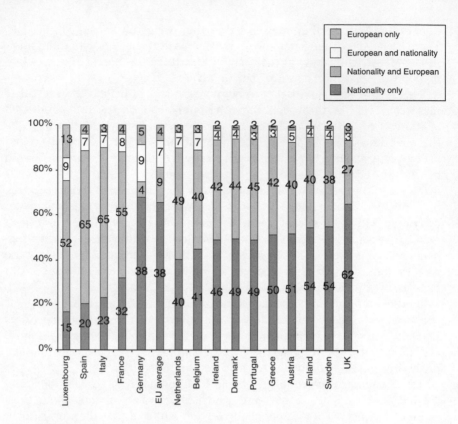

Figure 8.2. Percentages of respondents across the EU reporting European and national identity.
Source: Commission of the European Community, *Eurobarometer: Public Opinion in the European Union*, report number 54 (Brussels; Commission of the European Community, 2001).

market was at its height, there was more support for the EU and the perceived benefits that it had brought to Britain. As things stand, however, British public opinion is the most Eurosceptical in the EU. British people tend not to feel particularly European, do not particularly trust EU institutions and have self-confessed low levels of knowledge about the EU. The hostile coverage of the EU in some sections of the press may have played a part in this,[16] but it all goes to confirm the adjectives most frequently applied to UK membership of the EU, such as 'awkward', 'reluctant' or 'semi-detached'.

The post-election utterances of the Labour government also suggest caution on the euro. Gordon Brown's Mansion House speech on 19 June 2001 appeared to rule out an early referendum and to enshrine a 'considered and cautious' approach to the euro as official government policy. Briefings by the Chancellor's staff also suggested that an assessment of the five economic tests

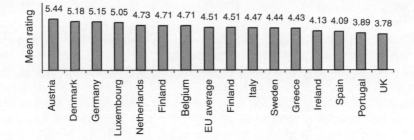

Figure 8.3. Levels of perceived knowledge of the EU, by member state nationality, rated on a ten-point scale from 1, 'Know nothing at all', to 10, 'Know a great deal'.
Source: Commission of the European Community, *Eurobarometer: Public Opinion in the European Union*, report number 54 (Brussels; Commission of the European Community, 2001).

was unlikely to occur before autumn 2003. If normal political rules were to be re-established – which depends on the Conservatives becoming a credible alternative government – then a referendum on the euro in 2004 could coincide with a mid-term period of government unpopularity and perhaps even fatally weaken the government. If pro-euro campaigners were looking for the government to take a lead on this momentous issue then they could be disappointed.

Conclusion

Opening clear blue water on Europe did not work for William Hague's Conservatives. The anti-EU and anti-euro message did not appeal to the electorate because it did not address their broader concerns about the state of public services. In 2001 the Conservatives appeared to be a single-issue party that was talking to itself and trapped in the debates that had bedevilled it during the 1990s. This does not mean that the re-elected Labour government has been let off the hook – far from it. It faces two important challenges.

First, it will have to contribute to the wider debate about the scope and shape of European integration that will culminate in further revisions to the EU Treaty in 2004. Key issues in this debate will be democracy and accountability and the attempt to reconnect a wider EU with its citizens. Tony Blair's Labour has advanced a vision of an integrated Europe with a continued strong role for the nation state and only limited transfer of powers to European institutions. In this preference Labour is not departing radically from the kinds of policies pursued by British governments in Europe for nearly thirty years: support for market integration and intergovernmental decision making combined with a suspicion of grand projects and big ideas.

Second, Labour will have to grapple with the issue of the euro. There is no great appetite in the UK for replacing the pound with the euro. When this lack of public support is combined with a circumspect government then 'considered and cautious' delay seems the likely outcome. Britain seems likely to watch from the sidelines as decisions about the future shape of the euro-zone are made. It could be suggested that a negative assessment of the five economic tests could allow the issue to be kicked into the long grass. Labour was, of course, re-elected to deliver improvements in public services rather than membership of the euro, so this scenario is not far fetched. This is especially pertinent when it is borne in mind that a euro referendum could sidetrack the government while attaching Labour's banner to a potentially unpopular cause with corrosive long-term effects. However, if Labour were to fudge this issue then Tony Blair's Warsaw speech may come back to haunt him. As he put it, 'The blunt truth is that British policy towards the rest of Europe over half a century has been marked by gross misjudgements, mistaking what we wanted to be the case with what was the case; hesitation, alienation, incomprehension'. The difficulty is that not many British people support deeper European integration; moreover, there also appear to be divisions within the Labour government about the relative prioritisation of the euro. Underlying all this, and perhaps the most worrying development, is the legitimacy gap separating the British public from a European political elite. Not many British people feel European, they do not tend to trust European institutions and have a self-confessed lack of knowledge about the EU. This is a real problem because the British people are in Europe, but do not seem to be particularly interested in Europe. This makes things difficult for a government that wants to be a 'leading player' in the EU.

Notes

1 On Britain's membership of the EU see, for instance, S. George, *An Awkward Partner: Britain in the EU*, 3rd edn (Oxford: Oxford University Press, 1998); A. Geddes, *The EU and British Politics* (Basingstoke: Palgrave, 2002 forthcoming); M. Rosenbaum (ed.), *Britain and Europe: The Choices We Face* (Oxford: Oxford University Press, 2001).

2 G. Evans, 'Euroscepticism and Conservative electoral support: how an electoral asset became a liability', *British Journal of Political Science*, 28:4 (1998), pp. 573–90.

3 See J. Turner, *The Tories and Europe* (Manchester: Manchester University Press, 2000), especially chapters 5, 6 and 7.

4 A. Geddes, 'Europe: Major's nemesis?', in A. Geddes and J. Tonge (eds), *Labour's Landslide* (Manchester: Manchester University Press, 1997).

5 Plans such as those outlined by German foreign minister Joschka Fischer. For Fischer's speech and responses to it see C. Joerges, Y. Mény and J. H. H. Weiler (eds), *What Kind of Constitution for What Kind of Polity? Responses to Joschka Fischer* (Florence: Robert Schuman Centre for Advanced Studies, European University Institute, 2000).

6 This is consistent with the findings of research analysing the comparative Europeanisation of national identities in Britain, France and Germany. This research found that 'Englishness' has been constructed as distinct from Europeanness, which is incompatible with supranational or federal visions of an integrated Europe. See T. Risse, 'A European identity? Europeanization and the evolution of nation state identities', in M. Green Cowles, J. Caporaso and T. Risse (eds), *Transforming Europe: Europeanization and Domestic Change* (Ithaca: Cornell University Press, 2000).

7 A. Gamble, 'The European issue in British politics', in D. Baker and D. Seawright (eds), *Britain For and Against Europe. British Politics and the Question of European Integration* (Oxford: Clarendon Press, 1998).

8 There was a blip during the fuel protests when the Conservatives went into an eight-point lead, which swiftly disappeared as the protests subsided.

9 *Independent*, 30 May 2001.

10 *Guardian*, 24 May 2001.

11 House of Commons Treasury Select Committee, fifth report, *The UK and Preparations for Stage Three of Economic and Monetary Union*, report HC 503–I (London: HMSO, 1998).

12 A. Rawnsley, *Observer*, 16 June 2001.

13 NOP for *Sunday Times*, 3 June 2001.

14 M. Franklin, M. Marsh and L. McLaren, 'Uncorking the bottle: popular opposition to European unification in the wake of Maastricht', *Journal of Common Market Studies*, 32:4 (1994), pp. 455–72.

15 Commission of the European Community, *Eurobarometer: Public Opinion in the European Union*, report number 54 (Brussels; Commission of the European Community, 2001). Also available from http://europa.eu.int/comm/dg10/epo/.

16 G. Wilkes and D. Wring, 'The British press and European integration: 1948–1996', in D. Baker and D. Seawright (eds), *Britain For and Against Europe. British Politics and the Question of European Integration* (Oxford: Clarendon Press, 1998).

Teignbridge

The unseating of Patrick Nicholls, MP for Teignbridge since 1983, emphasised the vulnerability of Conservative seats in the south-west to vigorous challenges from the Liberal Democrats. In a contest in which the Labour vote share fell by 5.6 per cent, the importance of tactical voting was also highlighted. Teignbridge had become a very winnable seat, the Conservative majority being cut from 9,000 to 281 in 1997, making the constituency the closest Conservative–Liberal Democrat marginal.

A former junior minister who resigned after a drink-driving incident, Nicholls appeared resigned to his electoral fate. During the campaign he publicly considered alternatives to parliament and appeared 'like a man on his last day at the office' (*Guardian*, 1 June 2001). Whatever the mood of resignation, Nicholls held his vote share, but fell to the 5 per cent rise in the Liberal Democrat vote, a figure approaching the drop in Labour's share. A Eurosceptic left alone by Sir James Goldsmith's Referendum Party in 1997, Nicholls was outflanked in his hostility to European integration by the UKIP's Lord Exmouth. Exmouth was the first peer, along with the Earl of Bradford, also for the UKIP, and Lady Sylvia Hermon (UUP) in Northern Ireland, to stand for parliament without renouncing the title; he offered an interesting vision of the future of the Teignbridge constituency, telling the *Guardian* (1 June 2001): 'I feel it's my duty to stand and defend my country. When there are French and German riot police goose-stepping down Newton Abbot high street, I'll at least be able to tell my grandchildren that I have put my case to the country. It's the greatest issue since 1939 quite frankly'. As the same newspaper reported, if Lord Exmouth was correct, it was 1938 and few people cared. The largest number of votes was cast for a party supportive of European integration. The Liberal Democrat candidate, Richard Younger-Ross, achieved a swing of 2.8 per cent, nearly six times the 0.5 per cent required.

Result

Teignbridge		
	No. of votes	*% of vote*
Younger-Ross, R. (Liberal Democrat)	26,343	44.4
Nicholls, P. (Conservative)	23,332	39.3
Bain, C. (Labour)	7,366	12.4
Exmouth, P. (UKIP)	2,269	3.9
Liberal Democrat majority	3,011	5.1
Liberal Democrat gain from Conservatives		
Turnout		69.3
Swing, Conservatives to Liberal Democrats		2.8

9

Environment and transport: a conspiracy of silence?

Stephen Ward

Introduction

It might seem that environmental and transport concerns ought to feature heavily on the parties' electoral agenda, not least because of the scale of the issues to be tackled. In the run-up to the 2001 general election, a range of problems emerged with environmental consequences, including: the worst flooding in living memory in Britain, attributed by ministers to global warming; a rail network close to collapse after the Hatfield disaster; fuel blockades over petrol taxes; and the foot-and-mouth crisis, which caused the postponement of the election and wider debate about the future of the countryside. There are also over 3.5 million members of national environmental organisations, which together comprise one of the largest social movements in the country. Therefore there ought to be a significant pool of voters who could be mobilised around green issues. The Prime Minister himself had raised expectations by making two major speeches on the environment in the eight months before the election, calling for a reawakening of the green challenge.[1] However, despite these apparent strengths, environment and transport have rarely overtly appeared as electoral issues and the 2001 election was no different in this respect. Few, if any, of the issues listed above received much of an airing. Charles Secrett, Executive Director of Friends of the Earth (FoE), referred to a conspiracy of silence by the main parties on green issues.[2] The task of this chapter, therefore, is to explain the apparent non-issue status of environment and transport during the election. It examines the conventional wisdom for their failure to break on to the electoral agenda, Labour's governmental agenda, the election campaign and its aftermath.

The conventional wisdom – non-issues? Elections and the green agenda

With the exception of the 1989 European elections, when the Green Party gained 14.8 per cent of the vote on a low turnout, the conventional wisdom is that parties forget environmental issues as soon as election campaigns begin.[3] The reasons offered are listed below.

- *Party consensus.* In an oppositional political system, unless the two main parties can have a significant argument over a policy area then it is unlikely to become an issue. Environmental concerns have often been seen as non-partisan, or somehow above party politics. This is partly because it is difficult to oppose environmental protection per se. They also cross-cut the traditional ideological debate between the main parties, who find it difficult to establish a distinct environmental issue profile with the voters.
- *Environment as a threat rather than an opportunity.* The main parties' attachment to continual economic growth as their major goal brings them into direct conflict with environmentalist messages about sustainable development and curbing the use of natural resources. A party adopting sustainable development as the central plank of its programmes would have to rethink many traditional economic commitments. Politicians often associate environmental protection programmes with public spending, additional taxation, increased regulation and, possibly, restrictions on personal freedoms – hardly a vote-winning combination.
- *Short-termism.* Arguably, parties are attracted to policy initiatives that can be expected to have paybacks within electoral cycles of four or five years. However, the environmental dangers are often not apparent for many years and any policy solutions can take decades to demonstrate benefits.
- *Not a national issue.* Elections tend to focus on national issues but, until the late 1980s, the environment had often been viewed as a concern of local government. When the environment became politicised in the past twenty years or so the agenda shifted to the international stage of the EU or United Nations. Around 80–90% of British environmental and countryside legislation has its origins in an EU framework,[4] so national politicians have less incentive to prioritise such issues in a national election campaign.
- *Too complicated and too scientific.* In the television age, the importance of summarising complex arguments in a few sentences has become para-mount. Environmental problems may create good photo opportunities but do they lend themselves to simple sound-bites? The scientific and technical nature of many environmental issues poses a problem for generally non-scientifically trained British politicians – they are hard to explain and it is difficult to provide easy solutions.
- *Lack of electoral salience.* Partly for the reasons noted above, parties are sceptical about whether there really is a green vote to be gained. They point to evidence of voters expressing high levels of concern about environmental issues but ultimately regarding them as less important than economic or welfare issues. This lack of salience is assisted by the weakness of the Green Party's challenge in Britain. In many west European countries

Green parties score 5–10 per cent of the vote in national elections and have representation in parliament. Consequently, for many established parties in continental Europe there are tangible votes to be won and lost on the environment, but this is not the case in Britain.[5]

Together, these factors suggest considerable in-built disincentives to promoting green issues at election time. Much of the remainder of this chapter seeks to explore how far this was the case in the 2001 campaign.

Labour's green agenda

British governments traditionally see environment and transport as matters of routine, technical, low politics. They have rarely prioritised environmental concerns and the style of environment and transport policy making has been one of reactive incrementalism, reaching the heights of the political agenda only in event of accidents or disasters.[6] Nevertheless, despite little mention of green issues in the 1997 campaign, Labour came to office with a significant rhetorical promise to put the environment at the heart of government. It talked of sustainable development and integrated policy making for transport. This was certainly a bolder set of promises than any government had given previously. How was such a promise to be delivered? In retrospect, four main mechanisms can be detected:[7]

- *Reforming the machinery of government.* Labour expanded the previous administration's 'greening government' initiative. The most important change was the creation of the new Department of the Environment, Transport and the Regions under the leadership of the Deputy Prime Minister, John Prescott. This was welcomed by environmentalists as having more political weight within Whitehall and providing the potential to integrate environmental considerations into one of the most ungreen parts of government – transport.
- *Prioritising environmental concerns in the international arena.* For example, the government proactively pushed the environmental agenda in both EU and global forums, such as Kyoto in 1997, and during in its presidency of the EU in 1998.
- *Integrated transport policy.* Two major reviews of transport policy were carried out: the 1998 White Paper and ten-year plan in 2000. In the main, these were about setting targets and enabling other agencies to act, rather than actual policy action from central government. The White Paper did suggest a shift in emphasis away from new road building towards improving the existing network and even hinted at road tolls and congestion charges. However, the government then gradually drew back from radical solutions in the face of considerable pressure from the roads lobby and fear of being labelled anti-car. The ten-year plan promised a sizeable injection of cash

for public transport, particularly rail, but also reintroduced a significant road-building programme.

- *Fiscal measures to change public and business behaviour*. The government introduced a number of so-called 'green' taxes and fiscal incentives. For example, revenue from the climate change levy, introduced to curb energy consumption and cut atmospheric pollution, and from an aggregates tax on quarrying in 2000 was to be ploughed back into environmental schemes. Vehicle excise duty was reformed to encourage motorists to use cleaner and more fuel-efficient vehicles. One of the government's main instruments was the fuel duty escalator, which had been introduced by the Conservatives, which led to petrol price increases of over 40 per cent between 1997 and 2000 (some of which was simply due to a rise in oil prices, but more than half of which was government taxes). Revenue here, however, went to the Treasury, rather than to promote transport or environmental schemes.

Overall, the consensus is that Labour achieved much more in rhetorical commitments and activities away from the domestic arena than it did in policy delivery. On transport, Prescott declared in 1997 that he would have failed if there were not fewer journeys by car and more by public transport in five years' time. In fact, although the numbers using public transport increased, so did the number of car journeys. Tony Blair himself admitted that the environment had dropped down the government agenda and Anthony Giddens, the Prime Minister's 'Third Way' guru, has described ecological policy as one of the biggest disappointments of the first term.[8] Perhaps the lack of delivery is not surprising given the scale of the agenda, but, after Labour's initial burst of activity, it seems to have lost momentum in the face of opposition. By the end of 2000 it appeared to be engaged in constant crisis management over transport and rural affairs.

Opposition and protest: cows, cars and crises

The government's difficulties spanned both external events and self-inflicted problems. Crises in transport and agriculture raised questions about the ability of government departments to manage problems and the direction of long-term policy.

A series of rail accidents, culminating with the Hatfield crash in October 2000, brought into question the whole basis of the privatised rail structure and the ability of government to direct or deliver change in the rail industry. Hatfield brought to light complex and inefficient management procedures, as well as inadequate and apparently declining safety standards; the emergency programme of track repairs brought chaos to the system. Rightly or wrongly, the Hatfield disaster appeared to be symbolic of the wider the failings of the privatised system.

Similarly, the ongoing problems in the UK agricultural sector were acutely highlighted by the foot-and-mouth crisis that began in February 2001. Again the competence of government in the face of crisis was questioned. The Ministry of Agriculture, Forestry, and Fisheries (MAFF) was accused of acting too slowly initially and then over-reacting through its contiguous culling policy. Confused presentation and the government's repeated claim that the crisis was under control as the problem spread undermined government credibility. One cabinet minister even described MAFF as 'utterly and totally useless'.[9] The rapid spread of the disease eventually forced Blair to delay his planned election in May, despite the majority of his colleagues wanting to go ahead. Worried about the image of campaigning against the backdrop of pyres, Blair cautiously decided to give the government more time to bring the problem under control.

The government was also caught out on a number of occasions by the strength of protest against some of its policies. The Countryside Alliance, using fox hunting as a catalyst, environmentalists campaigning against genetically modified crops and fuel tax protesters all forced concessions from government after direct action and popular protest.[10]

Potentially the most politically damaging of these was the fuel revolt of autumn 2000. From early 2000, an unholy alliance of the road lobby, the *Daily Mail* and the Conservatives had been arguing for a cut in fuel taxes. Ironically, the Chancellor had already ended the fuel escalator earlier in the year, but this failed to stop direct action by hauliers and farmers against fuel taxes. Blockades at oil refineries and go-slow conveys on motorways dramatically led to petrol stations running dry and supermarkets and other businesses running out of stock after just a few days. The protesters eventually gave government a sixty-day deadline to produce proposals for a reduction in fuel tax. In the 2001 budget the Chancellor provided concessions for the road lobby totalling around £1.7 billion in tax cuts.[11] However, perhaps the major impact was political rather than financial. For the first time in eight years Labour fell behind the Conservatives in the opinion polls in the autumn of 2000. It suggested that the seemingly invincible government could be beaten. The government deduced from this that the strength of popular feeling for the motorcar meant that environmental concerns should always come second to freedom of movement. In fact, during the protests, the government never really used the environmental case and the fuel tax was perceived as a mechanism for providing additional funding for the Treasury, not actually improving transport or the environment.[12]

The protests and crises highlight the uncertainties inherent in Labour's approach to both environmental and transport issues. Michael Jacobs, General Secretary of the Fabian Society, has argued that New Labour has never really been comfortable with environmental issues, for ideological reasons.[13] For some Blairites, it raises unpleasant reminders of old Labour – regulation and control of business, government prescription of citizen behaviour, tax and spend.

Number 10 has on occasion viewed the environmental movement as being anti-modernisation, anti-business and anti-rational science. Second, despite changing the machinery of government, the protests and crises emphasised that environment still lacked authority within government. Its importance within cabinet waned as Prescott was marginalised and Michael Meacher, the Environment Minister, remained outside the cabinet. Finally, while New Labour instinctively adopted a 'big tent' style of politics, trying to balance the interests of business, environmentalists and car users, Blair was continually conscious of undermining the fragile coalition put together in the 1997 election. The fuel protests in particular seemed to threaten the support of the voters in middle England who had switched to Labour in 1997 – so-called Sierra man – who could deliver Labour a second term.

The (non-)campaign: parties, policies and strategy

By the time the election was announced there was little expectation among the environmental lobby that environment and transport would feature highly in the campaign. Radical environmentalists have suggested that there was little to choose between the parties, but if one starts with more modest expectations then there were differences between the parties – not only in what they said but more often in what they did not (see Table 9.1).

Labour's environmental and transport commitments were generally viewed as rather uninspiring. Its manifesto contained no single environment section and there was only one mention in Blair's introduction. Nevertheless, it did contain more on the environment than the 1997 manifesto, but it was often difficult to pin down precise details or timetables. It was partly a continuation document, highlighting some things that Labour had already done in office. Many of the policy commitments had already been announced.[14] For instance, some of the transport pledges were restatements of the ten-year transport plan and the spending commitment for renewables had already been trumpeted before the election. It was hard to detect any overall strategy and interestingly this time Labour did not repeat its key 1997 commitment to place environment at the heart of policy making.

The Conservatives, by contrast, devoted a lot of space to what they were not going to do. Real differences in both philosophy and policies could be detected between the Conservatives and other parties. Indeed, much of the tenor of the main manifesto was deregulatory in tone, rather than making positive policy pronouncements.[15] Hence the Conservatives promised to abolish a number of green taxes introduced by Labour, including the climate change levy and the aggregates tax, and to reduce fuel duty by 6p per litre. The message appeared to be that Labour was anti-car and anti-business and, by implication, environmental control and regulation were part of Labour's attack on the motorist and British industry. The main manifesto was thin on substance and details relating to the environment and transport. It said little or nothing about pollution, globalisation and the environment, or administrative reform. The Conservatives were the only party not to promise to abolish MAFF, for example. Clear new commitments were difficult to find until, surprisingly, in the last week of the campaign the Conservatives suddenly produced a separate environment manifesto with a raft of new pronouncements, including: a recycling target of 50 per cent of household waste; a moratorium on the planting of genetically modified crops; and increased support for farmers wishing to convert to organic methods.[16] Although the new programme was welcomed by environmentalists as a real step forward, its promises ran counter to the approach of the main manifesto. More puzzlingly, having produced the document the Conservatives then failed to promote it, leaving critics to question its overall importance.

As in 1992 and 1997, in terms of green issues, the Liberal Democrats' manifesto was well received by both environmentalists and the media.[17] The party produced an environment mini-manifesto but, more radically, each policy area in the main manifesto contained an environment section,[18] in line with the claim to integrate environmental concerns into all areas of policy. It also contained more new and specific pledges than the manifestos of the two larger parties. Though the Liberal Democrats were deemed to have won the green manifesto award, cynics suggest two reasons for scepticism. The common charge is that the Liberal Democrats can afford to be radical since they, and the voters, know that they will not form the next government. Arguably, this frees the party of responsibility and subjects their proposals to less scrutiny from the public and media. Second, the green image of the Liberal Democrats is more about identity than substance. Repeated surveys have indicated that voters have difficulty identifying core Liberal Democrat values and how they are distinct from the major parties. Environmental issues, therefore, are a useful means of creating 'clear green water' between themselves and the two main parties.

In the 2001 campaign, environment and transport barely registered. Only the Liberal Democrats highlighted the issues, both at the launch of their mini-manifesto in early May and during the campaign. By contrast, the two main parties failed to hold any press conferences dedicated to the issues and their leading politicians made no major speeches on these themes. Similarly, press coverage was minuscule. A Loughborough University survey indicated that environment and transport accounted for less than 2 per cent of news coverage during the campaign, way behind the NHS, education, taxes, crime, asylum and Europe.[19] Indeed, when the broadsheets, or television, raised environment or transport it was usually to lament the lack of debate rather than to discuss substantive issues. Mostly, the environment, transport and countryside agendas remained at the margins. Some journalists and campaigners accused the government of delaying decisions on controversial projects with environmental ramifications, such as the fifth terminal at Heathrow and

Table 9.1. Main environment and transport manifesto commitments in the 2001 election

Policy area	Labour	Conservatives	Liberal Democrats
Climate change/energy	Meet Kyoto obligations Cut CO_2 emissions by 20% by 2010 Target 60% cut by 2050 Promise new agenda for a low-carbon economy £700 million for renewable energy sources 10% of UK electricity to be generated by renewables by 2010	Meet the commitments made by successive British governments using package of emission permit trading, energy conservation, tax incentives and encouragement of renewable energy and cleaner energy generation	Meet Kyoto obligations Cut CO_2 emissions by 20% by 2010 Switch from polluting to clean energy sources Comprehensive strategy to eradicate fuel poverty Support for combined heat and power 10% of UK electricity to be generated by renewables by 2010. Increasing by 1% a year afterwards Phase out nuclear power Mandatory energy-efficiency labels
Transport	£180 billion invested over 10 years, including £60 billion on rail network National bus fleet to be renewed by 2006 100 new bypasses to be built Walking and cycling to be encouraged in local transport	Promise to set out long-term investment plans for roads and public transport Create new roads standards unit Increase motorway speed limit where safe to do so Achieve airline standards of service and safety on the railways	New local/regional transport plans to reduce congestion and traffic growth Legislation to set stronger targets for local authorities to reduce road traffic Creation of a sustainable-transport authority Railtrack to become a not-for-profit organisation Reverse plans to build new roads in environmentally sensitive areas Increase public transport investment through bonds, congestion charges, parking tax revenues

Countryside/ rural affairs	Create a new Department of Rural Affairs	Planning streamlined to ease building on brown field sites	Create a new Agricultural Ombudsman and Department of Rural Affairs
	Independent commission to advise on sustainable competitive diverse farming sector within a thriving rural economy	Local authorities to be given new powers to declare new green belts	Reform the EU's Common Agricultural Policy to promote sustainability and organic farming
	Seek radical reorientation of the EU's Common Agricultural Policy	Establish blue belts to protect waterways	Seek EU moratorium on genetically modified crops until 2004 to allow environmental impact to be assessed
	High standards of safety for genetically modified products but science to establish opportunities		EU Common Fisheries Policy to be reformed to conserve marine environment
Waste management/ recycling	35% of household waste to be recycled by 2015	Doorstep recycling for all households – new funds to councils for such schemes	60% of household waste to be recycled by 2010
	Work with local authorities to establish kerb-side schemes wherever appropriate		National recycling programme with door-step collection within five years
			No new incinerators unless research indicates safe and best environmental option
Taxation	Tax policy to be geared to five factors including environment	Abolish climate change levy	Taxes to be levied on polluting vehicles and fuels
	Accelerate uptake of low-carbon technologies via carbon trust	Cut fuel duty by 6p a litre	Climate change levy replaced by carbon tax
	Local authorities to reinvest congestion charges	Abolish aggregates tax	Congestion and non-residential parking charges
	Continue differential in vehicle excise duty to support clean vehicles	Cut taxes on cleaner fuels and vehicles	Landfill tax to be increased
	Research and development tax credit	Introduce tax incentives to tackle climate change	Assessment of all budgets to help support environmental investment and revenues
			Green tax commission to advise on increases in environmental taxation, offset by tax cuts elsewhere

Source: Table adapted from party manifestos, ENDS Report, 316, May 2001.

expansion of military training in the Northumberland National Park, until after the election so as not to create debate.[20]

Yet, despite their low profile, environment and transport issues occasionally threatened to break out of the ghetto. In the opening stages of the campaign the Conservatives highlighted the issue of fuel taxes, and again sought to label Labour as the anti-car, high-tax party, perhaps hoping to reignite public anger over petrol prices.[21] As with the fuel protest in the autumn of 2000, Labour refused to engage in any environmental defence of high fuel prices and the debate largely moved to the familiar wider taxation issue.

Foot-and-mouth disease might have delayed the start of the campaign by a month but only briefly became a campaign issue when a renewed surge of cases appeared in north Yorkshire. In the latter stages of the election, Hague suggested that the government was suppressing the real impact of the disease and delaying a renewed mass cull of animals until after the election.[22] Notwithstanding evidence that the public was unhappy at the government's handling of the crisis, it was difficult to make much political capital out of the issue since for the most part the policy differences were small. The opposition had supported the government's contiguous slaughter policy. Attempting to score political points out of the situation was hardly likely to have attracted many votes.

Below the national-level campaign, transport was expected to be an issue in London, centring on the government's widely criticised public–private partnership investment initiative for the Tube. These proposals were opposed by a broad front, ranging from Socialist Alliance to the Conservatives, and were apparently deeply unpopular with the London public, who were suspicious of further privatisation after the experiences of the rail industry. In the run-up to the election, London Mayor Ken Livingstone threatened to make transport a key election issue when the government continued to press ahead with its plans, despite Livingstone having won the right for a judicial review. Equally, minor parties, such as the Greens and Socialist Alliance, made transport the centrepiece of their London campaigns. The latter's two candidates in London were trade unionists from the rail industry. Further opposition appeared when a business grouping (Get London Moving) announced plans to have three single-issue candidates, under the banner of London First, fighting solely on transport issues.[23] In one of the shortest-lived campaigns ever, London First abandoned its plans within a few days, fearing they could not make the deadline for registration of candidates. As at the national level, the issue fizzled but failed to ignite. Survey evidence in the *Evening Standard* suggested that the public opposed the government's privatisation policy but did not see it as one of main issues of the campaign. As one commentator noted:

> transport may enrage Tube travellers, but not everyone uses the Tube. Its constitution is immaterial to those who do not. Unlike hospitals, the condition of the Tube does not evoke deep public anxiety.[24]

Given that there were policy differences between the parties and that issues simmered in the background, why did the major parties not highlight the differences more actively? From the government's perspective, transport was not a strong campaign card. The public viewed public transport as having got worse under Labour. Furthermore, the fuel tax protest of the autumn had left its mark. For the past two years Labour had been increasingly concerned not to be seen as anti-car, fearing it would lose vital voters. Stephen Tindale, former government environment adviser, has claimed that Labour's own private polling and focus group evidence suggested that environment would not win Labour votes.[25] In short, there was more to lose than to gain by campaigning on a transport/environment platform. For their part, the Conservatives, though recognising government vulnerability on transport and the countryside, were in a weak position to counterattack. Their own record on public transport in office was hardly outstanding and their handling of the 'mad cow' crisis (bovine spongiform encephalopathy) was still lodged in the public memory. The harsh reality for transport and environment campaigners was, the parties calculated, that only a minority cared deeply about public transport and foot-and-mouth disease, unlike health and education.

Public opinion, the election and green issues

If the supply side (politicians and journalists) failed to provide much debate of the issues, was there any evidence of the demand side (voters) wanting such a debate? Conventional wisdom suggests that, in general, environment and transport are low on the list of public priorities. However, several surveys conducted just before and during the campaign provide less straightforward evidence. In April, the *Ecologist* published details of a large survey on environment, transport and countryside issues which revealed some surprising results and appeared to contradict conventional assumptions.[26] A startling 55 per cent of respondents indicated that environment would affect the way they voted and 65 per cent believed that Labour had done nothing to improve the environment since it came to power. The survey also showed large majorities favoured renationalising the rail network and investment in alternatives to road building, and opposed genetically modified foods. The support for such positions came from across the political spectrum. Other surveys also indicated concern over the lack of debate on globalisation, public transport and environmental issues. For example, a *Scotsman*/ICM poll suggested that four out of ten Scots believed the environment would affect the way they voted; the environment was the fourth most important issue, not far behind health, education and law and order, and countryside issues came sixth.[27] Predictably, environmentalists seized on such surveys to attack politicians. Zac Goldsmith of the *Ecologist* stated that their survey showed:

Table 9.2. Percentage of respondents to MORI's monthly polls rating issue most important

	Environment	Education	NHS
June 1997	10	45	54
December 1997	9	31	42
June 1998	8	33	44
December 1998	3	26	34
June 1999	5	29	35
December 1999	6	33	41
June 2000	4	32	55
December 2000	9	29	45
May 2001	2	35	40

there is an increasing gap between the aims of our political class and the views of the people. The overall impression is of a public much better informed than the politicians and the media give it credit for. A public which cares about issues that don't even appear on the radar screens of most politicians.[28]

The evidence was not all one way. One poll suggested that younger voters' much vaunted environmental concerns were a myth. A Radio 1/ICM poll indicated that their concerns were in line with those of the wider public, and environmental issues were not a significant priority. Longer-term studies, such as MORI's monthly survey of important issues facing Britain, support such a claim (see Table 9.2). On average only 3–8 per cent of voters consistently list the environment as an important issue; the peak was at 14 per cent, in November 2000, around the time of the abortive European summit in The Hague on global warming and following the floods and fuel protests of the autumn. By the start of the campaign it was back to 2 per cent, joint ninth on a list of issues and way below the NHS (41 per cent), education (32 per cent), law and order (19 per cent) and Europe (14 per cent).

Similarly, ongoing research for the British Social Attitudes Survey reveals more contradictory beliefs among the public.[29] For instance, while the public values countryside protection and believes that car usage is creating environmental and transport problems, preferred policy solutions are more ambiguous. The public favours the carrot approach to encouraging environmentally friendly behaviour. However, voters also display their 'Mr Hyde' tendencies over restrictions on car usage. They want to reduce congestion and pollution but also want the freedom to drive their cars. They are prepared for some restrictions as long as someone else is prepared to take the punishment. Hence, in short, though politicians have failed to give a lead, they are also receiving mixed messages from the public.

The green movement and the election

The green movement was active in the campaign, in particular trying to counter the lack of interest as it saw it from the media and politicians and to mobilise the public. The Green Party was keen to raise a wider, radical, issue-agenda based around globalisation. In the past the Greens have been derided as single issue and/or extreme. The Greens were certainly not single issue but were radical. On environment, transport and agricultural issues, as one would expect, they went further than the main parties, seeking increased targets for the reduction of greenhouse gas emissions, recycling and organic food production (see Box 9.1). They also promised to renationalise the railways, scrap the national road-building programme and increase fuel taxes. The manifesto received minimal attention and in an effort to generate publicity the Greens produced polling evidence which suggested that they had the most popular policies among the public.[30] They did at least gain grudging respect from the media: 'At the very least they are offering an alternative', was the view of one national newspaper.[31]

Box 9.1. Green Party's manifesto: key points[32]

Transport
Scrap the national road-building programme
Renationalise railways and air traffic control
Investment in rural public transport
'Safe routes to schools' programmes
Increase fuel tax but scrap car tax

Food and farming
A new ministry to ensure food safety
Thirty per cent organic food production by 2010
Importation and production of genetically modified food banned
End to genetic engineering and factory farming
Phase out the EU's Common Agricultural Policy

Energy and pollution
Cut greenhouse gas emissions by 80 per cent from 1990 levels by 2050
UK should have a 20 per cent reduction on 1990 levels by 2005
Energy demand should be cut to a level that can be met from renewable
    resources
Decommission nuclear facilities
Sixty per cent of domestic waste should be recycled by 2007
Landfill tax revenues to be used to expand local council recycling schemes

---

The problem for the Greens (and indeed other small parties) is coverage and resources. The media rarely provide coverage unless the party does something considered wacky or extreme. The problem of coverage was more acute in this election since not all television channels carried their election broadcasts. The Greens have tried to counter some of the lack of coverage with a relatively professional website through which they can deliver their message unedited to voters. However, they had an election budget of only £40,000–£50,000, compared with £15 million for Labour and Conservatives, and one volunteer press officer based in Manchester. General elections are something of a double-edged sword for the Greens: while they can bring some additional publicity and new members, they are also a considerable drain on resources through lost deposits and activists' time and morale.

As with the 1997 election, some of the leading environmental pressure groups, including the World Wide Fund for Nature, Greenpeace, FoE, the Council for the Preservation of Rural England, Wildlife Trusts, the Green Alliance and the Royal Society for the Protection Birds, campaigned together under an umbrella grouping entitled Vote Environment. The basic objectives were to try to increase their weight, produce a unified voice for the environmental movement and in doing so push environment and transport issues on to the election agenda. There was also a similar, larger alliance of twenty-four charities campaigning under the Global View 2001 banner, focusing on international development and globalisation. To increase interest, groups provided a wide range of information on parties' environmental stances, comments on the manifestos and highlights of their own key issue agenda. The lobby used the Internet and email extensively, creating election websites as a key resource for voters. FoE provided a detailed analysis of party manifestos against fifty important environmental yardsticks and assigned the parties scores. Not surprisingly, the Greens came top, with a score of forty-two out of fifty, closely followed by the Liberal Democrats, with thirty-seven and a half. Labour scored a modest twenty-three, while the Conservatives gained an abysmal six and a half.[33] Groups also tried to mobilise members to put pressure on candidates, by providing standard letters and suggesting questions they might ask. Perhaps the best example of this was FoE's Green Cross Code Campaign, whereby candidates were asked to support five pledges on business accountability, climate change, genetically modified food, transport and waste. Just under a third of candidates from the main parties replied, with Liberal Democrat candidates showing high rates of support for green positions: 93 per cent supported all five pledges. Labour and Conservative candidates had considerably lower rates, at 39 and 14 per cent respectively. The results were in line with general party stances, although some Labour candidates appeared to want to go further than their party on business and genetically modified foods in particular.[34] Finally, the leading environmental organisations, along with internal green pressure groups within Labour and the Liberal Democrats, arranged a rally and publicity stunt in London in the last week of campaign to coincide with World Environment Day. This was a final attempt to draw attention and generate interest, but coverage was limited mainly to the broadsheets and BBC Online.

One of the undoubted skills of the green movement has been the promotion of the environmental agenda and its use of the media. Yet its strength at election time seems to be eroded. Many groups tend to be wary of being too politically partisan because of their charitable status and because they have to work with, and lobby, any incoming government. Hence many groups, with the exception of FoE, which has tended to adopt an oppositionist stance towards Labour, remained cautious in their criticisms of the leading parties.

Impact and aftermath: business as usual?

Given the lack of coverage, it is not surprising that the impact of environment and transport issues on the results was minimal. Some have argued that the dramatic fall in turnout was partly a reflection of the failure of politicians to address issues such as the environment. Moreover, the Greens achieved their best ever general election result, doubling their share of the vote and

Table 9.3. Green Party national electoral performance, 1974–2001

Election	Number of candidates	Percentage share of vote (average)	Highest individual result
General election, February 1974	5	1.8	3.9 (Coventry North West)
General election, October 1974	4	0.7	0.8 (Coventry North West)
General election, 1979	53	1.5	2.8 (Marylebone and Worcester South)
European election, 1979	3	3.7	4.1 (London Central)
General election, 1983	106	1.0	2.9 (Ogmore)
European election, 1984	16	2.6	4.7 (Hereford and Worcester)
General election, 1987	133	1.3	3.6 (Weston-Super-Mare)
European election, 1989	79	14.9	24.5 (Sussex West)
General election, 1992	253	1.3	3.8 (Islington North)
European election, 1994	84	3.2	N/A
General election, 1997	95	1.4	4.3 (Hackney)
European election, 1999	84	6.3	8.3 (South West Region)
General election, 2001	145	2.8	9.3 (Brighton Pavilion)

Source: Table adapted from N. Carter, 'Prospects: parties and the environment in the UK', in M. Jacobs (ed.), *Greening the Millennium: The New Politics of the Environment* (Oxford: Blackwell, 1997), p. 197.

Table 9.4. The Green Party's best results, 2001 (saved deposits)

Constituency	Percentage share of vote
Brighton Pavilion	9.3
Leeds West	8.0
Hackney North	7.5
Bradford West[a]	7.0
Lewisham Deptford	6.5
Islington North	6.2
Holborn and St Pancras	6.0
Edinburgh Central	5.3
Dulwich and West Norwood	5.0
Hornsey and Wood Green	5.0

Note: [a]Finished third, pushing Liberal Democrats into fourth place.

managing to save ten deposits for the first time (see Tables 9.3 and 9.4). As one party official commented, 'since Tony Blair's underpants got more coverage than the Green Party this is a creditable showing'.[35] They also succeeded in gaining their highest ever constituency vote, of just under 10 per cent in Brighton Pavilion. However, all this needs to be put in context. Overall they averaged 2.8 per cent of the vote and without proportional representation their task of gaining a Westminster seat is currently impossible. It is likely, however, that they will continue to pick up protest votes in local and European elections and the results should allow the Greens to consolidate their growing local base as the fourth party.

Countryside groups hoped that rural discontent, especially in the wake of foot-and-mouth disease, would be a factor in some areas. Many rural constituencies gained by Labour for the first time in 1997 ought to have been vulnerable. Yet Labour's rural constituencies remained largely untouched. It even increased its majority in marginal seats such as Shrewsbury, and Atcham and Stroud. In areas where foot-and-mouth disease had the biggest impact – Cumbria, Devon, Northumberland/Durham and north Yorkshire – there were some swings to the Conservatives and they gained Galloway, although this was from the SNP (see Table 9.5). But in some of these seats Labour also increased its vote. Labour was punished more heavily in the local elections on the same day, with the Conservatives gaining control of Cumbria and Cheshire County Councils and making gains in many rural areas. It also has been suggested that her support for banning fox hunting may have been crucial in depriving Liberal Democrat Jackie Ballard of her seat in Somerset. Overall, foot-and-mouth disease failed to materialise as a decisive national issue and the results do not provide evidence of a widespread rural backlash.

Environment and transport had little impact on the direct result, but does this signify a business-as-usual approach? Day one of Labour's second term

Table 9.5. Voting in constituencies most affected by foot-and-mouth disease in the run-up to the 2001 election

Constituency	No. of confirmed cases	Winning party	Swing	Turnout
Penrith and Border	557	Conservatives	5.2% Labour to Conservatives	65.3%
Dumfries	131	Labour	0.6% Conservatives to Labour[+]	67.7%
Devon West	119	Liberal Democrats	0.6% Liberal Democrats to Conservatives	70.5%
Carlisle	73	Labour	6.0% Labour to Conservatives	59.4%
Workington	72	Labour	6.9% Labour to Conservatives	63.4%
Forest of Dean	47	Labour	4.0% Labour to Conservatives	67.3%
Bishop Auckland	44	Labour	4.8% Labour to Conservatives	57.2%
Skipton and Ripon	42	Conservatives	5.4% Labour to Conservatives	65.3%
Devon North	41	Liberal Democrats	2.6% Liberal Democrats to Conservatives[+]	68.3%
Durham North West	37	Labour	5.9% Labour to Conservatives	58.5%
Galloway	35	Conservatives	6.8% SNP to Conservatives[+]	68.1%
Hexham	32	Conservatives	2.7% Labour to Conservatives[+]	70.9%
Ribble Valley	32	Conservatives	5.6% Liberal Democrats to Conservatives[+]	66.2%
Hereford	31	Liberal Democrats	5.2% Liberal Democrats to Conservatives[+]	63.5%
Richmond	29	Conservatives	8.0% Labour to Conservatives	67.4%
Montgomery	27	Liberal Democrats	0.8% Conservatives to Liberal Democrats	65.5%
Brecon and Radnor	22	Liberal Democrats	4.9% Liberal Democrats to Conservatives	71.8%
Berwick	20	Liberal Democrats	0.9% Conservatives to Liberal Democrats	63.8%
Burton	20	Labour	0.6% Labour to Conservatives	61.8%

[+]Labour vote increased.
Source: Confirmed cases originally taken from MAFF website in the week following the election. The figures can now be found at the new Department of Environment, Food and Rural Affairs: www.defra.gov.uk/arimalh/diseases/fmd/cases/fmd cases/constituency.pdf.

brought a significant change to the machinery of government. To nobody's surprise, MAFF was abolished and its main functions went to the new Department of Environment, Food and Rural Affairs. One report in the *Independent* stated that 'Ministers have said it should be seen as a signal to farmers that they will have to change their role from food producers to custodians of the countryside'.[36] Environmental concerns should therefore be integrated more closely into agricultural affairs. Similar arguments about integrating environmental considerations into transport were heard in the wake of the creation of the Department of Environment, Transport and the Regions in 1997. In fact, greens have long pointed out that the problem in greening Whitehall lies with the economic departments, particularly the Treasury and the Department of Trade and Industry, and a lack of prioritisation from Number 10. Reshaping the Department of the Environment every few years does not necessarily overcome this. Yet much of the ability of the government to deliver meaningful policy reform will depend on its ability to reform the Common Agricultural Policy rather than changing the machinery of government.

Public transport, particularly the rail industry, will continue to dog Labour. Since the government has already staked much on delivery and improvement of public services in the second term, the issue has the potential to be even more problematic. The new head of Railtrack has already admitted that delivering noticeable changes is likely to take a decade, if not longer.

Once again, most large environmental political disputes are likely to take place away from Westminster and Whitehall, in the international arena, notably in battles between the EU and the Bush administration over global warming and between anti-globalisation protesters and European governments generally. How far this drifts down into the domestic arena remains to be seen but, on past evidence, while direct action may increase, the impact on elections and national policy is likely to be limited.

Conclusion

Environment and transport had little direct impact on the conduct or the outcome of the 2001 general election. For environmentalists, the campaign followed the same depressing pattern as in 1992 and 1997. Yet the conventional wisdom to explain this is not all confirmed. There were differences between the parties, the issues were not all international, and there were a good number of candidates with keen environmental and transport interests. There was the potential to have a debate. So did a conspiracy of silence prevent it happening? More likely it was fear of uncertainty – in a tightly controlled and on-message election, the main parties did not necessarily want to stray on to unfamiliar territory on which they were not getting clear messages from voters. One might argue that the Labour government, with its contradictory approach to green issues, actually mirrors the wider public quite well. It is easy to blame the politicians, but the response to fuel taxes and plans to curb car use have shown the difficulties of policy delivery. However, for those with a deeper commitment to environmental causes, elections and parties are an increasingly irrelevant means of achieving their ends. Increasing support for direct action and the continued growth of environmental organisations indicate that environmental concerns will arrive on the political agenda in other ways. There is a vicious circle in operation here: 'green' voters either do not perceive party differences or see means other than party politics as the solution, so parties detect no electoral advantage in beating the green drum. Consequently the options for voters are slow to improve and the parties see little need to change.

Notes

1 Having made no key speeches on the environment in his first three and half years in office, Blair made two major addresses in the run-up to the election: 'Richer and greener', to the Confederation of British Industry and Green Alliance Conference, 24 October 2000; and 'Environment: the next steps', 6 March 2001.
2 BBC Online, 5 June 2001. http://news.bbc.co.uk/vote2001/hi/english/newsid_1371000/1371110.stm.
3 For discussion of the environment at previous elections, see N. Carter, 'Whatever happened to the environment? The British general election of 1992', *Environmental Politics*, 1 (1992), pp. 442–8; N. Carter, 'The 1997 British general election', *Environmental Politics*, 6 (1997), pp. 156–61.
4 P. Lowe and S. Ward (eds), *British Environmental Policy and Europe: Politics and Policy in Transition* (London: Routledge, 1998).
5 N. Carter, 'Prospects: parties and the environment in the UK', in M. Jacobs (ed.), *Greening the Millennium: The New Politics of the Environment* (Oxford: Blackwell, 1997).
6 J. McCormick, *British Politics and the Environment* (London: Earthscan, 1991).
7 It is not the intention here to provide a full analysis of the Blair government and environment policy. For more in-depth analysis, see S. Young, 'New Labour and the environment', in D. Coates and P. Lawlor (eds), *New Labour in Power* (Manchester: Manchester University Press, 2000), pp. 155–6; P. Toynbee and D. Walker, 'Greening Britain', in P. Toynbee and D. Walker, *Did Things Get Better?* (London: Penguin, 2001); and A. Jordan, 'Environmental policy', in P. Dunleavy *et al.* (eds), *Developments in British Politics 6* (Basingstoke: Macmillan, 2000).
8 Blair, 'Environment: the next steps'; A. Giddens, 'Just carry on being new', *New Statesman*, 11 June 2001, pp. 29–31.
9 *Independent*, 1 April 2001.
10 Following the first Countryside Alliance march in 1997 the government created the Countryside Agency and produced extra money for a variety of rural services such as post offices, buses and the like. Toynbee and Walker, 'Greening Britain', p. 196.
11 *Guardian*, 8 March 2001.
12 Toynbee and Walker, 'Greening Britain'.
13 M. Jacobs, *Environmental Modernisation*, Fabian Pamphlet 591 (London: Fabian Society, 2000).

14 *ENDS Report*, 316, May 2001.
15 The Conservative manifesto, *Time for Common Sense* (London: Conservative Party Central Office, 2001).
16 Conservative environment manifesto (London: Conservative Party Central Office, 2001).
17 N. Carter, 'Prospects: parties and the environment in the UK'.
18 Liberal Democrat manifesto, *Freedom, Justice, Honesty* (London: Liberal Democrats, 2001).
19 *Guardian*, 25 May 2001.
20 *Independent*, 21 May 2001.
21 Minor fuel blockades did occur in the latter part of the campaign but with little impact.
22 *Independent*, 5 June 2001.
23 *Evening Standard*, 22 May 2001.
24 *Evening Standard*, May 2001.
25 *Independent*, 2 June 2001.
26 'The Great British Environmental Survey', *Ecologist*, May 2001.
27 *Scotsman*, 15 May 2001.
28 Z. Goldsmith, *Ecologist*, May 2001.
29 See N. Stratford and I. Christie, 'Town and country life', in R. Jowell *et al.* (eds), *British Social Attitudes: The 17th Report* (Aldershot: Ashgate, 2001).
30 'The Green Party: the strongest link', Green Party press release and report (London: Green Party, May 2001).
31 *Independent*, 18 May 2001.
32 Table from BBC Online Green manifesto at a glance – http://news.bbc.co.uk/vote2001/hi/english/newsid_1337000/1337720.stm.
33 FoE, *2001 General Election: 4 Party Manifesto Analysis – The Environmental Agenda* (London: FoE, May 2001).
34 FoE press release, 6 June 2001.
35 *Independent*, 9 June 2001.
36 *Independent*, 10 June 2001.

Penrith and the Border

When the foot-and-mouth outbreak began in February it appeared to add further weight to the claims of a crisis in the countryside and it was suggested that the government could face electoral backlash in rural areas. Penrith and the Border, a safe Conservative seat, and the largest constituency in England, dramatically illustrates the regional nature of the foot-and-mouth crisis. It had four times as many outbreaks as the next most affected constituency. The government's contiguous slaughter policy meant that cattle and sheep were destroyed in large parts of Cumbria. Moreover, the closure of footpaths and countryside walks in the Lakeland fells led to a severe decline in tourism, on which the area is also heavily dependent. Although the government delayed the election by a month while trying to bring the crisis under control, the Conservative opposition and some countryside campaigners suggested that people in rural areas did not want an election and some would be unable to participate. In the end, foot-and-mouth disease made a negligible impact on the campaign and little significant impact on electoral outcomes. There was no large-scale rural backlash, although there were some above-average swings against the government in some constituencies, including Penrith and the Border. However, these were not in the crucial marginal constituencies. In Penrith, David Maclean was a popular local candidate certain to hold a safe Conservative seat. Given the scale of the foot-and-mouth epidemic, perhaps the most startling feature of the constituency campaign was its lacklustre nature.

Result

Penrith and the Border		
	No. of votes	% of vote
Maclean, D. (Conservative)	24,302	54.9
Walker, G. (Liberal Democrat)	9,625	21.8
Boaden, M. (Labour)	8,177	18.5
Lowther, T. (UKIP)	938	2.1
Gibson, M. (Legalise Cannabis)	870	2.0
Moffat, J. (Independent)	337	0.8
Conservative majority	14,677	33.2
Conservative hold		
Turnout		65.3
Swing, Liberal Democrats to Conservatives		6.1

10

Law, order and race

John Benyon

Introduction

Crime and policing were among the top issues in the 2001 election. Gallup's respondents placed law and order as the third most urgent problem, after health and foot-and-mouth disease and above immigration and education, while MORI also found it came third, but after health and education. The voters' views were broadly reflected in the extent of the media coverage. In an analysis of over 3,000 election news items by Peter Golding and David Deacon, excluding stories about the conduct of the election and politicians, crime and policing ranked equal fourth with education in terms of media coverage, after Europe, health and taxation.[1] William Hague's chief press adviser, Amanda Platell, confirmed that crime was the third issue on the Conservatives' list, following Europe and taxation.[2] As Hugo Young put it: 'The Tories are determined to make crime one of the biggest issues. It's one of the few they've got.'[3]

Clearly, despite its rather uninspiring record on crime and policing during the first Blair government, the Labour Party had no option but to campaign on law and order as well as on its more favoured issues, such as health and education. And so in 2001 the party again turned to the declaration that had proved so effective in the run-up to the previous election – it would be 'tough on crime and tough on the causes of crime'. The phrase was cited in the party's manifesto as the centrepiece of Labour's 'clear and consistent' strategy.[4]

The statement was originally coined in February 1993 by Tony Blair, then the shadow Home Secretary, as a means to overcome the Labour Party's image of being 'soft' on criminals. The mantra 'tough on crime and tough on the causes of crime' was intended to challenge the Conservatives for the mantle of the 'party of law and order'. It was brilliantly effective – as was evident in polls before the 1997 election, which showed a Labour lead of around 15 per cent as the party with the best policies on law and order.

Of course, the difference in 2001 was that Labour had been in power for four years. Overall levels of crime had continued to fall, but violent crimes had risen considerably and government policies had been criticised by both the police and civil liberties groups and penal reformers. Within the party hierarchy, the Home Office was seen as one of the failures of the first term, although Home Secretary Jack Straw seemed to be largely exonerated, as he had stood his ground and had ensured that Labour was portrayed as tough and uncompromising on crime in the media.

The level of discussion in the 2001 campaign on crime and policing, and on the associated Home Office issues of immigration and race and ethnic relations, was generally superficial. The Labour and Conservative parties vied with each other to occupy the same ground, while the Liberal Democrats advocated the most radical policies but went largely unheard in much of the media 'debate'. This chapter outlines the manifesto commitments and the key points of the campaign, before briefly examining possible future developments. First, however, it is necessary to consider the legacy from the eighteen years of Conservative rule, which continues to affect contemporary debate, and the approach and record of New Labour.

The Conservatives' legacy

In the postwar years there had been a broad bipartisan consensus on policing and criminal justice, and general agreement on the causal relationship between 'anti-social conditions' and 'anti-social behaviour'. However, this social democratic approach was increasingly questioned as rising incomes, improved welfare provision and full employment coincided with a steady increase in the levels of crime. This undermined the social democratic arguments that reductions in poverty and disadvantage would lead to decreases in crime.

Crime, public order and policing emerged as a major field of party conflict in the 1970s. The Labour Party continued to emphasise the rehabilitation of offenders, diversion from custodial sentences and the need to remove the social conditions in which crime flourished. On the other hand, Margaret Thatcher called for 'less tax and more law and order' and the 1979 Conservative manifesto argued that the 'rule of law' had been undermined by the Labour government. The Conservatives linked rising levels of crime with public disorder during industrial disputes, particularly the 'winter of discontent' of 1978–79, and with violence at political demonstrations and sporting events, and blamed a weak government and the 'permissive society'. During the 1979 election, crime and disorder featured as one of the main issues and one on which the Conservatives had a 30 per cent lead according to the polls – their largest on any policy issue.[5]

The effects of the new right's ideological framework were dramatic for law-and-order politics. 'Authoritarian populism' meant abandoning the postwar consensus and embracing the 'classical' conceptions of discipline, deterrence and punishment. Law and order maintained a high political salience throughout the Conservative administrations of 1979–97. The Thatcher and Major governments struggled to contain rising crime and disorder, but with limited success, and the annual number of crimes rose steadily, from 2.38 million in 1979 to an all-time peak of 5.67 million offences in 1993, while the proportion of offences which were solved (the 'clear-up rate') fell from 41 per cent to 26 per cent.

There were three phases of Conservative law-and-order policy during their eighteen years in power.[6] The first of these, 'Restoring the rule of law', lasted from 1979 until 1987 and entailed an authoritarian strategy with an emphasis on deterrence and retribution. Expenditure on law enforcement increased considerably, with a rise in the cost of the police service from £1.6 billion in 1979 to £3.4 billion in 1984 and expenditure on prisons up by 85 per cent.

By 1987, despite the large increases in expenditure, levels of crime and disorder had continued to rise and government policies appeared to be an expensive failure. The result was a new emphasis on 'Enlisting the community'. Government ministers began to stress the need for the active participation of private citizens and communities in crime prevention, through schemes such as neighbourhood watch, increased focus on reducing opportunities for offending and greater value for money in expenditure on policing. The community also featured large in the new approach to punishment. Custody should be imposed only for the most serious offences – 'otherwise it can be an expensive way of making bad people worse'[7] – and there should be a greater use of community service orders.

The third phase of the Conservatives' law-and-order policy, 'Back to basic law enforcement', lasted from 1993 until 1997. This period was characterised by crisis management of the law-and-order agenda and growing electoral competition with the Labour Party, against a background of rising public concern about crime and falling opinion poll figures on public confidence in the Conservatives' policies. In 1993 the new Home Secretary, Michael Howard, signalled a complete reversal of policy. Outlining a 'twenty-seven-point plan for law and order', he stated: 'Let us be clear: prison works'.[8] These policies produced a rapid expansion in the prison population, from its licensed capacity of 46,994 in late 1993 to nearly 58,000 in early 1997.

New Labour – new approach

During the 1990s there was a growing opportunity for the Labour Party to challenge the Conservatives on crime and public order, but to do this it needed to dispel its lingering image of being 'soft' on crime. The party began to advocate the need for increased penalties for certain offences, as well as enhancement of community policing, physical security improvements and greater police accountability. Personal and family morality and responsibility were seen as the foundations of 'strong communities'. Thus, in 1997, Tony Blair stated: 'I am utterly convinced that the only way to rebuild a strong civic society for the modern world is on the basis of rights and responsibility going together'.[9]

The need to clamp down on 'anti-social behaviour' was stressed, in calls for 'tough' action against beggars and the introduction of 'zero-tolerance' policing. This approach, popularised in New York, was based on the 'broken-windows thesis', which argued that one broken window leads to further vandalism and then to more serious criminal acts.[10] Intervention against apparently mundane acts of anti-social behaviour, such as begging, street prostitution and graffiti, can arrest a neighbourhood's downward spiral of increasing criminality and disorder. These ideas were again evident in Labour's 2001 manifesto.

Despite proposals to tackle homelessness and youth unemployment, and to develop community partnerships, New Labour's approach to law and order had a decidedly authoritarian ring, which contrasted sharply with former Labour Party thinking. Indeed, during run-up to the 1997 election the parties vied with each other to appear the most tough and uncompromising on crime and public disorder. Jack Straw and Home Secretary Michael Howard seemed to be trying to outbid each other in advocating high-profile policing and new punishments for anti-social behaviour, and Straw even accused the Home Secretary of 'stealing' Labour's ideas on crime reduction and zero-tolerance policing. To some this smacked of Tweedledum and Tweedledee! However, New Labour was able to go into the 1997 election with the bold statement in its manifesto 'Labour is the party of law and order in Britain today' and this undoubtedly paid worthwhile electoral dividends.

Soon after its victory in 1997 the party introduced a major piece of legislation which covered a large range of issues, including youth justice and young offenders, anti-social behaviour orders, parenting orders and child curfews, racial harassment, reparation orders, and other sentencing reforms. At the centre of the Crime and Disorder Act 1998 was a series of measures intended to promote community safety and crime prevention. A statutory duty was placed on local authorities and the police to develop a partnership to implement 'crime and disorder strategies' in each local government area. A stream of other legislation and reports followed, on the police, courts, prosecutions, the criminal justice system, the probation service, prisons and sentencing. A particularly important report was that from the Stephen Lawrence Inquiry, chaired by Lord Macpherson, which made a large number of recommendations on ways to overcome racism within the police service.

There were mixed results from the Labour Party's new approach, and these formed the basis of the battleground on which the 2001 election campaign was waged. Problems with recruitment and retention meant that the numbers of police remained well below the 127,000 that Labour had inherited. In line with demographic trends, and as a result of improved crime prevention initiatives, including 'target hardening', total recorded crime continued to fall under the Labour government annually, with the exception of 1999, with burglary and vehicle crime falling each year. More ominously, violent crime, including robberies, rose sharply in each year, other than 1998, and there was continuing media concern about guns and drugs. Clear-up rates fell to 25 per cent, and only 9 per cent of recorded crimes ended in a conviction. Under the Labour government the prison population rose to nearly 65,000 at the time of the 2001 election, giving England and Wales one of the highest rates of imprisonment of any country in the developed world. The findings from the International Crime Victims Survey indicated that the crime rate in England and Wales was the worst in any industrialised country, with fifty-eight offences for every 100 inhabitants.

The 2001 manifestos

In the build-up to the election, the Labour Party emphasised tough crime control rather than tough action to tackle its causes. In keeping with this, the party's manifesto devoted six pages to 'Strong and safe communities' and set out a 'ten-year vision' of 'the sort of Britain we want to live in'.[11] Within the strategy of being tough on crime and its causes, crime reduction would be put 'centre stage'. The proposals included a rise in funding for the police of £1.6 billion, to £9.3 billion, over three years, an increase of 6,000 in police numbers, and modernisation of the service, with an emphasis on specialist training, enhanced leadership, improved equipment and a new independent Police Complaints Commission.

Not surprisingly, crime, policing and punishment also featured strongly in the Conservatives' manifesto. In a section entitled 'Living safely', the manifesto declared: 'Common sense means having enough police to keep our streets safe and a criminal justice system that reflects our values rather than undermines them'.[12] The Conservatives promised to raise the number of officers, free them from paperwork and increase their morale, and said the creation of parish constables would be encouraged. The police would be given new powers to deal with drug dealers, especially those who sold drugs to people aged under sixteen.

The Liberal Democrats' manifesto stressed that the best way to beat crime was to tackle its causes. They criticised the Conservatives for their 'superficially populist yet highly ineffective' approach, and Labour for 'trying to sound as tough, or tougher, than the Conservatives', but with no more effect.[13] The Liberal Democrats provided detailed proposals on a range of issues. The manifesto promised funds for 6,000 additional officers, for 2,000 part-time community officers and for setting up a Community Safety Force, which would promote cooperation between the police and groups such as traffic wardens and parks officers. The Liberal Democrats also pledged improvements in police accountability and complaints procedures, in international co-operation on law enforcement, and in making local partnerships more effective against crime.

Labour's manifesto promised to tackle persistent offenders – the 100,000 people who commit about half of all serious crimes. Measures included increased levels of punishment, better supervision on release, further development of a national DNA database and increased activity by youth offender teams. The Labour Party declared: 'Our proposals are based on a simple principle: stay straight or you will stay supervised or go back inside'.[14] The Conservatives' manifesto also directed particular attention towards 'persistent young offenders' and proposed to increase tenfold the places in secure training centres, to abolish the early-release scheme and to require prisoners to do a proper day's work. Saying 'many prisons are colleges of crime', the Liberal Democrats proposed to focus more expenditure on crime prevention rather than 'very expensive' prisons, with a greater emphasis on community sentences and restorative justice. The manifesto promised to make prisons more effective and to cut reoffending by ex-prisoners, by placing more emphasis on training and rehabilitation in gaol, with the aim of improving the resettlement in the community of released prisoners.

All the parties stressed the importance of victims' rights. The Conservatives proposed that both the police and the Crown Prosecution Service would be required to keep victims informed of progress with their case. They would also 'overhaul the law so that it is on the side of the victim not the criminal'.[15] The Liberal Democrats promised to provide more support for the victims of crime, including the rights to be heard in court and to be kept informed about the case. Labour said it would introduce a Victim's Bill of Rights and a right to be heard in court before sentencing occurred.

The Labour Party's manifesto called for further modernisation of the criminal justice system, setting a target of 100,000 more crimes ending in a criminal being brought to justice. The proposals included the recruitment of 300 new specialist prosecutors, changes to the court system to make the process quicker and more flexible, and reform of the rules of evidence, for example to allow greater disclosure of previous convictions. Proposals in the Liberal Democrats' manifesto included restoring the right to silence, an end to mandatory sentencing, an overhaul of the youth justice system and the creation of a Department of Justice.

Echoing theories of zero-tolerance policing, the Labour Party manifesto stated that 'Broken windows, graffiti and litter all send a signal about lawlessness'.[16] Proposals included new powers to tackle unruly behaviour, kerb crawlers, alcohol-related disorder and anti-social behaviour. The Conservatives promised to tackle the problem of 'neighbours from hell' and also loutish behaviour, graffiti and vandalism, 'which destroy the quality of everyday life for millions of people'. Labour promised further investment in high-crime areas, drugs education in schools and action to mobilise every neighbourhood against drugs. The Liberal Democrats' manifesto included several detailed proposals for tackling the causes of crime, including more support for sport, recreation and the youth service, expanded facilities for drug and alcohol abusers, the setting up of a standing royal commission on drugs and alcohol abuse, and the establishing of a national crime reduction agency.

On racial discrimination and equality, the Liberal Democrats pledged to introduce an Equality Act and a new Equality Commission 'to fight unfair discrimination on whatever grounds'. Declaring that 'civil liberties are at the core of our critique of the other parties', the manifesto asserted that 'asylum seekers, in particular, have been treated in a disgraceful manner by both Labour and the Conservatives'.[17] The Liberal Democrats promised to ensure that immigration policy was non-discriminatory, and to review the system of handling asylum applications, to make it quicker and fairer. Under the heading 'A safe haven, not a soft touch', the Conservatives' manifesto stated: 'our ability to be a safe haven for the genuinely oppressed is severely hampered by the virtual collapse of our asylum system'.[18] Blaming 'Labour's mismanagement', the Conservatives said they would speed up the system, normally refuse to accept applications from safe countries and ensure rapid deportation of those whose claims were rejected. In its manifesto, the Labour Party said its aims were to process asylum cases swiftly and fairly, to assist refugees to settle in smoothly, and to apply tough penalties to the traffickers of migrants. Supporting an inclusive, multiracial society, the manifesto promised to promote equal opportunities and to reduce barriers which hold people back.

The campaign

The 2001 election campaign on law and order really began as early as 26 February, when Jack Straw, the Home Secretary, unveiled a ten-year plan entitled *Criminal Justice: The Way Ahead*.[19] A central theme in the plan was tougher sentences for the 100,000 persistent offenders alleged to commit half of all crime, 'rigorous' supervision of those released after short sentences and more funds for rehabilitation while in gaol. The plan set the aim of halving the burglary rate and included proposals for more involvement in crime prevention for groups such as security guards, park keepers and night-club bouncers, and ways to keep more experienced police on the beat rather than behind desks. As part of this relaunch of Labour's policy, Tony Blair toured Pentonville, becoming the first serving Prime Minister to visit a British prison. He described the proposals as 'root and branch changes in the way our system of fighting crime works'. William Hague, however, said that Britain was 'on the brink of losing the war against crime' while Ann Widdecombe, the shadow Home Secretary, saw it as 'a desperate attempt' to cover up Labour's failure. The Liberal Democrats were equally critical, with

Simon Hughes, their home affairs spokesman, saying the last four years had been 'paved with broken promises' on crime.

The ten-year plan broadly succeeded in its aim of drawing the sting from criticisms of Labour's record during the four years after 1997. The Labour leadership frequently returned to the themes in the plan in the run-up to the election. In early May Jack Straw again indicated that he was prepared to drive up the prison population to tackle the hard core of persistent offenders. On 8 May the results of a year-long review of sentencing, under the chairmanship of John Halliday, were announced. The new approach reflected Straw's views that the approach set out in the 1991 Criminal Justice Act, of making the punishment fit the crime, needed to be replaced. He said in a speech to the Justice Clerks' Society: 'Persistent offenders need to know that if they persist in their crimes they will receive increasingly severe punishment'.

Immigration and race were also raised as issues in advance of the election campaign itself. First, there was some controversy over a speech by William Hague in Harrogate in March, in which he warned of the danger of Britain becoming a 'foreign land'. Subsequently, Tory MP John Townend claimed that 'Commonwealth immigration' was destroying Britain's Anglo-Saxon heritage and then several Conservative candidates refused to sign a pledge from the Commission for Racial Equality, which had invited all candidates to promise to eschew racism. With the number of asylum cases rising fast, and a growing backlog of unresolved applications, there was increasing debate in the media about immigration, and attempts were made by some to link crime and disorder with refugees from various countries. Government ministers, notably Barbara Roche, began to speak in uncompromising – some said illiberal – terms about immigration and asylum seekers, and the application procedures were visibly tightened. Thus, it could be said, Labour was being tough on asylum seekers but not tough on the causes of asylum seekers.

Law and order came to the fore on 15 May, when the Conservatives used their first election broadcast to attack Labour's record on crime and linked government policies with two rapes committed by prisoners released early under the home-detention curfew scheme. The broadcast, described as 'dire and desperate' by Home Office minister Paul Boateng, claimed that Labour had let 35,000 criminals out of prison early and that they had committed 'more thefts and robberies, more burglaries, more drug offences and two rapes'. A day later the Tories stepped up their attack when William Hague claimed that a Labour victory could lead to 80,000 prisoners being released early during the next parliament. He said: 'There will be no get out of jail early card when Ann Widdecombe is Home Secretary'. The *Observer* reported that a Home Office study indicated that the prison population would rise by a third, to 83,500, within six years if current policies continued.[20]

Also on 15 May, Jack Straw received a hostile reception when he addressed the Police Federation conference in Blackpool. The Home Secretary was rudely heckled and jeered as he outlined Labour's policies, unlike Widdecombe, who, the next day, received applause. At this point in the campaign law and order was indeed centre stage, with Widdecombe leading the charge:

> Jack Straw has failed to keep the promises on police numbers, to crack down on assaults against officers, to address declining morale in the service and to deliver tougher sentences for criminals.

The issue of law and order was again in the headlines when, on 'black Wednesday', 16 May, John Prescott was hit from close range by an egg and responded by punching the assailant. The media coverage was initially largely negative and Prescott's behaviour was criticised by William Hague and others. However, a number of polls found that some 60 per cent of the public appeared to support Prescott's reaction and the incident faded from discussion.

On 24 May the Conservatives screened a further controversial election broadcast which showed various groups of truanting school children shop-lifting, setting fire to a car, selling and buying drugs and defacing a railway bridge with graffiti. The broadcast, designed to attack Labour's record on education and particularly teacher shortages, also highlighted teenage delin-quency and crime.

The law-and-order and racial dimensions of the campaign took a new turn on 26 May, when major public disorder occurred in Oldham. According to witnesses the riots involved several hundred Asian youths, who caused extensive damage in the town. The BNP had candidates standing in two of the Oldham constituencies and in nearby Burnley, and they were able to capitalise on the disorder, eventually picking up more than 12,000 votes in the two Oldham constituencies alone. The BNP also exploited anger among some white voters at what they perceived to be special treatment for people from a Pakistani background in the provision of council housing and other local government services.

Lord Tebbit spoke of clashes between 'tribal factions' while a number of Labour and Liberal Democrat politicians made it clear that they considered that Conservative references to Britain being seen as a 'soft touch' for asylum, and Hague's 'foreign land' speech in March, had been designed to heighten fears of immigration and multiculturalism among white people. Simon Hughes said:

> If politicians talk up things that encourage the view of racial difference then there is an indirect likelihood that will resonate with people, particularly with young people, and increase prejudice ... some of us have been very critical of some of the language William Hague and his colleagues have used over the last two years.

But Ann Widdecombe responded by accusing Hughes of a 'scurrilous smear' and Hague said that 'Asylum is an entirely different issue to race'.

Just two days before polling day, serious disorder broke out in the Harehills area of Leeds, involving a few hundred youths. The catalyst for the riot appeared to be the arrest of a Muslim man for a suspected tax disc offence, but there were clearly more fundamental underlying causes, not least in terms of relations between the Asian youths and the police.

Despite the significance attached to the issue of law and order by the Conservatives in their election strategy, and its continuing high rating in the opinion polls, crime and policing did not receive as much detailed attention during the campaign as one might have expected. The level of the debate that occurred was generally poor and limited in depth and scope. Some claimed this was a result of a new bipartisan consensus on crime and public disorder, although this was not apparent in the exchanges between Home Secretary Jack Straw and his opposition counterpart Ann Widdecombe, or between the party leaders themselves. Some support for the view of convergence of the two main parties on law and order was, though, subsequently offered by Sir David Ramsbotham, the Chief Inspector of Prisons, who said: 'There was nothing between Jack Straw and Ann Widdecombe ... there was no difference in views'.[21]

From this perspective, the Liberal Democrats were the radicals, as they emphasised the need to be tough on the causes of crime, while the Conservatives and Labour vied for the populist common ground. However, although the manifestos of these two parties did show quite a number of similarities, there were also some important differences. In practice, the contemporary politics of crime and public disorder is a complex mixture of continuity and change. The apparent agreement on stressing individual responsibility and punishment is accompanied by longer-standing disputes over the social causes of crime and civil unrest and what should be done to tackle them.

Conclusion

In 2001, as in 1997, the Labour Party effectively stole the issue of law and order from the Conservatives. They successfully neutralised the Tory threat on crime and policing, where Labour was traditionally vulnerable and where the Conservatives considered they could score an advantage. But Labour actually did more than this, and turned crime and policing to their own benefit, showing a lead over the Conservatives of several percentage points. Jack Straw may not go down in history as a great Home Secretary, but he performed a major service for his party by planting Labour's flag on the Tory high ground of law and order, standing firm and preventing the Conservatives from recapturing it.

Why did the Tories fail to make any real headway on law and order? First, the Labour Party was assisted by the Conservatives' rather thin and predictable manifesto proposals, which lacked detail and substance. They offered few new ideas and little to capture public imagination. Second, the government's ploy of announcing a ten-year plan on criminal justice in February seems to have paid dividends. Labour strategists believed the party was vulnerable to criticism on crime and policing but calculated that this could be deflected if the image of being committed and uncompromising were to be reinforced. The ten-year plan was designed to do this: it argued for tougher sentences, focused on 100,000 persistent offenders, and set targets for crime reduction. The plan, coupled with the announcement of a significant increase in police recruitment, helped to reinforce the image of being 'tough on crime' and thereby blunted the Tory attack. Finally, evidence from polls and in the media indicated that while many thought the government's track record on crime was lacklustre they doubted whether any other party could do better. The level of realism on this issue may be greater than is often supposed: a significant proportion of voters believe that progress in crime reduction will be a slow and uphill task. It may be that 'common sense' on this issue did not favour the Conservatives.

It was clear, though, that Tony Blair was not happy with what had been achieved in this field during his first term. He acted decisively after the election, removing the entire outgoing ministerial team and trimming Home Office responsibilities 'to enable it to concentrate on the fight against crime' without distraction. David Blunkett was installed as Home Secretary with the brief of modernising the police and criminal justice system, strengthening crime prevention initiatives, tackling drugs and violence, and improving race and ethnic relations. On the last, the new Home Secretary said he would seek to provide a more effective route for those with skills who wished to enter Britain but also to clamp down on unfounded claims for refugee status and particularly on the traffickers of migrants. Obviously, the disorder in Oldham, Burnley, Bradford and elsewhere had to be taken seriously, as did the size of the vote for the BNP in Oldham West and Royton (16.4 per cent), Burnley (11.2 per cent) and Oldham East and Saddleworth (11.2 per cent). In total, the BNP contested thirty-three seats, while the National Front put up four candidates. These aspects of the 2001 election indicated the levels of the racial, religious and ethnic tensions in a number of cities, in need of attention by national and local government.

One of the effects of the increased significance of law and order in the last two decades or more is that public pressure for action has risen considerably. With insufficient Treasury money to meet this demand, concern over 'value for money' is likely to grow. Further efforts to increase efficiency and effectiveness in the police service seem certain, with tighter performance indicators, increased reliance on computers and other technology, and further 'civilianisation' of posts. Shortly after becoming Home Secretary, David Blunkett made it clear that he intended to overhaul police working practices, and to introduce a national 'standards unit', while promising that there would be a real rise in police numbers from 125,537 to at least 130,000 within fours years.

There will also be continuing pressure for increased efficiency in the rapidly expanding prison system, and further experiments with prison privatisation and community-based crime prevention and punishment seem likely. During the election campaign there was little serious discussion of these and other issues associated with the effects of incarcerating growing numbers of people. It is worth noting that a recent study for the Home Office showed that at least one-third of prisoners are unable to read, nearly half cannot write and 40 per cent of juvenile offenders are innumerate.[22] Findings such as these, and others on the bullying and abuse which occur in prisons, possibly indicate ways of seeking to tackle some of the causes of crime.

Achieving 'strong and safe communities' requires rather more than appearing to be tougher on criminals than the Conservative Party. The reasons for racism and conflict and rivalry between some members of different ethnic groups need to be acknowledged and removed. The various causes of the growth in violent behaviour among certain groups of young men need to be understood and tackled. In the 2001 election campaign there was a good deal of huff and puff about law and order but little real discussion of substance. The new Home Secretary and his team need to move away from slogans and get to grips with the underlying causes of the problems if the Labour government is going to deliver on its promises in the field of home affairs in its second term.

Notes

1 *Guardian*, 12 June 2001, p. 5.
2 *Unspun*, Channel 4, 15 July 2001.
3 *Guardian*, 27 February 2001, p. 22.
4 Labour Party, *Ambitions for Britain: Labour's Manifesto 2001* (London: Labour Party, 2001), p. 31.
5 D. Butler and D. Kavanagh, *The British General Election of 1979* (London: Macmillan, 1980), pp. 37–8.
6 J. Benyon and A. Edwards, 'Crime and public order', in P. Dunleavy *et al.* (eds), *Developments in British Politics 5* (London: Macmillan, 1997), pp. 328–35.
7 Home Office, *Crime, Justice and Protecting the Public*, Cm 965 (London: HMSO, 1990), para. 2.7.
8 J. Benyon, *Law and Order Review 1993* (Leicester: Centre for the Study of Public Order, 1994), pp. 44–8.
9 Benyon and Edwards, 'Crime and public order', p. 335.
10 J. Q. Wilson and G. L. Kelling, 'Broken windows', *Atlantic Monthly*, 249:3 (1982), pp. 29–38.
11 Labour Party, *Ambitions for Britain*, p. 31.
12 Conservative Party, *Time for Common Sense* (London: Conservative Party, 2001), p. 10.
13 Liberal Democrats, *Freedom, Justice, Honesty: Liberal Democrat Manifesto 2001* (London: Liberal Democrats, 2001), p. 6.
14 Labour Party, *Ambitions for Britain*, p. 32.
15 Conservative Party, *Time for Common Sense*, p. 12.

16 Labour Party, *Ambitions for Britain*, p. 32.
17 Liberal Democrats, *Freedom, Justice, Honesty*, p. 15
18 Conservative Party, *Time for Common Sense*, p. 31.
19 Home Office, *Criminal Justice: The Way Ahead*, Cm 5074 (London: TSO, 2001).
20 *Observer*, 27 May 2001, p. 6.
21 *Independent on Sunday*, 15 July 2001, p. 11.
22 *Observer*, 10 June 2001, p. 10.

Oldham West and Royton

Environment Minister Michael Meacher safely retained his Oldham West and Royton seat, albeit with a reduced majority in the face of low turnout. The story, however, was the performance of Nick Griffin, the leader of the extreme right-wing BNP. The extreme right has never managed to win a parliamentary seat in Britain. By 2001 many assumed that the extreme right had become an irrelevance. This assumption was challenged in Oldham West and Royton, where Griffin got 16.4 per cent of the vote. The Oldham West and Royton vote was, perhaps, the biggest shock of election night. The BNP managed to exploit simmering tensions in the town and play on divisions between the white and Asian (predominantly Pakistani-origin) communities. It did so, for instance, by launching its own 'Oldham in Harmony' website, which was claimed to demonstrate 'how the multi-racial fanatics turned a decent, proud, working class community into a mini Bosnia'. The BNP was keen to exploit a sense among some sections of Oldham's white population that Asian people received special treatment. This it managed to do, although Oldham's problems, such as poor employment opportunities, tend to be common to white and Asian people.

The BNP also did well in the neighbouring Oldham East and Saddleworth constituency, where its candidate amassed 5,091 votes (11.2 per cent). Across Oldham the BNP received 11,643 votes – 16 per cent of the total. Griffin, who had served a prison sentence for publishing racist material, claimed that 'there will be disorder in the weeks ahead. But this is not so much to do with our vote but the way multiracial Oldham has irrevocably broken down.' The BNP was keen further to entrench divisions within Oldham, with proposals for Northern Ireland-style peace lines between the white and Asian communities.

The BNP also did well in Burnley, where it took 11.2 per cent of the vote, and in neighbouring Pendle, where it got 5 per cent. BNP candidates retained their deposits in seven seats, which was seen as the basis for gains in forthcoming local elections, in which turnout tends to be even lower. The BNP was also keen to establish a cyber presence for itself, and claimed that its site was attracting more than 500,000 hits per week after the general election.

Results

Oldham West and Royton		
	No. of votes	% of vote
Meacher, M. (Labour)	20,441	51.2
Reed, D. (Conservative)	7,076	17.7
Griffin, N. (BNP)	6,552	16.4
Ramsbottom, M. (Liberal Democrat)	4,975	12.5
Roney, D. (Green)	918	2.3
Labour majority	13,365	33.5
Labour hold		
Turnout		57.6

11

Scotland and Wales:
the first post-devolution general election

James Mitchell and Jonathan Bradbury

Introduction

General elections in Scotland and Wales have always been different. Even at the height of Conservative success under Margaret Thatcher the Labour Party dominated Scotland and Wales. The party system was further differentiated by the successes of the SNP and Plaid Cymru since the 1960s. The Liberal Democrats, moreover, have looked upon the Celtic periphery as a source of support, particularly in rural and Nonconformist areas. The Conservative Party has gained representation, but its position has differed significantly from that in England. This distinctiveness of Scotland and Wales was reinforced in 1997 when Labour swept the board in each country, with the nationalists and the Liberal Democrats picking up the scraps, and each country becoming a 'Tory-free zone'.

Since 1997 the distinctiveness of Scottish and Welsh politics has been heightened further by devolution. The first elections to the Scottish Parliament and Welsh Assembly were held in 1999, using a mixed-member electoral system. They resulted in a Labour–Liberal Democrat coalition in Scotland, and a minority Labour administration in Wales, which was superseded by coalition with the Liberal Democrats in October 2000. The SNP became the largest opposition party in the Scottish Parliament and Plaid Cymru had its best ever election result and also took second spot in the Welsh Assembly. Devolution thus created new inter-party relations, different forms of electoral arithmetic, and raised questions about how parties would conduct elections in the context of multi-level politics in the future. The 2001 general election was the first to be held since devolution and is thus of historic interest in Scotland and Wales.

To assess the significance of the general election against this background we consider two key issues. First, we examine the election results in 2001 in the context of both the 1997 general election results and the 1999 Parliament/Assembly results. Here we are concerned to ascertain electoral trends and the implications for party strategies. Second, we examine the parties' behaviour during the 2001 general election in Scotland and Wales. Here we assess the approach taken to leadership, campaigning and policy to see how party behaviour in 2001 was affected by the fact of devolution and what implications this has for electoral politics. We argue that, as for the general election overall, the experience in Scotland and Wales in terms of both election results and party behaviour was marked more by continuity than change. Tensions in party approaches to general elections were, however, clearly visible, which suggests that in part the 2001 general election was transitional, before the effects on party behaviour of devolution come to be fully realised.

Election results and party fortunes

Scotland

Only one seat changed hands in Scotland in the general election. Galloway and Upper Nithsdale was recaptured by the Conservatives from the SNP to provide the Scottish Tories with a presence in the new Westminster parliament. Labour remained Scotland's dominant party, winning 43.2 per cent of the vote and fifty-five of the seventy-two seats (see Table 11.1, p. 204). The SNP confirmed its position as Scotland's second party, with 20.1 per cent of the vote, though only five seats. The Liberal Democrats overtook the Conservatives for third place, winning 16.4 per cent and ten seats, while the Conservatives, on 15.6 per cent, now have one Scottish MP. In addition, the Scottish Socialist Party (SSP) contested all of Scotland's seventy-two constituencies and received 3.1 per cent of the vote. Michael Martin, the Speaker and former Labour MP, was safely returned in Glasgow Springburn, though the SNP and SSP broke with tradition and contested the Speaker's seat.

As ever, measurements of 'success' in an election need to be treated with care and in these elections we had the added complication of the elections to the Scottish Parliament two years before. Should the 1997 general election or the 1999 Scottish Parliamentary elections (see Table 11.2, p. 205) be the benchmark against which the 2001 results should be measured? Other measures of 'success' were the expectations of the parties and commentators. In the past, the SNP under the leadership of Alex Salmond had 'talked up' its support in the hope of gaining media exposure and thereby increasing its vote. The cost of doing this had often been disillusionment when the party had failed to make anything like the breakthrough promised. SNP hardliner Alex Neil had declared 'Scotland Free by '93' in the run-up to the 1992 general election, which had created unrealistic expectations. Despite the fact that the SNP's vote rose by 7.5 per cent in 1992, it was interpreted as a setback given the expectations that had been raised.

The SNP strategy in 2001 appears to have been to play down expectations. There were no predictions of a great breakthrough. Indeed, the message from the party was that it would be content to hold its existing seats. This was hardly surprising. First, all but one of its sitting MPs was standing down, having won seats in the Scottish Parliament. Alex Salmond, the former SNP leader, had decided to stand down from the Scottish Parliament and contest his Westminster seat, Banff and Buchan, which he had held since 1987. Allied to this, the Scottish media – less hostile to the SNP than in 1999 but still no friend – persistently argued that the party was irrelevant in these elections. In the event the SNP vote fell 2.0 per cent but more significantly its loss of Galloway and Upper Nithsdale, by seventy-four votes, was a great disappointment.

The expectation that the SNP would struggle to do well did not, however, sit comfortably with poll findings suggesting that it might pick up a few percentage points. However, as has now become standard in Scotland, the polls overstated the SNP's (and Labour's) strength. The *Herald*'s System Three poll suggesting that Labour was on target to win 50 per cent of the vote attracted some excitable comment, to which Labour was wise not to pay much attention.[1] Despite a poor record, there was too much faith in the polls or at least a tendency to overinterpret polls by media pundits as far as the Tories were concerned. The *Scotsman* made the mistake of assuming that the best hopes for the Conservatives lay in Pentlands and Eastwood.[2]

Another consideration is the extent to which any party can expect to do well in a four-party system such as operates in Scotland. With the intervention of Tommy Sheridan's SSP claiming to be Scotland's fifth party, indeed outpolling the Liberal Democrats in by-elections, the competition for votes is intense in Scotland. Labour's 43.2 per cent share of the vote may appear unimpressive by the standards set in the past but in the modern Scottish party system this is indeed impressive. This leads on to measurement by seats rather than votes won. The efficiency of Labour's support – it won 77 per cent of Scottish seats (excluding the Speaker's) – is extremely impressive. However, as the results of the Scottish Parliamentary elections demonstrated, this success owed much to luck or the party has yet to devise a strategy anywhere near as efficient in the additional member system that operates for Holyrood. Labour's vote fell by 2.4 per cent, marginally more than the SNP's vote fell, but it held on to all of its seats. The intense media coverage of Labour–Conservative marginals – Eastwood, Edinburgh Pentlands, Ayr – during the campaign ensured that Labour's success in holding these seats was portrayed as a remarkable achievement.

The SNP vote in 1999 had been higher than in the 1997 general election and one of the key questions was whether this would provide it with a base on which to make electoral progress at Westminster or whether voters who had switched to the SNP would revert to old loyalties in a British general election. The common view, as articulated in the Scottish media, was that the SNP would not only have difficulty in building on its 1999 performance but that the party would struggle to retain its 1997 level of support. The

Table 11.1. Votes and seats in Scotland and Wales in the 2001 (1997) general elections

	Conservatives	Labour	Liberal Democrats	SNP/Plaid	SSP/other
Scotland					
Vote (%)	15.6 (17.5)	43.2 (45.6)	16.4 (13.0)	20.1 (22.1)	3.1 (1.9)
Seats	1 (0)	55 (56)[a]	10 (10)	5 (6)	1[a] (0)
Wales					
Vote (%)	21.0 (19.6)	48.4 (54.7)	13.8 (12.4)	14.2 (9.9)	2.3 (3.4)
Seats	0 (0)	34 (34)	2 (2)	4 (4)	0 (0)

[a]The Speaker holds one seat.

media overwhelmingly accepted the argument that the SNP would struggle to be relevant after devolution in a general election.

The Liberal Democrats held on to each of their Scottish seats and saw their share of the vote rise by 3.4 per cent, to 16.4 per cent. Alone among Scotland's four main parties, the Liberal Democrats saw a rise in the actual number of votes cast for it, despite the drop in turnout. The party had not expected to make any gains and polls suggested that its share of the vote would likely be under 10 per cent. Measured against expectations, especially set by the polls, and against its 1997 general election performance, the Scottish Liberal Democrats came out on top. As measured by the simple and ultimately the most important test, of comparing the parties in this election, Labour was the winner. However much comfort the Conservatives took from regaining one seat, now its most marginal in Britain, this was a very poor election for a party that has sunk to fourth place for the first time in terms of both votes and seats. The SNP's performance was no disaster, but it was a disappointment especially for John Swinney, fighting his first election as leader.

The most remarkable figure was that for turnout. This fell by 13.2 per cent in Scotland compared with 1997 (12.3 per cent across Britain as a whole). Speculation that devolution would lead Scots to doubt the value of the House of Commons and result in a low turnout might have appeared to have been justified but for the exceptionally low turnout recorded across Britain. However, the low turnout does raise questions about the perceived relevance of the Scottish Parliament and Westminster. The turnout in elections to the Scottish Parliament in 1999 (58.8 per cent) was almost identical to the turnout in the 2001 general election (58.2 per cent). The highest turnout in Scotland was in Eastwood. At 70.7 per cent this was below the average for Scotland in 1997. In a number of seats the turnout was abysmally low:

Table 11.2. Votes and seats in Scotland and Wales in the 1999 elections

	Conservatives	Labour	Liberal Democrats	SNP/Plaid	Others
Scotland					
Constituencies					
Vote (%)	15.5	38.8	14.2	28.7	2.7
Seats	0	53	12	7	1
Regional lists					
Vote (%)	15.4	33.6	12.4	27.3	11.3
Seats	18	3	5	28	2
Wales					
Constituencies					
Vote (%)	15.8	37.6	13.5	28.4	4.7
Seats	1	27	3	9	0
Regional lists					
Vote (%)	16.5	35.4	12.5	30.5	5.1
Seats	8	1	3	8	0

in six of Glasgow's ten constituencies, turnout was under 50 per cent, falling as low as 39.7 per cent in Shettleston.

After the 1999 elections it was widely assumed that the low turnout reflected the significance voters attached to the Scottish Parliament. These were 'second order' elections. But the low turnout in 1999 may simply have reflected a more general and worrying trend as electors switch off from politics.

Wales

In Wales there was perhaps more reason for expecting electoral change from 1997. Although Labour's dominance in Wales had been strong since the First World War, the result in 1997 was a particularly stunning success. The party took over 50 per cent of the vote and thirty-four out of forty seats (see Table 11.1). Labour won not only in its south and north Wales heartlands but also in the former Conservative strongholds of Vale of Glamorgan, Cardiff North and Monmouth in the south, and Clwyd West, Vale of Clwyd and Conwy in the north. This indicated Labour's ability in Wales to broaden its electoral coalition, not only holding on to traditional Labour voters but also gaining 'New' Labour voters, which allowed victory in such seats as Conwy. In the 2001 election the six seats captured by Labour on this basis were the seats the Conservatives needed to win to erode Labour's Westminster majority and few expected Labour to hold all of them. The remaining seats were split between Plaid Cymru's four seats in north-west and west Wales and the Liberal Democrats' two seats in rural mid-Wales. Other things being equal one might have expected little change in these parties' fortunes.

However, the politics of devolution recast expectations and suggested that Labour faced concerted challenges from all the parties. In contrast to Scotland, the first elections to the National Assembly in 1999 resulted in an apparent 'electoral earthquake'.[3] Labour's vote slumped while Plaid Cymru took nearly a third of the vote (see Table 11.2). In the constituency contests Labour took just twenty-seven seats, losing seven that they held at Westminster. Of these Monmouth went to the Conservatives, Cardiff Central to the Liberal Democrats and Carmarthen East, Conwy, Llanelli, Rhondda and Islwyn to Plaid Cymru. For the 2001 general election, therefore, Labour faced a Conservative Party holding particularly strong hopes of capturing Monmouth, the Liberal Democrats with a major part of their party resources focused on Cardiff Central, and further Plaid Cymru aspirations in north and west Wales as well as across the south Wales Valleys. Plaid Cymru, in particular, while not expecting a Westminster election to replicate the 1999 result, was confident of significant gains in both vote share and seats.

In practice, however, 7 June 2001 proved again to be Labour's day. Although its share of the vote declined, Labour reaffirmed its dominance over vote share in Westminster elections and somewhat remarkably still won thirty-four constituencies. It lost Carmarthen East and Dinefwr to Plaid Cymru but to everyone's surprise took Ynys Mon from Plaid Cymru. These were in fact the only two seats to change hands. Elsewhere, Labour consolidated control in former Conservative seats with popular local MPs in Cardiff North and Conwy. They even hung on in Monmouth by 384 votes despite strong criticism over the government's handling of the foot-and-mouth crisis, and in Cardiff Central by 659 votes, despite Liberal Democrat attempts to mobilise the large student population on the issue of tuition fees. Given the context it was a stunning return to form for Labour, and indicated Labour's ability to repeat the trick of 1997 in holding together a broad electoral coalition of traditional and New Labour voters.

In contrast it was a major disappointment for the other parties, although this varied in character. For the Conservatives the Welsh contests represented a microcosm of the election as a whole. Given the success of Charles Kennedy's national campaign, the Welsh Liberal Democrats probably considered that they fell a bit below par. Not only did they not win Cardiff Central but their majority in Brecon and Radnor was significantly reduced to just 751 following a strong Conservative challenge. However, it was Plaid Cymru for which the results proved most disappointing. While it achieved its highest ever share of the vote in a Westminster election, results fell well below expectations of making at least two net gains. Its hopes of expanding winnable territory into the Valleys were spectacularly dashed, even in the Rhondda, where Labour ran with an openly gay candidate and won with a majority of over 16,000. Even more worrying, however, were the problems in Plaid Cymru's heartlands. Not only did it lose Ynys Mon but it gained a substantially reduced majority in Caernarfon, the seat where Dafydd Wigley was standing down.[4]

The reasons for the particular fortunes of Labour and Plaid Cymru can partly be related to the changing politics of Welsh devolution. Labour had had a particularly bad performance in the 1999 Assembly elections. This was strongly related to having Alun Michael parachuted in by Tony Blair as its Welsh leader. While opinion polls suggested that, even during that period, support for Labour in a UK election would still be high, many remained concerned that the sustained unpopularity of Michael, who insisted on running a minority administration, could have broader implications for Labour electorally, largely to Plaid Cymru's advantage. The 2001 result, therefore, reflected the turmoil in Labour Party politics that surrounded the forced resignation of Alun Michael as First Secretary in the Welsh Assembly and his replacement by Rhodri Morgan in February 2000 as well as Morgan's decision to create a coalition administration with the Liberal Democrats in October 2000. Not only was Morgan a more popular politician in Wales but he rebranded Labour in Wales as Welsh Labour at the spring 2000 conference. The coalition arrangements also facilitated the appearance of an Assembly administration that had direction and a sense of purpose. In other words, Labour's 2001 result was in part attributable to the Welsh party's efforts to remove the negatives for the party that had built up initially in the context of devolution.

In contrast the considerable achievement that Plaid Cymru had in not only sustaining its appeal in core Welsh-speaking areas but also in south Wales in 1999 was undermined over the next two years. Dafydd Wigley, who by 1999 had achieved high voter recognition and regard, stood down under considerable pressure from party colleagues and was succeeded in 2000 by Ieuan Wyn Jones. Wyn Jones, however, failed to establish a reputation for charismatic leadership or popularity with voters that could enhance the party's appeal in south Wales. More damagingly, Ynys Mon was the seat he had previously represented in Westminster and now represents in the Assembly. Here there were distinctive local problems caused by a bitter candidacy selection contest between the party organiser for Ynys Mon, Robat Trefor, and the outsider, Eilian Williams, the former candidate in Clwyd West in the 1999 Assembly elections. Williams won the ticket, which led to inaction in the campaign by several leading activists. Wyn Jones was clearly damaged by his inability to use his authority to maintain local party members' support for the candidate finally chosen and by the perception that this contributed to the election defeat in Ynys Mon.[5]

Beyond this, Wyn Jones' authority was seriously undermined by his handling of the Simon Glyn affair. In late 2000, a Gwynedd councillor raised concerns over the rights of Welsh-speaking communities and the need for control of in-migration of English-speakers in north and west Wales. Wyn Jones failed either to support Glynn or conclusively to slap him down, thus underlining perceptions that he lacked clear views on matters of central importance to heartlands voters. The results in Ynys Mon and Caernarfon thus reflect unresolved dilemmas in Plaid Cymru about how to sustain its core vote while trying to broaden its appeal in English-speaking areas, dilemmas exacerbated by the perceived public dissembling of their leader.

The results of the elections in Wales obviously have few immediate implications for Westminster politics. The most significant impact at the reconvening of parliament will in fact be the number of new faces. For while the election saw few seats change hands between parties, there was a 28 per cent turnover of personnel. Five long-serving MPs retired, five MPs stood down as a result of their decision to serve in the Assembly, and Albert Owen, Labour's victor in Ynys Mon, was fresh to parliament.

The implications for Assembly politics, however, are considerable. In the short term, Labour's retention of its thirty-four-seat haul of 1997 and the Liberal Democrats' maintenance of their two mid-Wales seats silences doubters who argued that the Liberal Democrat–Labour coalition in the Assembly was a gift to the electoral prospects of Plaid Cymru and the Conservatives in picking off respectively Labour seats in south Wales and the Liberal Democrats in Brecon and Radnor. Hence the coalition is likely to stay together until the 2003 Assembly elections. Moreover, the electoral strategies of the coalition parties for those elections have been well served. Labour ambitions to win back several of the Westminster seats it lost in the 1999 Assembly elections, and thus achieve an overall majority in the Assembly, now look credible. Equally, even if they are ousted from Assembly government, the Liberal Democrats can take comfort in the relative safety of their constituency seats and the receding popularity of Plaid Cymru, which may well deliver more votes and seats to the Liberal Democrats on the regional party lists. By the same token, Plaid Cymru came out of the 2001 election with dashed expectations and is now under considerable pressure to rebuild the momentum gained in 1999 for the 2003 elections. The Conservatives were left once again to their post-mortems on failure.

The elections also had implications for democracy. Turnout in Wales was, as usual, slightly above the UK average, at just under 62 per cent, and six closely fought seats saw turnouts of over 67 per cent. Generally, however, the concerns over voter disengagement from the electoral process across the UK were shared in Wales. Swansea East, the constituency with the lowest turnout in 1997, repeated the trick with a turnout this time of just 51 per cent. At the polling station in Caerethin turnout was just 34 per cent. Local MP Donald Anderson blamed the apathy of the young and suggested the need for a concerted effort to reinstil ideas of citizenship.[6] Looking around this constituency, however, as it sprawls down the Swansea Valley, where village communities once thrived on the basis of heavy industry and metal trades, one is struck by how some places have simply been left behind by de-industrialisation. The disillusionment of the old and low waged, uncertainty in the job market, and high rates of offending and alcohol and drug usage in the young have all combined to destroy a sense of community and a sense of the worth of voting. That such grim realities and the policy failures they suggest eat into the very fabric of electoral democracy itself is probably one of the most significant results of the general election in Wales on 7 June 2001.

Party behaviour and election campaigning

The leader, as a personification of the party's image, has assumed an importance in electoral politics. This presents challenges in post-devolution politics, though these should not be exaggerated. Devolution complicates matters in that there is considerable media focus on the leaders of the parties in the devolved institutions. The electorate's focus shifts between leaders in London and in Edinburgh/Cardiff and even the nationalist parties now have both a London and Scottish/Welsh party leader. Acting together, the London leader and leader in the devolved institution can project complementary images that, combined, act to the advantage of the party. However, differences between the two may have the opposite effect. In addition to the images as portrayed through the leaders of the parties, the policies of the same party may diverge and cause difficulties. Devolution may have been the institutional embodiment of a more pluralist form of politics but any differences between London, Cardiff and Edinburgh have been seized upon by opponents and the media. The political culture remains to a very large extent that of a unitary state even after devolution.

Scotland

The main theme of Labour's campaign in Scotland was 'partnership'. Though First Minister Henry McLeish was kept well away from the media, he was frequently referred to as part of the partnership with London. McLeish gained notoriety for gaffes – 'McLeishies' or 'McCliches' – though these were generally a source of personal rather than political embarrassment. Nonetheless, in Labour's 'safety first' campaign, keeping the First Minister away from the camera was thought best. This strategy proved sensible given that, a day after the election, McLeish was unwittingly recorded in conversation with Helen Liddell, Scottish Secretary, describing John Reid, the former Scottish Secretary, as a 'patronising bastard' and Brian Wilson, former Scottish Office Minister of State, as a 'liability'.[7] The partnership between London and Edinburgh had not been as smooth as Labour succeeded in projecting it, but this conversation, picked up by a radio journalist, came after the election was safely over.

Another theme of Labour's Scottish strategy was to stress that it was a two-horse race between Labour and the Conservatives. At first sight this might have seemed odd, given that the Conservatives had no seats in Scotland before dissolution and that the real threat to Labour comes from the SNP. However, the intention was to remove the nationalist threat by simply ignoring it. One consequence was that it would involve 'talking up' the Conservatives as a threat and thereby potentially aiding that party in its efforts to win back seats. In the event, the strategy appears to have worked without the cost of aiding the Tories to any great extent. Indeed, from Labour's perspective, the Tory victory in Galloway at the expense of the SNP was a good result, as became clear in Labour's post-election comments.

The SNP strategy was first to find some means of entering the race and laying down markers for the Scottish Parliamentary elections in 2003. It was also an opportunity of projecting John Swinney, its little-known new leader, to the public. Though Swinney was standing down from the Commons, he was pictured on the front cover of the party's manifesto and led the campaign. Alex Salmond, his predecessor as leader with a high profile, played an uncharacteristically secondary role in the campaign, though he was standing again for the Commons. The issue that might legitimately have allowed the SNP to enter the race was the complex and disputed Barnett formula – how Scottish public spending is determined. A number of politicians in England, including each of the candidates who stood for London Mayor and senior local politicians across England, maintained that Scotland is given more than its fair share. The SNP, on the other hand, maintained that Scotland contributes more than it receives from the Treasury. Barnett presents Labour with some tricky territorial management issues. Under pressure from the SNP, Labour seeks to show that Scotland does well while in England simultaneously arguing that Scotland is not favoured.

Before the announcement of the election, Deputy Premier John Prescott and Peter Mandelson, both representing constituencies in the north of England, argued for a review of the territorial distribution of public spending. Early in the election campaign a group of twelve prominent Scottish economists wrote to the *Scotsman* arguing for a debate about whether Scotland ought to have fiscal autonomy. This was a gift to the SNP, though the debate that ensued was largely conducted in the columns of the paper in which the economists had originally set out their case. The *Herald*, reacting with the petulance of a newspaper that failed to get a scoop, gave little serious coverage to the issue and the ensuing debate hardly excited public attention. Despite the best efforts of the economists to encourage a serious debate the juvenile response from one academic antagonist, the dismissive tones of senior Labour politicians and the difficulty of translating a technically complex matter into a popular vote winner proved difficult to overcome. Nonetheless, an issue of central importance in Scottish and British politics has been placed on the political agenda.

For the Liberal Democrats, the central aim had been to convince voters that they were relevant. They made much of their involvement in the Scottish coalition, claiming policies as their own and exaggerating their impact. Scottish university tuition fees were said to have been abolished when in fact payment of fees had really only been postponed until after a student graduated. As coalition partners, Labour and its supporters in the media found it difficult to challenge the Liberal Democrats. The SNP and Conservatives targeted Labour rather than its coalition partner. The Liberal Democrats were in the unusual position of being able to make the running almost unchallenged. As a Scottish MP, Charles Kennedy had fewer problems than either William Hague or Tony Blair in projecting himself as in touch with his Scottish colleagues. If at times Jim Wallace, Scottish Liberal Democrat leader, irritated opponents with pompous references to his position as Deputy First Minister it succeeded in creating an impression that the Liberal Democrats were serious players in Scottish politics.

The Tories played down expectations that they would make many gains in the election. In common with the pundits, the Tories were unclear as to which seats they were most likely to gain. There was little talk of winning back Galloway and Upper Nithsdale and the result was reminiscent of Ian Lang's 1992 victory when the Scottish Secretary appeared amazed that he had held on to Galloway for the Tories. While the Scottish Conservatives have come to terms with devolution, in some respects better than any of the other parties, this cannot be said for the party at UK level. The perception that the Conservatives are an English party with little sympathy or understanding of Scotland was not altered under William Hague's leadership. The UK manifesto commitment to stop Scottish MPs voting on exclusively English matters may have been seen as a reasonable response in England but it confirmed a long-standing impression in Scotland that the Tories had not changed.

Wales

As in Scotland, Labour focused on the idea of partnership between Labour in Westminster and Welsh Labour in the Assembly. Rhetoric emphasised the need to deliver a Labour government in Westminster in order to underpin a successful Labour administration in the Assembly. Nothing was said about any future plans for constitutional change, which suggested Welsh Labour's endorsement of the manifesto priorities of the British-wide campaign. To front this approach Paul Murphy as Secretary of State for Wales and Rhodri Morgan as First Minister in the Assembly routinely appeared and were photographed together. The appeal of the two men was complementary. Murphy lacked charisma but was held in high respect in Welsh public life for his years as a Northern Ireland minister at the heart of the peace process.

His gravitas combined well with Morgan's appeal as the most popular Welsh politician.

To give substance to this partnership approach, Labour published a Welsh Labour manifesto, called appropriately *Ambitions for Wales*, which neatly dovetailed the main substance of the UK manifesto with specific Labour policies in the Assembly on devolved matters such as education, health and transport. As a result the biggest compliment one might pay to the Welsh dimension of Labour's general election campaign was that it was trouble free. It took John Prescott's visit to Rhyl on 16 May to create the only potentially damaging episode, when he hit a protestor, and even here subsequent reactions at worst neutralised its importance, and at best actually enhanced Labour's appeal.

By comparison all the other major parties had significant problems. The Conservatives faced major problems of division. First, it was clear that the emphases in William Hague's British-wide campaign found little favour among Welsh Tories. In particular there was clear irritation among members of the nine-strong Conservative Assembly group, led by Nick Bourne, that they had not been consulted fully over strategy, and that the issues on which they could campaign authoritatively during the election, such as education and health, were drowned out amid the obsession with the European issue. Second, there was also clear irritation with Hague's decision to appoint Nigel Evans, the Swansea-born MP for Ribble Valley, as the Welsh campaign organiser. This was problematic because there was no attempt to put Evans and Bourne up as joint figureheads. As a result Bourne appeared to be personally slighted and it looked like the Conservative campaign was being run by someone with only an accidental interest in Wales.

Evans' appointment was also problematic because he was a 'devo-sceptic'. He presented the party's constitutional proposals, which included flagging up the continued importance of the post of Secretary of State and denying Scottish and Welsh MPs a vote in the House of Commons on specifically English issues, with great enthusiasm. In contrast the bulk of the Conservative Assembly group, including Bourne, had become pro-devolution, even sympathetic to the granting of more powers. The Hague–Evans approach to Wales flew in the face of attempts to reposition Welsh Conservatism.

General Conservative campaigning themes which had specific reference to Wales bred some unity of effort. Both the Evans team and the Welsh party were keen to campaign on the tax platform and to highlight the problems of the rural economy. However, the overall problems of the Welsh campaign in coming to terms with the changed context of fighting the 2001 election were summed up by the problems in publishing a Welsh party manifesto. Its launch ended up being delayed as a result of translation errors into Welsh, including the mis-spelling of the words for Conservative and Assembly. Rhodri Morgan quipped that Hague's Welsh-speaking wife, Ffion, would have been better deployed in the party's translation unit than accompanying her husband on his many travels.[8]

The Liberal Democrats fared rather better in adjusting to campaigning in the new context. The UK-wide campaign was considered extremely helpful. Charles Kennedy's leadership had been praised generally and the Celtic empathy worked well in the Welsh context. Equally, there was little division over policies. Given Wales' identification with left-of-centre politics, the party's policies of a penny on the basic rate of income tax, a new higher income tax rate of 50 per cent on those earning over £100,000 and changes to capital gains tax were useful where the party was in competition with Labour and Plaid Cymru, though less so when competing locally with the Conservatives. At the same time there was an easy accord over campaigning for the abolition of student tuition fees, free personal care for the elderly and free eye and dental checks. In doing so Kennedy highlighted his party's influence in the coalition government in the Scottish Parliament. As part of the partnership agreement that took them into coalition with Labour in October 2000, the Welsh Liberal Democrats had also revised the policy on prescription charges and check-ups, as well as forcing the reintroduction of school milk. The Welsh party therefore could argue too that it was having a practical influence on these issues specifically in Wales.

Against this it faced a number of difficulties. A key problem was that of specifically Welsh leadership of the party. Richard Livsey was still the parliamentary leader of the Welsh party and served in this capacity during the election. However, he was in fact standing down to become a peer. He was leading a Welsh party campaign in an election in which he was not standing. At the same time the idea of a leadership partnership between Livsey and the leader of the Welsh party in the Assembly was impossible. This was because the leader in the Assembly, Mike German, was still facing serious allegations of mismanagement of public funds and improper use of a corporate credit card when formerly working for the European division of the Welsh Joint Education Council. German was still Deputy First Minister in Rhodri Morgan's coalition, but it was thought best if he kept a low profile. As it was, promotion of what the party had achieved as part of the Lib–Lab coalition was somewhat blunted by the immediate reminder to voters of the cloud hanging over the party's Assembly leader. The Liberal Democrats in Wales became embroiled in a number of allegations of negative campaigning, which sat uneasily alongside the emphasis placed on 'honesty' in the party's rhetoric. It was heavily criticised for setting up a number of dubious websites, including www.plaid-cymru.co.uk, which turned out to be a website devoted to criticising Plaid Cymru's policies.

Finally, when one turns to Plaid Cymru, some problems with Ieuan Wyn Jones as party leader have already been alluded to, but there were wider problems of the party leadership with which to contend. Wyn Jones is formally the party President and leader of the party in the Welsh Assembly. Although he kept his seat in the House of Commons until the 2001 election, he had handed parliamentary leadership to Elfyn Llwyd, MP for Meirionnydd Nant

Conwy. Technically one might have expected Llwyd to lead Plaid Cymru's campaign for a Westminster election but there was never any serious chance of this given Llwyd's relative obscurity in the eyes of the public and Wyn Jones' and the party's expectation that Wyn Jones would take the lead. Yet Wyn Jones suffered the same problem as Livsey for the Liberal Democrats. He was leader for an election in which he was not standing. It made little sense to voters.

Beyond this, Plaid Cymru was alone among the parties in fighting an election on familiar terms, simply to gain representatives in a UK parliament to influence the political agenda on how Wales would be dealt with. The party chose to campaign in the election on three substantive issues. First, it called for a Westminster Act to raise the Assembly to the same status and powers as the Scottish Parliament. Second, it campaigned as an explicitly socialist party on an election manifesto that contained a commitment to a new top-rate tax of 50 per cent for those earning over £50,000. On the basis of this, like the Liberal Democrats, it listed a wide range of public spending commitments that it could enter into above and beyond Labour. Finally, it campaigned for a reform of the Barnett formula, by which public spending is allocated to the Welsh Assembly: that it should be changed from its population basis to a more needs-based formula. On this basis, the party suggested, Assembly funding would be increased and be capable of a much wider range of spending commitments than had been the case under Labour and the coalition since 1999.

The first of these commitments proved to be relatively unproblematic, largely because it went undiscussed. Plaid Cymru has an Achilles' heel in suggesting that in the long term it is committed to 'full national status'. Wyn Jones would no doubt have experienced the same discomfort as his predecessor Dafydd Wigley in explaining what that meant. As it happened, he was not really called upon to do so and in the context of it being a Westminster election, and Labour saying nothing about the future development of the Assembly, the constitutional proposals never became an issue. The second commitment was specifically designed to peal off Labour voters in the Valleys. It simply failed to work. Given Wigley's successes in the Valleys in the 1999 elections, one might again point to a failure of leadership to get this socialist appeal through in the same way.

Finally, discussion of the Barnett formula also made little impact, largely because to many voters it was a technical issue beyond their understanding. Again, Wyn Jones' failure to impress on the revision of the Barnett formula in the apparently manageable context of the *Jimmy Young Show* on Radio 2 was perhaps indicative of a failure to gain lift-off in Plaid's campaigning themes. Rhodri Morgan struck a chord with voters when, after listing the Labour government's successes in gaining EU funding for Wales through Objective One status for the Valleys and west Wales, and complementary funding after the 2000 CSR, he labelled Plaid Cymru the 'Oliver Twists of Welsh politics'.[9]

Overall, analysis of the other main parties' campaigning provides a fairly bleak picture of how they went about storming Labour's electoral fortress, and how problematic they found the changed context of multi-level electoral politics. Labour, it appears, had learned some pretty stiff lessons from the 1999 Assembly elections. Having been confronted with the voters' wrath at the imposition of Alun Michael, and the centralisation and party disunity that that suggested, Labour by 2001 had learned to show a very clear public unity and mutual respect between British and Welsh dimensions of the party. It will be interesting to see whether that is replicated in the context of the 2003 Assembly elections. All political logic suggests that it should be. The other parties, particularly Plaid Cymru, having all gained in the 1999 Assembly elections at Labour's expense, had different experiences of multi-level politics in 2001. Following the elections the Welsh Conservative Party moved to consider plans for legal separation and a greater degree of autonomy in operation. Both the Liberal Democrats and Plaid Cymru went into immediate post-mortems over why they did not achieve expected breakthroughs.

Conclusion

In both Scotland and Wales Labour retained its lead despite the dramatic fall in turnout. Though the share of the vote for each party fell, and by quite a margin in Wales, Labour's ability to hold on to seats will have satisfied party strategists. Labour's main challengers, the nationalists, had disappointing results. In Wales, Plaid Cymru suffered a similar fate to that of the SNP in 1992. Having built up unrealistic expectation, its significant improvement in the share of the vote was generally dismissed as a poor result. Labour's partnership message was central to its strategy in both Scotland and Wales, though local circumstances demanded different tactics. There were differences in the approaches of the two nationalist parties. In Wales, Plaid Cymru has traditionally fought general elections on a platform offering a 'voice for Wales' in Westminster and, while this has also been a theme of SNP campaigns, the SNP has also pressed the case of a vote for it as a vote for independence. In 2001, Plaid Cymru's strategy was in this sense little different from that used in the past but the SNP's emphasis on winning independence via elections to Edinburgh rather than Westminster meant that its approach was more similar to Plaid's than in the past. Voting for the SNP to ensure that Scotland's interests were protected at Westminster became a theme, though less explicit than Plaid's, in this election. For internal management reasons, the SNP leadership could not afford to ignore its independence message.

In Scotland, more than in Wales, the Liberal Democrats emphasised their part in the coalition. As relative latecomers to power in Wales, the Liberal Democrats there could make fewer claims to have influenced policy and therefore fell back on the familiar message of the party of local heroes. Liberal

Democrats in both Scotland and Wales have long based their appeal on being strong representatives for their constituencies. With coalition politics, they are now able to add real influence to their appeal and this was done, with remarkably few challenges in Scotland.

Neither Labour nor the nationalists can read too much into these results as far as elections to the Scottish Parliament and Welsh Assembly are concerned. Voting patterns appear to be different for the two levels of government and, while this does not mean that there is no relationship between the devolved and UK elections, it does mean that at this stage we must be careful in our interpretation. Turnout in 1999, for example, appeared to suggest that the Scottish and Welsh elections were second order when compared with previous general elections. However, the low turnout in 2001 might contradict this and suggest that 1999 marked a general downward trend. If Scottish and Welsh elections are second-order elections we should expect that turnout will fall even further in 2003.

The Conservatives could take little comfort from the 2001 results – the local parties in both Scotland and Wales complained bitterly that they had been let down by a British leadership that failed to take account of devolution. Despite William Hague's period as Welsh Secretary and Michael Ancram, Party Chairman, having formerly been a Scottish MP and Scottish Office minister, the London leadership ran a campaign that appeared no less unsympathetic to Scottish and Welsh distinctiveness than in the past.

Labour in Wales appears to have recovered well from its troubles in 2001. Across Britain as a whole, and with apparently little difference in Scotland and Wales, the coalition of old and new Labour support held together well. There was little evidence that pressure from the SNP and Plaid Cymru attacking from the left undermined this coalition of voters. However, the context of an election fought during a period of economic optimism and general 'feel good' tell us little about what might happen in different circumstances. Labour's remarkable performance may owe much, indeed most, to an electoral system that exaggerates its voting strength in number of seats, but first past the post remains the system under which elections are held. The best hope for its opponents in two years may continue to be the alternative devolved system with its proportional element.

Notes

1 See the *Herald*, 'Labour truly lifted on way to achieving 50% share of actual vote', 23 May 2001.
2 J. Curtice, 'Election 2001 Conservatives can't win a Scottish Seat, say polls', *Scotsman*, 4 June 2001.
3 D. Trystan and R. Wyn Jones, 'A quiet electoral earthquake', *Agenda* (summer 1999), pp. 26–8.
4 *Western Mail*, results edition, 9 June 2001.

5 *Western Mail*, 17 May 2001.
6 *Western Mail*, 9 June 2001.
7 *Herald*, 9 June 2001.
8 *Western Mail*, 16 May 2001.
9 *Western Mail*, 10 May 2001.

Galloway and Upper Nithsdale

The capture of Galloway and Upper Nithsdale represented a rare bright spot for the Conservatives, and assumed special significance because it revived Scottish representation for the party at Westminster after the wipe-out of 1997. The very close result in favour of businessman Peter Duncan caused some surprise, as most commentators expected any Scottish Conservative revival to occur in Eastwood or, perhaps more plausibly, Edinburgh Pentlands, contested by a former minister, Malcolm Rifkind. In capturing the Ayrshire seat, the Conservatives highlighted the weakness of the electoral performance of the SNP. Not only had the nationalists failed to make inroads into Labour's majorities, but in Galloway and Upper Nithsdale they had also lost a relatively comfortable seat to a party widely regarded as 'finished'. The SNP had captured the seat in 1997 from the Conservative minister Ian Lang. In 2001 the SNP campaign was criticised nationally and locally. The party failed to persuade its supporters of the continued importance of Westminster elections. Locally, the party ran a lacklustre campaign. The retirement of the SNP's MP, Alasdair Morgan, did not assist. While the vote share of the SNP fell by 10 per cent, all other parties enjoyed an increase in their share. Any Conservative recovery in Scotland since 1997 has been a modest affair, the party only holding seats in the Scottish Parliament through the proportional party list system. It was unclear how greater autonomy for the Scottish Conservatives from the national party, demanded by some members, would act as a panacea.

Result

Galloway and Upper Nithsdale		
	No. of votes	*% of vote*
Duncan, P. (Conservative)	12,222	34.0
Fleming, M. (SNP)	12,148	33.8
Sloan, T. (Labour)	7,258	20.2
Wallace, N. (Liberal Democrat)	3,698	10.3
Harvey, A. (Scottish Socialist Party)	588	1.6
Conservative majority	74	0.2
Conservative gain from SNP		
Turnout		68.1
Swing, SNP to Conservatives		6.8

12

Northern Ireland:
a different kind of election

Jonathan Tonge

Introduction: a unique contest

The 2001 general election in Northern Ireland was a radically different affair from that contested elsewhere, not mercly in the fact that it engendered interest. The vibrancy of the contest was reflected in a turnout of 68 per cent, which, although unexceptional, exceeded the average elsewhere in the UK by 9 per cent. The election for the eighteen Westminster seats departed from most previous contests. Within the Unionist community, the election adopted the form of a second referendum, albeit a complicated one, upon the 1998 Good Friday Agreement, which had created devolved government for Northern Ireland. Among Nationalists, there was uncertainty over the outcome of the battle for supremacy between the Social Democratic and Labour Party (SDLP) and Sinn Fein.

Given the absence, three Conservative candidates apart, of the main British parties, there was a traditional form of exceptionalism to this Northern Ireland contest. However, whereas previous elections had been sectarian headcounts in which few seats changed hands, the 2001 version, in which a remarkable seven seats changed party control, offered considerable variation. Intra-ethnic, rather than inter-ethnic, bloc rivalries were of huge importance. Traditional sectarian divisions were undermined by the support for the Good Friday Agreement from the Ulster Unionist Party (UUP), SDLP and Sinn Fein. The main opposition to the Agreement came from the Democratic Unionist Party (DUP), led by Ian Paisley. As a consequence, parallel contests took place. Among Unionists, the election offered a choice between pro- and anti-Agreement parties, although division was blurred by the individual opposition to the Agreement of several UUP candidates. Within the Nationalist 'family', intra-ethnic bloc rivalry centred upon which party could best convince Northern Ireland's Catholics that it was more likely to advance their interests. These contests were extended into the local council elections held on the same day, which, under the STV system of proportional representation, also offered some prospect of pro-Agreement voting across ethnic blocs. The elections took place against a background of unrest over the lack of progress towards the decommissioning of paramilitary weapons. Before the elections, in March, the problem of decommissioning had been 'parked'. Negotiations on this aspect of the Agreement were scheduled to resume very shortly afterwards, on 18 June. All parties were keen to improve their electoral mandate to strengthen their positions in the negotiations, or, in the case of the DUP, to end the Agreement in its existing form.

The results analysed

The most striking feature of the election was the loss of seats for the UUP, reduced to its lowest Westminster total since the divisions over the Sunningdale Agreement in early 1974. The *Belfast Telegraph* argued that the First Minister and leader of the UUP, David Trimble, was a mere '128 votes from disaster', referring to the majority the party enjoyed over the DUP in Antrim East.[1] The loss of that seat would have seen the DUP emerge, for the first time ever, as the strongest party in Northern Ireland in terms of Westminster representation. In terms of vote share, the UUP performed respectably (see Table 12.1). Indeed, its percentage share exceeded that it received in the 1998 election to the Assembly (22 per cent) and in the 1999 European elections (18 per cent), a point made forcefully by Trimble on the BBC's *On the Record* programme three days after the election. The UUP gained North Down from the anti-Agreement incumbent, Robert McCartney, of the United Kingdom Unionist Party (UKUP) and recaptured South Antrim from the DUP. Both gains were somewhat hollow. South Antrim was previously safe UUP territory until its loss in a by-election in 2000 and the successful UUP candidate, David Burnside, was anti-Agreement. The capture of North Down was assisted by the centrist Alliance Party's withdrawal, with most of its 1997 vote of 7,554 transferring to create the UUP's 7,324 majority. Against these gains lay losses to the DUP in North Belfast (where the UUP vote collapsed by 40 per cent) and Londonderry East, and to Sinn Fein in West Tyrone and Fermanagh and

Table 12.1. Westminster election results in Northern Ireland, 2001

Party	Seats	Change	Vote share (%)	Change in vote share from 1997
UUP	6	−4	26.8	−5.9
DUP	5	+3	22.5	+8.9
Sinn Fein	4	+2	21.7	+5.6
SDLP	3	0	21.0	−3.1
Others	0	−1	8.0	−5.5

South Tyrone. Trimble's own majority in Upper Bann collapsed alarmingly, to a mere 2,058 votes. The only safe seats left for the UUP appeared to be South Belfast and Lagan Valley, held by the *anti-Agreement* MPs Martin Smyth and Jeffrey Donaldson respectively.

Meanwhile Sinn Fein, for the first time ever, became the largest Nationalist party in Northern Ireland. The party gained 50.9 per cent of the Nationalist vote, compared with the SDLP's 49.1 per cent. The rise of Sinn Fein, still committed to abstentionism from Westminster, made inroads into the SDLP's overall percentage share in Northern Ireland, hitherto largely protected by the growing number of Catholics. Gerry Adams held West Belfast, capturing two-thirds of the entire vote; Martin McGuinness comfortably retained Mid-Ulster. The party captured Fermanagh and South Tyrone, by fifty-three votes on a 78 per cent turnout, and West Tyrone, on an 80 per cent turnout, both from the UUP. The latter was gained in a three-way contest. Aside from unseating the incumbent, Willie Thompson, Sinn Fein also had to defeat the SDLP's popular Minister for Agriculture, Brid Rodgers, widely praised across parties for her handling of the foot-and-mouth crisis. In fielding Rodgers the SDLP hoped for a decisive halt of Sinn Fein's advance, particularly in the west of Northern Ireland, with the West Tyrone contest described by BBC Northern Ireland as the SDLP's 'Stalingrad'. Both these gains were bitterly contested. Rodgers' team alleged intimidation by Sinn Fein party workers, while the defeated UUP candidate in Fermanagh and South Tyrone claimed electoral malpractice, arguing that a polling station had been allowed to remain open until 10.45 p.m. The successful Sinn Fein candidate, Michelle Gildernew, had nonetheless long been confident that her party would take the seat.[2] Along with the UUP's Lady Sylvia Hermon and the DUP's Iris Robinson, Gildernew became among the first women to be elected to Westminster for a Northern Ireland seat for twenty-five years. The turnouts in the west of Northern Ireland reflected the closeness of the contests and the ability of Sinn Fein to mobilise its vote, although historically the area enjoyed high turnouts, the figure of 93.4 per cent for Fermanagh and South Tyrone in 1951 remaining a Westminster election record. In 2001 Sinn Fein achieved the party's best election result since partition. Successful in West Tyrone, Pat Doherty indicated the divisive nature of the contest when he declared in his victory speech that 'West of the Bann is now green'.

Those political forces eschewing green versus orange politics did not have a good election. The contest confirmed the continuing collapse of the existing political centre in Northern Ireland, as represented by the Alliance Party. From a Westminster election peak of 11.9 per cent in 1979, Alliance's vote share has been in steady decline. The party polled a mere 3.2 per cent of the general election vote in 2001. The only prior occasion when Alliance had slumped to this level was in February 1974, after the Sunningdale Agreement provided Northern Ireland with a short-lived experiment in devolved, consociational government not entirely dissimilar to that created

Table 12.2. Local election results in Northern Ireland, 7 June 2001, and change from 1999 local elections

Party	Seats	Change	First preference vote (%)	Change
UUP	154	−31	23.0	−7.0
DUP	131	+40	21.5	+5.5
Sinn Fein	108	+34	20.7	+3.7
SDLP	117	−3	19.4	−1.5
Others	72	−19	15.4	+2.3

by the Good Friday Agreement. Alliance also lost thirteen council seats and 2 per cent of its vote share in the local elections. Indeed, the movement towards the 'polar extremes' of the DUP and Sinn Fein was confirmed in the simultaneous local elections (see Table 12.2). The DUP substantially increased both its vote share and number of councillors. Sinn Fein won 51.6 per cent of the Nationalist vote, against 48.4 per cent for the SDLP.

A small body of evidence gathered on the 1998 Assembly elections had indicated an increase in the willingness of pro-Agreement electors to transfer votes across the sectarian divide. Kelly and Doyle found a 5 per cent increase in pro-Agreement Unionist transfers to the SDLP.[3] Evans and O'Leary found that 10 per cent of the electorate transferred from Unionist to Nationalist and vice versa.[4] Sinnott found that 36 per cent of final UUP vote transfers went to the SDLP where an Alliance candidate was unavailable.[5] Furthermore, among even the 860-strong Ulster Unionist Council, the ruling body of the UUP, 15 per cent of members said that they 'definitely' or 'might' consider transferring lower preference votes to the SDLP, with a further 26 per cent describing such a prospect as a 'slight possibility'.[6]

Obviously, under the first-past-the-post Westminster election system such transfer possibilities were irrelevant, although there was no initial evidence of widespread cross-community tactical voting to bolster pro-Agreement candidates in the 2001 general election. The initial message from the 2001 local elections, worthy of further research, appeared to be that any cross-community vote transfers appeared to be minuscule in comparison with shifts within the Nationalist and Unionist blocs, the DUP and Sinn Fein benefiting from substantial increases in first preference voting and from lower preference vote transfers from UUP and SDLP voters respectively. The trend for SDLP voters has been increasingly to transfer lower preference votes to Sinn Fein. Two-thirds did so in the 1998 Assembly elections, whereas in the past the strength of Sinn Fein's associations with the Irish Republican Army (IRA) led a substantial body of SDLP supporters to vote transfer to the centrist, avowedly non-sectarian Alliance Party.

Analysis of the election results thus shows movement away from the centre towards historically 'harder' parties, although the changed political context of Northern Ireland, notably the new moderation of Sinn Fein, means that such votes should not be interpreted as a manifestation of political extremism.

The problem of decommissioning

The apparent shift in Northern Ireland's electorate to tougher forms of Unionism and Nationalism was associated, within the Unionist community, with the failure of the IRA to decommission its weapons (despite Sinn Fein's continuing presence in government) and, on the Nationalist side, with the vibrancy of Sinn Fein's electoral strategy, the energy of which made the SDLP appear tired and dated. The election campaign had a dramatic start when Trimble declared that he would quit as First Minister on 1 July 2001 if the IRA had not begun decommissioning its weapons by that date. Trimble's move was dismissed as a 'pathetic and cynical election stunt' by the DUP, concerned that Trimble's gesture would reassure wavering 'yes' Unionist voters.[7] Trimble handed a letter to the Speaker of the Northern Ireland Assembly, Lord Alderdice, confirming his intention to resign. This was the second threat of resignation from Trimble. An earlier threat to quit if decommissioning failed to occur, offered to his party chairman, had been superseded by the temporary suspension of the Northern Ireland Executive by the Secretary of State, Peter Mandelson, from February until May 2000. The renewed threat reflected electoral calculation and Unionist frustration at the lack of movement on decommissioning, a consequence of the ambiguity on the issue within the Good Friday Agreement. The minimalist demands of the Agreement required merely that parties use 'any influence they may have' to facilitate paramilitary decommissioning.[8] Nonetheless, decommissioning became the issue upon which anti-Agreement Unionists rallied.

In June 1998, the leader of the IRA in the Maze Prison, Padraig Wilson, had insisted that 'voluntary decommissioning' would be a 'natural development of the peace process'.[9] For Unionists, however, there were three essential requirements to decommissioning. First, it had to be accepted by republicans as an essential part of the process. Second, Sinn Fein should not be permitted to accept places in the Northern Ireland Executive in advance of IRA decommissioning. Third, decommissioning must mean the handover of 'product', that is the relinquishing of weaponry.

The decommissioning controversy remained unresolved despite a series of efforts by the British and Irish governments. As the Good Friday Agreement was forged, the British Prime Minister offered written pledges to Trimble that decommissioning was an essential element. In July 1999, the two governments offered *The Way Forward*, a choreographed set of proposals, by which the process of decommissioning would begin in conjunction with the formation of the Northern Ireland Executive. Progress reports were to be issued by the

International Commission on Decommissioning (ICD) headed by John de Chastelain, in September and December 1999, with decommissioning to be completed by May 2000. With the IRA yet to appoint a representative to meet the ICD, the UUP Executive rejected *The Way Forward* and the Northern Ireland Executive could not be formed. By November 1999 the Ulster Unionist Council had softened its line in voting by 58 per cent to 42 per cent to allow the UUP to join Sinn Fein in a Northern Ireland Executive. An Executive was finally formed and the IRA appointed a representative to deal with the ICD.

Although the UUP had 'jumped first' in abandoning the requirement for decommissioning as a prerequisite for Sinn Fein's entry into government, a default mechanism had been added, in the form of Trimble's threat of resignation as First Minister if the IRA failed to proceed with decommissioning. Trimble's threat produced movement from the IRA before the restoration of the Executive in May 2000. The Provisional IRA agreed to open arms dumps to regular inspection by the former Finnish President Martti Ahtisaari and the former Secretary-General of the African National Congress Cyril Ramaphosa. Although the inspections restored devolved government to Northern Ireland, Unionists still wanted weapons to be put permanently beyond use. The debate had moved from sequencing towards substance: what exactly did decommissioning mean? 'Yes' Unionists appeared ready to accept the placement of weapons beyond use; 'no' Unionists demanded the handover of weaponry.

Despite the enduring party rows over decommissioning, it appeared there was broad political consensus among the wider population that decommissioning was an essential aspect of the political process, as indicated in an Ulster Marketing Surveys/*Belfast Telegraph* opinion poll taken during the election campaign, the results of which are shown in Table 12.3. Nearly three-quarters

Table 12.3. Attitudes to decommissioning among party supporters[a]

	Party supported				
	DUP	UUP	SDLP	Sinn Fein	Total
IRA					
Yes – all weapons	93	93	73	44	81
Yes – some weapons	6	6	21	28	12
No	1	1	6	28	7
Loyalist paramilitaries					
Yes – all weapons	87	91	76	60	82
Yes – some weapons	9	7	19	23	12
No	4	2	5	17	6

[a]The question was phrased 'Should paramilitaries decommission weapons?'
Source: Ulster Marketing Surveys/*Belfast Telegraph*, May 2001.

of Sinn Fein supporters believed that the IRA should get rid of at least some of its weaponry. The extent of Unionist belief that the organisation should remove its weapons was clearly evident. The IRA issued a statement during the election campaign confirming that a third examination of its arms dumps had been concluded and indicating that four meetings between the IRA and the ICD had taken place since March 2001. In a separate statement, the ICD confirmed its satisfaction with the inspection and declared that the IRA had 'fully honoured their commitments'.[10] The onus was on David Trimble to convince a Unionist population much more divided on the Good Friday Agreement that its Nationalist counterpart that decommissioning could finally be delivered in a manner that would win permanent confidence.

Creating Northern Ireland's new consociational democracy

The interminable row over decommissioning overshadowed Northern Ireland's transition to a relatively peaceful, consociational democracy. Now the polarisation evident in the election results threatened to make a permanent accommodation of elites even more problematic. The Good Friday Agreement met the criteria of cross-community power sharing: proportionality in government; equality; and minority veto rights consistent with consociational principles.[11] It created an interlocked set of institutions: a Northern Ireland Executive and Assembly; a North–South Ministerial Council, presiding over the work of all-Ireland implementation bodies; a confederal Council of the Isles, linking devolved institutions throughout the UK and the Republic of Ireland; and the east–west dimension of the British–Irish intergovernmental conference. To supporters, it was an imaginative agreement, amounting to an 'exemplary constitutional design'.[12] Undoubtedly it was a far more inclusive settlement than its consociational predecessor, the 1974 Sunningdale Agreement, which had little hope of success given its abject rejection by paramilitary groups.[13] This time the paramilitaries, small dissident groups excepted, were onside, their ceasefires consolidated. The 1998 referendum on the Agreement confirmed that Northern Ireland's population was supportive. The Agreement offered the longer-term possibility that the confessional party system in Northern Ireland might be transcended by new pro-Agreement alignments. Direct rule was replaced by local democracy and, by December 1999, all the political institutions were functioning.

On the debit side, at least two of the new sets of institutions, perhaps the most important, were clearly not working properly at the time of the 2001 general election. The Executive, comprising members of the UUP, DUP, SDLP and Sinn Fein, adopted little sense of collective responsibility, appearing, in the words of one critic, as little more than a 'holding company for a collection of Ministers with different party affiliations than a collective decision-making body'.[14] The DUP declined to work with Sinn Fein in the Executive, while

Assembly parties represented in the Executive attempted to undermine decisions taken by that Executive, including budgetary items. The 108-member Assembly appeared much too large, compared, for example, with Scotland's 129-seat Parliament with tax-raising powers. If the House of Commons were based on the representation ratios used for the Northern Ireland Assembly it would contain over 5,000 MPs. That only the UKUP demanded reductions in the size and cost of the Assembly was indicative of the vested interest of all sides in maintaining devolved government. The suspension of Sinn Fein from North–South ministerial meetings by the First Minister, on the basis of a lack of IRA decommissioning, was indicative of how the development of political institutions was not only seen as interlinked with other institutions but was also conditional upon particular interpretations, in this case clearly an incorrect one, of the Agreement.

Meanwhile the Agreement appeared merely to hasten the demise of the existing centre in Northern Ireland. The strongest intellectual criticism of the Good Friday Agreement was that it legitimised zero-sum-game Unionist versus Nationalist politics. The Alliance Party's Members of the Legislative Assembly, long attempting to overcome such division, were reduced to the designation of 'other' amid the weighted majority rules of the Northern Ireland Assembly, designed to achieve a sufficiency of consensus among Unionists and Nationalists. Supporters of the Agreement could of course point out that the Agreement hardly invented Unionist and Nationalist politics. The greening of the SDLP, for example, was a consequence of the failure of a consociational solution in 1974, not a product of its implementation.[15] The Good Friday Agreement diverted antagonism towards 'attrition rather than aggression'.[16] Moreover, successful management of division offered the prospect of long-term reconciliation. Against this there lay the argument that post-Agreement politics best served those playing green or orange cards, proving themselves the stronger Nationalists or Unionists, and the 2001 election results offered evidence of reward.

For supporters of the Agreement there loomed the prospect of further problems in the 2003 Assembly elections (which would take place earlier, if ministerial resignations forced fresh elections) if ethnic bloc politics continued to polarise. With Sinn Fein having overtaken the SDLP, the party could expect to claim the post of Deputy First Minister. Yet, unless full decommissioning took place, it was scarcely conceivable that the cross-community consensus required for an election would be forthcoming, given the implacable opposition of the DUP to Sinn Fein. The problem of sufficiency of consensus looms large if the DUP vote continues to increase. The declining centre could redesignate itself as Unionist to save the Agreement. Although the other centre party, the Women's Coalition, would be most unlikely to adopt this position, it remains a possibility for Alliance, 40 per cent of its members believing it would be worthwhile to adopt a Unionist designation to save the Agreement.[17] At times the Agreement appeared to survive by default, due to the lack of alternatives, than through effective development and implementation, although it retained considerable popular support.

The Unionist campaign

The successes for the DUP belied predictions during the campaign. In the months before the announcement of the election it had been forecast that the DUP and Sinn Fein would make substantial gains at the expense of the UUP and the SDLP respectively. The loss of 'safe' South Antrim to the DUP's William McCrea in a Westminster by-election in 2000 wounded the UUP, prompting fears of electoral meltdown for the pro-Agreement party. During the election campaign itself, however, it appeared that support for the UUP had stabilised. A majority of Unionist electors had, after all, backed the Good Friday Agreement and were therefore likely to cast their vote to reflect this position. In May 2001, 61 per cent of Protestants said that they would vote 'yes' to the Agreement if asked to endorse it again, an increase on the level of support in the referendum three years earlier.[18] Less than one in five Protestants backed a return to direct rule from Westminster and only just over one-quarter disagreed with the proposition that the Agreement was 'improving conditions in Northern Ireland'.[19] Unsurprisingly, even 'yes' Unionists had qualms concerning what they saw as the moral equivocations of the Agreement, notably paramilitary prisoner releases, the presence of former IRA personnel in government and the reforms of the Royal Ulster Constabulary (RUC) introduced following the Patten Report. Nonetheless, the pain of prisoner releases had begun to fade, after the programme had been completed in summer 2000.[20] Many of the changes proposed within the Patten Report had been diluted by the then Secretary of State, Peter Mandelson, when given legislative effect.[21] Although the decommissioning row rumbled on, the assertions of successive Secretaries of State – Mowlam, Mandelson and Reid – that the Good Friday Agreement was the 'only show in town' appeared to be gaining credence within the Unionist community.

Trimble's position appeared even more secure when an Ulster Marketing Surveys/*Belfast Telegraph* poll during the election campaign placed UUP support at 25 per cent, with the DUP trailing at 14 per cent.[22] Moderate Unionists could also be reassured by the same poll's findings that Sinn Fein's support (at 16 per cent) trailed that for the SDLP by 9 per cent.[23] Perhaps such optimistic forecasts led David Trimble to make the rash assertion that the election would determine the future of Northern Ireland. The opinion poll proved highly inaccurate as a guide to actual voting, not in its findings in respect of UUP support (it was within 1.8 per cent of the UUP total) but in its underestimation (by nearly 9 per cent) of DUP support. The polling organisation blamed shifts in support and electoral fraud, but neither offered sufficient explanation.[24] Allegations of fraud were confined mainly to aspects of Sinn Fein activity, levelled by defeated political opponents suspicious of the high turnouts in the seats gained by Nationalists. Late shifts in opinion were unlikely, given that there had been no developments in respect of the Good Friday Agreement since March, when the controversies surrounding implementation were 'parked' until after the election.

The threat of resignation from David Trimble exacerbated the hostility within the Unionist campaign. The DUP's manifesto, *Leadership to Put Things Right*, offered a predictably strident critique of the UUP's 'endorsement of the republican agenda'.[25] The manifesto concentrated upon those aspects of the Agreement most distasteful to Unionists, summarised as 'terrorists in government; the RUC destroyed; murderers released and executive all-Ireland bodies set up'.[26] The main theme of the manifesto was to highlight the 'broken promises' of the UUP in allowing Sinn Fein's entry into government in advance of IRA weapons decommissioning. There was also condemnation of the manner in which 'everything Gaelic, republican and Irish is promoted while everything British, unionist or Orange is derided' under the Agreement.[27] The document did not offer any alternative to the Agreement. Instead it confined its policy agenda to other issues, including farming, pensions and health. On education, the DUP accused the Minister for Education, Sinn Fein's Martin McGuinness, of favouring Catholic schools in terms of capital expenditure. The DUP's avowed left-of-centre position on non-constitutional issues was reflected in its expansionist agenda on health and transport, alongside a pledge to abolish university tuition fees, although the party also supported the retention of selection in schools. This social agenda led *The Times* to claim that the DUP and Sinn Fein's populist agendas were 'more compatible than either would care to admit'.[28] Such social agendas nonetheless played little part in an election campaign dominated by stances on the Good Friday Agreement.

Sensitive to charges of negativity, not least because of the lack of a positive constitutional agenda in its manifesto, the DUP stressed its devolutionist credentials. The party had always supported devolved government for Northern Ireland. This, however, had to be an internal affair, devoid of attached cross-border bodies and minus Sinn Fein unless the IRA handed over weapons. Renegotiation of the Agreement would need to be based upon the principle of IRA decommissioning before Sinn Fein's entry to the Executive. The other main negotiating 'principle' was full accountability of the Executive and cross-border bodies to the Assembly.

The DUP's critique of the Agreement was shared by the UKUP in its manifesto.[29] The UKUP argued that the consent principle, under which Northern Ireland would remain part of the UK for as long its people chose, applied only to the legal transfer of Northern Ireland to the Irish Republic, but did not protect the Unionist population from the 'formation of institutions and policies that will make the giving of consent either inevitable or unnecessary'.[30]

Whatever the limitations of its agenda, the DUP (and the tiny UKUP) could at least claim party unity. Such a luxury was not afforded to the UUP leadership, obliged to support pro- and anti-Agreement candidates. The presence of Agreement rejectionists within its own ranks diluted the UUP's criticisms of the DUP's negativity, although the retiring UUP MP, Ken Maginnis, did assert that 'The DUP has rejected international support just as it has rejected every Secretary of State, every Chief Constable, every Protestant church leader, the Ulster Unionists, Jim Molyneaux and David Trimble – not to mention line dancing', the final aside based on the recent prohibition issued on the hitherto seemingly inoffensive activity by the Free Presbyterian Church, headed by Paisley.[31] Within his party, Trimble was obliged to back, for example, the Reverend Martin Smyth, having fended off a leadership challenge from the same MP by the narrow margin of 57 per cent to 43 per cent during the previous year. The party manifesto encouraged a semblance of election unity by including photographs of pro- and anti-candidates and, more extraordinarily, omitting all reference to the Good Friday Agreement. Other than one reference to a 'genuinely British–Irish Agreement' replacing the 'flawed Anglo-Irish Agreement', the accommodation yielding the most important set of political arrangements in Northern Ireland since partition was the Agreement that dare not speak its name.[32] Instead, the UUP manifesto (leaked in advance by the DUP) concentrated upon one product, albeit the major item, of the Agreement, the Northern Ireland Assembly, while also mentioning the other Unionist institutional gain, the Council of the Isles. Correctly, the UUP insisted that the Assembly offered Unionists a 'veto over policy decisions in Northern Ireland and over cross-border co-operation', the latter seen as beneficial provided it was not based on 'ideological nationalist schemes'.[33]

During the campaign, the UUP was dismissive of the DUP's insistence that it would not 'work with terrorists', pointing to the presence of DUP and Sinn Fein members on Assembly committees. In stark contrast to the DUP's offering, the UUP listed the positive benefits of recent political accommodation: abolition of the Anglo-Irish Agreement; application of the 'consent principle'; self-determination in respect of Northern Ireland's constitutional future; the ending of the Irish Republic's territorial claim; the replacement of direct rule with devolved government, via a directly elected assembly; the maintenance of paramilitary ceasefires; and the inspection of arms dumps. The message was that the Unionists had won the war and secured the Union. That some unfinished business remained was acknowledged, notably the need for decommissioning, stable government and greater devolved powers, particularly to cover policing. The manifesto attempted to portray the UUP as the creators of a more liberal, pluralist and tolerant Unionism, now possible given the eradication of the threat to the state. This led to significant omissions from the manifesto, particularly the issue of Orange parades, despite the party's criticisms of the Parades Commission in previous years. Overall, the UUP approach was in step with Trimble's determination to end any lingering perception of Northern Ireland as a 'cold house' for Nationalists. It reflected

Trimble's belief, outlined in his opening addresses to the Northern Ireland
Assembly, that what was needed was a 'pluralist parliament for a pluralist
people' to effect liberal, tolerant governance.

Not all the members of the Ulster Unionist Council agreed that the Good
Friday Agreement offered the most appropriate framework for progress. Forty-
four per cent of them agreed with the set of institutional arrangements
created by the Good Friday Agreement, in that they believed that the best
solution for Northern Ireland was devolved power sharing between Unionists
and Nationalists, with cross-border bodies attached. However, the same
percentage believed that the best solution was power sharing *without* cross-
border bodies, even though such internal arrangements would be unacceptable
to Nationalists.[34] Furthermore, despite the UUP's claim that devolved government had been a success, 48 per cent of its Council members clung to a
desire for the full integration of Northern Ireland into the UK, however
unrealistic given devolution elsewhere.[35] Perhaps worse for Trimble was that
less than half the members of his party's ruling Council indicated that they
would support the Good Friday Agreement if another referendum were held.

Whatever the bitter rivalry between the two Unionist parties and the
internal divisions within the UUP, a sizeable section of the Unionist electorate
desired increased Unionist cooperation against what was sometimes seen as
vibrant pan-Nationalism. Almost half of UUP supporters believed that there
should be an electoral pact with the DUP, a feeling reciprocated by 41 per
cent of DUP supporters, although 46 per cent opposed the idea.[36] A realignment of Unionist party politics remained a possibility, albeit an unlikely one,
on the basis of support or opposition to the Good Friday Agreement. Only
Robert McCartney's anti-Agreement UKUP called for a pan-Unionist alliance.[37]
Important support for the Agreement had been offered among working-class
loyalists by the Progressive Unionist Party (PUP), linked to the paramilitary
Ulster Volunteer Force. It feared a loss of its limited electoral support as a
consequence of the deadly loyalist feud of the previous year and disillusionment
with the Agreement. The party's vote did decline in South Belfast, but David
Ervine's candidature in East Belfast (uncontested by the PUP in 1997) yielded
a respectable 10 per cent of the vote. Although the PUP remained a significant
voice of 'yes' Unionism, its aim of providing a new working-class loyalism
to displace Paisleyism remained ambitious.

The Nationalist campaign

The contest within the Nationalist community concerned which party was
best placed to achieve the most gains for its electorate from the Good Friday
Agreement, supported in the 1998 referendum by 96 per cent of Nationalists.
Not everyone welcomed the electoral battle for the Nationalist vote, as almost
half of Sinn Fein supporters argued that there should be an electoral pact

between their party and the SDLP, although fewer than one-third of SDLP supporters were prepared to reciprocate.[38] SDLP members were divided on the merits of such an alliance, 47 per cent agreeing, but 36 per cent dissenting.[39] Those most hostile tended to be older party members, implacably opposed to the form of republicanism offered by Sinn Fein during the previous thirty years.

Sinn Fein, fielding candidates in all eighteen constituencies for the first time, concentrated upon its support for full implementation of the Good Friday Agreement. The party also demanded: further all-Ireland political and electoral arrangements, including the advancement of all-Ireland bodies; the right of those elected in parliamentary contests in Northern Ireland to participate in the Irish parliament; and Northern Ireland's citizens to be given the right to participate in presidential elections and referendums in the Irish Republic. Sinn Fein demanded further changes in policing, with full implementation of the Patten Report constituting the minimum demand. The party also desired alterations to the criminal justice system and offered support for 'restorative justice' schemes. Sinn Fein's social, economic and cultural proposals included: more investment in integrated and Irish-language schools; the abolition of the eleven-plus examination and university tuition fees; the establishment of a Social Care Council for vulnerable NHS patients; the creation of a Ministry for Children; and tax-raising powers for the Northern Ireland Assembly. Although committed to abstention from Westminster, due to the requirement to swear the oath of allegiance to the Queen, Sinn Fein demanded use of Westminster facilities.

Sinn Fein's electoral strategy, emphasising support for the Good Friday Agreement, was always likely to pay dividends among an electoral base strongly favouring the accord and searching for 'strong' political representatives. Sinn Fein's electoral rise had been unchecked since the reverse of the 1992 general election, when the party had lost Gerry Adams' West Belfast seat to the SDLP. Committed to its peace strategy, Sinn Fein had long moved from its early electoral position of the 1980s, when its *ard-fheis* (annual conference) instructed all candidates to declare unequivocal support for the IRA's armed struggle. With that struggle increasingly confined to memory, the party, while emphasising its continuing republican objectives, offered a participatory form of politics starkly at odds with the support for the armed destruction of the state favoured in previous eras. The disavowal of the small number of republicans preferring more traditional methods of 'liberation' was emphasised by the criticism offered by Martin McGuinness of the shooting of two RUC officers by republican 'ultras' in an attack at a polling station on election night, an action reminiscent of much Provisional IRA activity between 1970 and 1994, but now deemed unacceptable.

For the few republican critics of Sinn Fein's changed approach, the party's electoral success could not disguise the failure of the party to achieve its objective of a united Ireland, now displaced by participation within a Northern

Ireland state previously held to be illegitimate.[40] Sinn Fein's manifesto assertion
that the Good Friday Agreement 'transcends partition' was ranged against
the Agreement's stark message that Ireland remains divided and Northern
Ireland part of the UK, for as long as the people of Northern Ireland so
choose.[41] Yet even those critics eschewing a return to armed struggle failed
to advance a coherent alternative strategy, although lamenting the alleged
promotion of green, Catholic Nationalist politics at the expense of 'true'
republicanism. Sinn Fein's continued insistence upon eventual British withdrawal and Irish unity reassured many republicans. Any widespread lingering
sympathy for militarism, as found among the tiny Real and Continuity IRAs,
disappeared with the killing of twenty-nine civilians in the 1998 Omagh
bombing.

For the SDLP there was the irony that its electoral problems coincided with
the realisation of many of its political ambitions through the Good Friday
Agreement. The Agreement lay much closer to SDLP thinking than to
traditional republican objectives.[42] Despite its considerable political achievement, the SDLP nonetheless had organisational and image problems. The
party leader's willingness to take initiatives for peace had, it was argued even
by sympathisers, led to his neglect of internal party matters.[43] Equally
problematic was that the party's internal reviews revealed concern about its
ageing electorate, while its ageing membership (with an average age of fifty-
seven) was confirmed by an external survey.[44] With the party no longer able
to condemn Sinn Fein's associations with violence, it needed to convince the
Nationalist electorate that it could offer the same benefits from the Agreement
as could be extracted by Sinn Fein's vigorous form of politics. The SDLP
attempted to portray itself as the party best placed to deal with post-
constitutional issues through its longer experience of politics than its Nationalist
rival. In an attempt to reinforce the idea of progressiveness, the party also
emphasised its pro-European credentials. Although its campaign appeared
lacklustre alongside that conducted by Sinn Fein, this was partly explained
by the lack of serious possibilities, Brid Rodgers in West Tyrone apart, of
gaining or losing seats. For the SDLP, there remained the ongoing difficulty
of whether its best tactical approach was to reinforce pan-Nationalist common-
alities with Sinn Fein, or attempt to forge a new centre with pro-Agreement
elements within the UUP. Neither strategy could be guaranteed to stem the
flow of votes to Sinn Fein.

Conclusion

Unsurprisingly, various interpretations were placed on the election results.
Sinn Fein saw its gains as a vindication of its 'peace strategy'; the DUP
believed its increased popularity was a clear rejection of the 'appeasement'
of republicans by its main Unionist rival. The Secretary of State, John Reid,

offered a verdict not dissimilar from the UUP's conclusion in stating that there was an enduring commitment to the Good Friday Agreement, but that there was concern to see 'all its aspects ... implemented as fully as possible', a barely disguised reference to the need for further movement on decommissioning.[45] There were three broad conclusions in much of the immediate post-election media analysis, all of which require disaggregation: first, the Good Friday Agreement was in difficulty; second, the entire peace process was in jeopardy; third, politics in Northern Ireland had become more polarised. Much of the argument behind these contentions did not bear closer inspection.

First, it was certainly true that the Good Friday Agreement would be in difficulty if there was not further movement by the IRA on decommissioning. The setting of a 1 July deadline by David Trimble failed to bolster his party's electoral fortunes and, arguably, drew further attention to the impasse on decommissioning. If it remained unlikely that IRA weapons would ever be handed over, as demanded by the DUP, further movement was nonetheless likely from the IRA, including the possibility of the destruction of weapons, as most republicans eschewed and indeed condemned violence.

Second, therefore, the election results did not necessarily jeopardise the peace process. The IRA remained committed to its ceasefire, now in place for seven years, temporary fracture in 1996–97 notwithstanding. Sinn Fein's faith in the vibrancy of its electoral strategy had paid dividends and made the already remote prospect of a return to violence by the Provisional IRA even less likely. Loyalists remained committed to their ceasefires. Low-level violence from 'ultras' apart, a return to the 'armed struggle' appeared highly unlikely. As such, the threat to the peace process remained minimal.

Finally, the argument that politics had polarised was based upon a dated conception of 'polar extremes' within Northern Ireland politics. The argument does contain some merit in respect of developments within Unionism, as the DUP's approach to politics has changed little, but the party nonetheless supports devolved power sharing. The vote for Sinn Fein was a product of the party's new respectability far more than its capacity for extreme politics. A vote for Sinn Fein fifteen years earlier could readily be interpreted as a vote of support for the IRA's 'armed struggle'. A modern vote for Sinn Fein instead represented a view that the party could achieve substantial gains for the Nationalist community. While desirous of a united Ireland, the party uses constitutional politics within the state to achieve change, tacitly accepting the principle of consent for change within Northern Ireland in a manner unthinkable in previous decades.

The election did, however, confirm the risks attached to a consociational settlement such as the Good Friday Agreement. Inter-ethnic bloc rivalries (Unionist versus Nationalist) have been legitimised, although not, as critics of the Agreement claim, increased. Intra-ethnic rivalry between parties can increase, as each faction attempts to prove to its electorate that it is the stoutest defender of the interests of that bloc. That rivalry has not yet been accompanied by sufficient thawing of inter-ethnic bloc relations between Unionists and Nationalists for Northern Ireland to become a consensual society – or for a 'normal' election, based on social and economic issues, to take place.

Acknowledgement

The author acknowledges the assistance of ESRC awards R000222668, New Nationalism in Northern Ireland, L327253058, The Role of 'Extra-Constitutional' Parties in the Northern Ireland Assembly (with Professor James McAuley) and R000223414, Third Traditions in Northern Ireland, in the construction of this article.

Notes

1 *Belfast Telegraph*, 13 June 2001.
2 Interview with author, 27 June 2000.
3 M. Kelly and J. Doyle, 'The Good Friday Agreement and electoral behaviour – an analysis of vote transfers under PRSTV in the Northern Ireland Assembly elections of 1992 and 1998', paper presented to the Political Studies Association of Ireland's Annual Conference, University of Cork, October 2000.
4 G. Evans and B. O'Leary, 'Northern Irish voters and the British–Irish Agreement: foundations of a stable consociational settlement?', paper presented to the Political Studies Association's Elections, Parties and Opinion Polls Annual Conference, University College Northampton, September 1999.
5 R. Sinnott, 'Centrist politics make modest but significant progress: cross-community transfers were low', *Irish Times*, 29 September 1998.
6 Survey of the Ulster Unionist Council conducted by author, 2000.
7 Peter Robinson, DUP Deputy Leader, quoted in the *Guardian*, 9 May 2001.
8 *The Agreement* (1998), p. 20.
9 *Financial Times*, 17 June 1998; J. Tonge, 'The formation of the Northern Ireland Executive', *Irish Political Studies*, 15 (2000), pp. 153–61.
10 www.irlnet.com, 29–31 May 2001.
11 B. O'Leary, 'The nature of the British–Irish Agreement', *New Left Review*, 233 (1999), pp. 66–96.
12 B. O'Leary, 'The Belfast Agreement and the Labour government', in A. Seldon (ed.), *The Blair Effect: The Blair Government 1997–2001* (London: Little Brown, 2001), p. 460.
13 J. Tonge, 'From Sunningdale to the Good Friday Agreement: creating devolved government in Northern Ireland', *Contemporary British History*, 14:3 (2000), pp. 39–60; S. Wolff, 'Context and content: Sunningdale and Belfast compared', in R. Wilford (ed.), *Aspects of the Belfast Agreement* (Oxford: Oxford University Press, 2001).
14 M. Laver, 'Coalitions in Northern Ireland: preliminary thoughts', programme for government conference, Belfast, 2000. See also R. Wilford, 'Northern Ireland one year on: a discursive narrative', paper presented to 'Transitions to Devolution', Political Studies Association UK Territorial Politics Conference, University of Wales Cardiff, January 2001.
15 J. Evans, J. Tonge and G. Murray, 'Constitutional nationalism and socialism in Northern Ireland: the greening of the Social Democratic and Labour Party', in

P. Cowley, D. Denver, A. Russell and L. Harrison (eds), *British Elections and Parties Review Volume 10* (London: Frank Cass, 2000).

16 R. Wilson, 'Introduction: politics or polarisation?', in R. Wilson (ed.), *Agreeing to Disagree? A Guide to the Northern Ireland Assembly* (Belfast: Stationery Office, 2001).

17 Author's membership survey, 2000–01.

18 Ulster Marketing Surveys/*Belfast Telegraph* poll, May 2001.

19 *Ibid.*

20 *Guardian*, 5 June 2001.

21 O'Leary, 'The Belfast Agreement and the Labour government'.

22 Ulster Marketing Surveys/*Belfast Telegraph* poll, May 2001.

23 *Ibid.*

24 *Belfast Telegraph*, 13 June 2001.

25 Democratic Unionist Party, *Leadership to Put Things Right*, parliamentary and district council election manifesto 2001 (Belfast: DUP, 2001).

26 *Ibid.*, p. 2.

27 *Ibid.*, p. 4.

28 *The Times*, 29 May 2001.

29 UKUP, *Facing the Truth*, election manifesto (Belfast: UKUP, 2001).

30 *Belfast Telegraph*, 30 May 2001.

31 *News Letter*, 29 May 2001.

32 UUP, *Manifesto* (Belfast: UUP, 2001), p. 20.

33 *Ibid.*, p. 7.

34 Author's survey of Council members, 2000.

35 *Ibid.*

36 Ulster Marketing Surveys/*Belfast Telegraph* poll, May 2001.

37 *News Letter*, 30 May 2001.

38 *Ibid.*

39 Evans, Tonge and Murray, 'Constitutional nationalism and socialism in Northern Ireland'.

40 See A. McIntyre, 'Modern Irish republicanism and the Belfast Agreement: chickens coming home to roost or turkeys celebrating Christmas?', in R. Wilford (ed.), *Aspects of the Belfast Agreement* (Oxford: Oxford University Press, 2001); S. Breen, 'On the one road', *Fortnight*, 388 (2000), pp. 18–19.

41 Sinn Fein, *Manifesto 2001* (Belfast: Sinn Fein, 2001).

42 G. Murray, *John Hume's SDLP* (Dublin: Irish Academic Press, 1998).

43 *Ibid.*

44 J. Tonge, and G. Murray, ESRC SDLP membership survey, 1999. See also Evans, Tonge and Murray, 'Constitutional nationalism and socialism in Northern Ireland'.

45 www.irlnet.com, 9 June 2001.

West Tyrone

Pat Doherty's triumph for Sinn Fein in West Tyrone highlighted the increasing dominance of Sinn Fein in the west of Northern Ireland. The party lay a close third behind the UUP and the SDLP after the 1997 election and had been confident of taking the seat. However, capture of the seat, contested by only three candidates, the fewest of any contest in Northern Ireland, appeared less certain after the SDLP's decision to field Brid Rodgers, the highly respected Agriculture Minister. Her competence in dealing with the foot-and-mouth crisis was thought likely to be a highly useful asset in a predominantly rural constituency and led to her being billed as the 'People's Champion' on election posters. Vice-President of Sinn Fein since 1988 and chair of the Northern Ireland Assembly Economic Committee, Pat Doherty had been a prime mover in Sinn Fein's 'peace strategy' during the 1990s. His brother had been imprisoned for over two decades as an IRA member of the 'Balcombe Street gang' operating in London during the 1970s. Doherty's republican credentials were seen as impeccable, but his campaign emphasis was upon the needs to attract jobs and investment to one of the poorer areas of Northern Ireland. Doherty also insisted upon the need for fundamental changes to policing in Northern Ireland, although Rodgers' own public concerns over the 'lack of an acceptable police force' attempted to prevent Sinn Fein gaining ground on this issue (*Irish News*, 29 May 2001). The incumbent UUP MP, Willie Thompson, was a staunch opponent of the Good Friday Agreement. His opposition was based not merely on the presence of Sinn Fein in government in advance of IRA decommissioning but also upon a belief that the Agreement could not work.

Sinn Fein's confidence was partly a product of analysis of the 1998 Assembly elections, in which the party captured 34 per cent of the vote, compared with 25.7 per cent for the SDLP and a poor 15.7 per cent for the UUP. However, during that contest the Unionist vote was divided by the presence of the DUP. In 2001, with no Nationalist electoral pact (despite half of Nationalists favouring such a development) there remained a risk that intra-Nationalist rivalry would allow the UUP to retain the seat. Doherty nonetheless improved Sinn Fein's vote share from 1997 by a remarkable 9 per cent, against 2 per cent and 5 per cent falls for the SDLP and UUP respectively. Assessing the result, Sinn Fein's President, Gerry Adams, drew wider implications, dismissing the SDLP's post-Nationalist approach as 'factually and politically wrong', pointing to the simultaneous rejection of the Nice Treaty by the voters of the Irish Republic (www.irlnet.com, 15 June 2001). The result was above all, however, a triumph for Sinn Fein's well organised local campaigning.

Result

West Tyrone		
	No. of votes	*% of vote*
Doherty, P. (Sinn Fein)	19,814	40.8
Thompson, W. (UUP)	14,774	30.4
Rodgers, B. (SDLP)	13,942	28.7
Sinn Fein majority	5,040	10.4
Sinn Fein gain from the UUP		
Turnout		79.9
Swing, UUP to Sinn Fein		7.1

13

Women representatives and women voters: taking account of 'Worcester woman' in the 2001 general election

Rachel J. Ward

Introduction

The general election of 1997 appeared to herald a new era in British politics in all kinds of different ways. One aspect was that the gender gap in voting – the difference between the votes cast by men and women – narrowed to 2 per cent as many women floating voters voted for Labour.[1] Previously women were more likely to support the Conservative Party than were men, especially among older groups, which led Pippa Norris to refer to a 'gender-generation gap'.[2] Norris also found that younger women were more likely to vote Labour than younger men in the 1997 election, but that the obverse still held true for older men and women and votes for the Conservative Party. Moreover, another dimension of the gender gap relates to voter turnout. More women than men have voted in general elections since 1979. In 1997 this amounted to 1.9 million votes.[3] Therefore appealing to women voters has become an important aspect of party competition.

There is also evidence of a gender gap in political priorities, with women more concerned about such issues as health and education.[4] Policies related to equality in employment, child care, reproductive rights and the family, which affect women in particular, have been on the political agenda since the 1970s, along with pressure from women political activists for equality in political representation.[5]

Another major change at the 1997 election was the large increase in the number of women MPs, from sixty (9 per cent) in 1992 to 120 (18 per cent) in 1997. This was hardly revolutionary, but as 101 of them were Labour MPs, thus comprising 24 per cent of the parliamentary Labour party, a difference in the policy agenda was anticipated. Indeed, this anticipation was fuelled by the words of Prime Minister Blair when he said that greater numbers of women would lead to a change in the culture of politics at Westminster. Rather depressingly, elements of the British media then sought immediately to belittle the influx of women Labour MPs by designating them

'Blair's Babes'. That there was no ground-breaking feminist-inspired legislation in the early days of the new Labour government appeared to justify the jibe.

We can thus see in the 1997 results a closing of the gender gap, increased representation of women and evidence to suggest that the parties have an incentive to pay attention to issues that matter to women voters. In this chapter I draw these factors together and consider the extent to which the increased number of women MPs has made a difference to politics. In doing this, I reflect upon the significance of the term 'Worcester woman'. This label was first used in 1997 by Conservative Party strategists to describe the 'middle England' female floating voter and thus a key target group. 'Worcester woman' is defined as being in her late thirties, in the C2 social category, with two children, a part-time job, a husband employed in skilled manual work, and a penchant for holidays in Florida. How did the parties seek to appeal to 'Worcester woman'? To answer this question, I first explore the context by assessing the impact of the increased representation of women in the 1997–2001 parliament. The chapter draws upon the distinction between *descriptive* and *substantive* representation made by Pitkin, who distinguished between the way in which representative institutions may 'look' like the people they are supposed to represent (descriptive) and the ways in which they represent the interests of the people who elected them (substantive).[6] I then consider the role of women in the 2001 general election. Aside from the Conservative shadow Home Secretary, Ann Widdecombe, women were largely invisible during the campaign, to the extent that it even became something of a campaign joke. The chapter then examines how the parties targeted women's votes. It explores the reasons why the 2001 election saw a drop in the number of women elected for the first time since 1979 and argues that a change in the electoral system to proportional representation may well be necessary if women are to attain a substantial presence in parliament. In conclusion, I argue that chasing the votes of 'Worcester woman' could be seen as reflecting a 'dumbing down' of politics whereby parties seek to appeal to a stereotype and thus obscure either the detail of party policy or radical policies that could address substantive representational deficiencies.

New Labour women and the policy record – bringing gender into the mainstream?

This section considers the difference made by the increased representation of women in parliament after the 1997 election. It looks at the impact of legislation on women and on changes to the culture of politics at Westminster.

The initial euphoria surrounding the increased female representation in parliament faded into disillusion as 'Blair's Babes' appeared excessively loyal to the government. For instance, the vast majority of women Labour backbench

MPs were not moved to rebel when, in the early days of the new administration, legislation was passed to remove the premium from lone-parent benefit. Rather than dismissing these women as 'Stepford Wives',[7] however, it is possible to look beyond the more obvious signs of a lack of dissension to give a more charitable account of their performance.

Arguably the disappointment with the new Labour women was due in part to differing expectations of women as representatives. Pitkin's approach to the concept of representation shows that a representative can be viewed as 'standing for' or 'acting for' her constituents. 'Acting for' constituents can be done in one of three ways: as an 'agent', acting on behalf of; as a 'trustee', acting for the benefit of; or as a 'deputy', acting instead of. Whether the representative is understood as acting independently or on a mandate is, of course, mediated by the political parties to which almost all representatives belong.

It is interesting to note how the women MPs viewed their representative role. Research by Sarah Childs demonstrates that the new intake of Labour women MPs perceived their representative role in terms of acting for party or constituency but that a 'substantial minority' included the representation of women in their understanding.[8] She found that nearly a third of these women MPs had experienced women constituents contacting them to raise issues they would not have felt comfortable discussing with a male MP, and that half of them believed that they could bring women's concerns to the political agenda. Hence the new Labour women MPs interviewed in Childs' study viewed their presence at Westminster as both descriptive and substantive in that they were acting for party, constituency and women. These findings are reflected in research on women MPs carried out by the Fawcett Society, in which the representation of women's interests was viewed as 'not very important' by 50 per cent of Conservative respondents, but by only 6 per cent of Labour respondents.[9] Voting with the party line was considered 'very important' by 52 per cent of Labour women and by only 25 per cent of Conservative women. Of Conservative women MPs, 13 per cent believed voting with the party line to be 'not at all important'. These figures suggest that for Labour women party takes precedence over women's interests. The Conservative women's responses demonstrate the limits of descriptive representation – greater numbers of women representatives do not necessarily translate into a gendering of the political agenda.

Party discipline also needs to be taken into account. New MPs may hold high hopes for political advancement. These hopes can come crashing down if a new MP establishes a reputation for unreliability in the voting lobby. A long career as a political maverick may beckon. Indeed, the message conveyed to the new intake of MPs by the party whips was that to rebel against the government line would be political suicide.[10] In the debates on lone-parent benefits, Harriet Harman, the Social Security Minister with additional responsibility for women in the first cabinet, defended the policy. Only Ann Cryer of the new intake of Labour women dissented. Hence there was a perception that women Labour MPs had betrayed the women who would be affected by this policy. New Labour women were also criticised for not joining forces to lobby for a higher minimum wage.[11] There have been a number of policy successes, however, for which women Labour MPs failed to claim the credit.[12] Harman, who was demoted to the back benches in the first cabinet reshuffle, contends the women MPs should have claimed credit for the increase in child benefit, which was a response to the short-sighted reduction in lone-parent benefit.[13] For Yvette Cooper, new Labour women have had an impact in many areas of government policy:

> Particularly the '98 budget which benefited women five times more than men, or the work that went into designing the Working Family Tax Credit so that it helps women, or the amount of family friendly policies in the Fairness at Work Bill, which could have been all about boys' stuff.[14]

In response to much negative media coverage, the Labour MP Fiona MacTaggart wrote a paper defending the record of new Labour women MPs.[15] She argued that they achieved a great deal but that they have a different style of politics to male MPs. MacTaggart asserted that to vote against the party line is an exercise in futility unless sufficient numbers vote to change the legislation. It is more effective to work to change policy in other ways. Labour women MPs have performed the functions of an MP in the same way that male politicians do, much of which is out of the public eye. This includes speaking to ministers to request policy amendments, signing early-day motions, introducing private members' bills, sitting on standing and select committees, asking questions on the floor of the House, gaining adjournment debates, developing cross-party alliances and working for their constituencies. Hence the assertion that women MPs are engaging in a different way of doing politics is questionable. However, their presence, along with having Ministers for Women and a Women's Unit, has ensured a gendered dimension to policy development, with the impact on women and children taken into account.

The notion that women politicians have a different approach to politics has been questioned by Philip Cowley.[16] He noted that the lack of rebellion among the newly elected women in 1997 cannot be attributed to gender alone due to the similar number of rebellions by women and men elected before 1997. Furthermore, explanations such as parliamentary inexperience, the effect of all-women short-lists (AWS) and the age of the MP are not valid. This is because inexperienced, newly elected MPs usually rebel more than their peers, some women MPs who came in on AWS have been the most rebellious, and newly elected women and men are similar in age. Looking beyond the lack of rebellion, there is some support for the view that behind-the-scenes lobbying is an effective method of influencing government policy, which negates the need to rebel in the division lobbies. While both male and female MPs utilise this method, Cowley noted that an established female MP dismissed the notion that women MPs are 'better' at it than men.

Although a question mark remains over whether the new Labour women MPs had a substantially different political style and critics doubt their effectiveness, measures were achieved that have had a positive effect on women's lives. These concerned the family, employment, child care, health and pensions. In the pre-election budget of March 2001, Chancellor Gordon Brown acknowledged that the needs of women and children had been largely overlooked by the tax system and so the budget would put 'families first'. Changes announced in the budget included increased statutory maternity pay and duration, two weeks' paid paternity leave, a new children's tax credit, an increase in the minimum wage to £4.10 and investment in schools and hospitals. Hence the focus was on the balance between work and family life. This concern had informed the earlier introduction of the New Deal for lone parents, which was brought in to help lone parents to get out of the 'benefits trap' and into work. Other changes included: the same rights for part-time workers as for full-time workers; the WFTC, over which the parliamentary Labour party women's group lobbied to ensure it is paid to the mother; child-care tax credit; increased child benefit; and increased child-care places. There was also a minimum-income guarantee for pensioners, paid adoption leave and a reduction in VAT on sanitary products from the 17.5 per cent luxury rate to the 5 per cent minimum, effective from January 2001. The last measure was the result of a campaign by Christine McCafferty. It was announced by the Paymaster General, Dawn Primarolo, rather than the Chancellor, who reportedly could not be persuaded to utter the words 'sanitary protection' in the Commons chamber.[17]

Women representatives

I now move on to consider women's candidacy in the 2001 election. This section discusses the reasons for the low numbers of women candidates and argues that the selection mechanism and electoral system could be the key to changing the gender balance of the legislature.

Analysis of the gender of prospective parliamentary candidates (PPCs) shows that in 2001 there were more women candidates overall but that fewer Labour women were standing (Table 13.1). In 1997, 47 per cent of constituencies had no women candidates. This rose to 63 per cent in 2001. Only two, Liverpool Garston and Amber Valley, were contested by women only. However, as Studlar and McAllister have found, the gender of the candidate makes little difference to voting behaviour. Rather it is the type of seat and the political party the candidate is standing for that is important: the electorate are not less likely to vote for a woman candidate.[18]

Table 13.1. Numbers of women prospective parliamentary candidates (PPCs) and women MPs by political party, 1997–2001

	1997		2001	
	PPCs	*MPs*	*PPCs*	*MPs*
Conservatives	67 (10%)	13 (8%)	93 (14%)	14 (8%)
Labour	158 (25%)	101 (18%)	146 (23%)	95 (23%)
Liberal Democrats	122 (19%)	3 (7%)	139 (22%)	5 (10%)
Totals	347 (18%)	117 (18%)	378 (20%)	114 (17%)

Sources: M. A. Stephenson, *The Glass Trapdoor: Women, Politics and the Media During the 1997 General Election* (London: Fawcett Society, 1998); A. Eagle and J. Lovenduski, *High Tide or High Time for Labour Women* (London: Fabian Society, 1998); and author's own calculations.

The reasons for the continuing low numbers of women candidates can be viewed in terms of a combination of demand-side and supply-side factors, although of course these market relations are embedded in a social context that gives meaning to discussions of equality and representation and shapes the discussion of alternatives. On the supply side, key factors are culture, child care, cash and confidence.[19] It has been argued that the culture of British politics is masculine and the family responsibilities of MPs often go unrecognised. The new intake of women MPs experienced sexist behaviour from their male colleagues who 'are like little boys, often reduced to giggles when a woman speaks, and obsessed with breasts'.[20] The House of Commons itself has been shown to be incompatible with family life. MacTaggart has referred to:

> gasbags who this week prolonged debates until after 2 am on matters where there was no disagreement and no vote.... [They] have a padding of self-importance which insulates them from contact with real life and increases with each year of continuing service.[21]

The long hours of business make arranging child care difficult and put pressure on family relationships. Tess Kingham, Judith Church and Jenny Jones, who had young children, resigned after one term because of the late-night sittings and were replaced by men. Over 300 men and women backbench MPs signalled their support for 'family-friendly' hours in a petition organised by the Cambridge MP Anne Campbell.[22] The Commons Modernisation Committee, which was charged with considering reforms, heard from the Prime Minister that he was in favour of changes such as shorter working days. However, no changes to procedure were introduced because of opposition.[23] In July 2000 the Commons had its first children's playgroup for children of parliamentary staff. This, along with the success of Caroline Flint, chair of the All Party Group on Child Care, in persuading officials in the House to consider a nursery, a holiday play scheme and a change in working hours, signals some attempt to dent the masculine culture.

An attempt to address the lack of facilities for parents in the House of Commons was seen in the cross-party cooperation of some women parliamentarians: Margaret Hodge and Tessa Jowell from the Labour Party, Caroline Spelman from the Conservatives and Jackie Ballard from the Liberal Democrats. They met with the Speaker, Betty Boothroyd, to ask for reform. Previously the Speaker had ruled out breast-feeding in the Commons committee rooms, thus failing to take account of the problems faced by women MPs with young families. Boothroyd's successor, Michael Martin, is not opposed to breast-feeding, however, and has asked the Commons Administration Committee to decide whether to lift the ban.[24] Indeed, in his discreet lobbying before his election as Speaker, Martin actively courted the votes of women MPs by letting it be known he would take a more liberal stance.

In addition to these factors, it is also important to consider the impact of child care on the selection processes for potential MPs. Attendance at evening meetings can make the cost and logistics of child care prohibitive. In turn, this relates to the third supply-side factor – cash. This is an important issue for prospective candidates, who can expect to have to cover costs such as travel to the constituency, overnight accommodation and child care. It also means that potential candidates from poorer backgrounds may find it more difficult to put themselves forward for selection.

Finally, the issue of confidence means that some women may be reluctant to put themselves forward for selection as they doubt their abilities. In fact women MPs are similar to men MPs in terms of their social, educational and occupational background that allows them the time and money to participate and may equip them with the skills – such as public speaking – that give them more chance of success.

On the demand side, parties can signal their commitment to equality by exhorting women to stand for election, by employing positive action such as providing training and assisting with child-care expenses, and by instigating positive discrimination measures such as internal quotas, AWS and twinning constituencies. The Labour Party used AWS for the selection of candidates for the 1997 election but ceased doing so on 8 January 1996 because an industrial tribunal found this method to contravene sex discrimination legislation. Labour still required that where women had put themselves forward for selection at least one should end up on a short-list, but this was no guarantee of selection. After its 2001 victory, the re-elected Labour government announced its intention to change the law so that positive discrimination could be used in the future.

To what extent are the possibilities for change circumscribed by an existing system that tilts the balance against resolution of representational deficiencies in British politics? It could be argued that the only way a radical change in the gender balance will occur is through the introduction of proportional representation. Indeed, the elections to the Scottish Parliament and Welsh Assembly, at which 37 per cent and 40 per cent of members respectively are women, demonstrate how effective proportional representation can be in ensuring a more representative body. In Scotland and Wales the choice of selection mechanism was also important. Labour was the only party to adopt a positive action mechanism. The 'twinning system' employed in the constituencies ensured that equal numbers of men and women were selected. This resulted in a 50:50 gender ratio among the Labour members of the Scottish Parliament and slightly more women than men among Labour Assembly members. In contrast the Conservative Party had no women elected to the Assembly and only three women members of the Scottish Parliament out of eighteen.[25]

Since their 1997 election disaster and the closing of the gender gap in voting, the Conservatives have sought to encourage more women to stand for election. This is a tricky issue for a party that disavows any form of positive discrimination. The Conservative Central Council rejected a proposal from William Hague in 1998 that there should be at least 25 per cent women on final selection short-lists.[26] The Conservative Party's stance on AWS was made very clear by their most prominent female politician, the shadow Home Secretary, Ann Widdecombe, who was scathing about the quality of the Labour women MPs elected via this 'patronising' mechanism.[27] According to Widdecombe, some New Labour women 'even whinged that Madam Speaker is too hard on them and indeed has caused more than one to burst into tears. Can anyone imagine Bessie Bradock, Barbara Castle or Margaret Thatcher dissolving at a ticking off from the Speaker?'[28]

Yet Widdecombe's traditional brand of Conservatism may be under threat within a Conservative Party forced to respond to low levels of popularity and a membership that is falling and becoming ever more elderly. The Centre for Policy Studies produced a report called *Conservative Women* in November 1999, which warned the Conservative Party that it was not keeping up with changes in society and had lost the support of women voters. The report suggested that the party may even have to introduce quotas to revitalise its image with young women voters. Speaking at the Conservative Party conference in 2000, Tessa Keswick, Director of the Centre for Policy Studies and one of the authors of *Conservative Women*, asserted that the party needed a new approach to policy, to recognise women's place in the workforce and in society. Policies should reflect issues of equality, community, the family and employment so that women were not 'second among equals'.[29]

The strategy employed by the Conservatives to get more women representatives has been predominantly one of exhortation. The party has, of course, announced that it is keen to have more women representatives and it is 'trying hard to make it the kind of selection process that does not discriminate'.[30] However, it has been reported that Central Office has failed to change the attitudes of local selection committees that are 'repeatedly turning down women'.[31] Despite this, the party's Campaign for Women into Public Life aims to win back women's votes and to encourage women to stand as councillors, MPs, MEPs and for public bodies. The campaign includes a mentoring scheme for PPCs along with media and presentational skills training. This training and mentoring can be seen as positive action of sorts, although the hurdle of the selection process must be tackled first.

The issue of discrimination by selection committees has been raised as a problem that may take some time to overcome because of differences in attitude between the generations. The average age of Conservative members is sixty-seven. It has been argued that there is a generational effect from older men and women who sit on these committees and have 'traditional' attitudes towards the role of women in society.[32] A female candidate is more susceptible to questions about how she plans to manage her family commitments and/ or what her partner thinks about her candidacy than would a male candidate. The Bow Group studied selections in the run-up to the 1997 election and found that sexist questions were asked, such as: 'It's the party of the family – shouldn't you be at home looking after your children?' Such questions were more likely to come from men and women over the age of fifty. It is often the older women who will give women candidates a hard time.[33]

It is not just the Conservative Party that has been guilty of prejudice in the selection of PPCs. The Fawcett survey of women MPs showed 77 per cent of Labour women respondents believed the party's selection committees do not give women the opportunity to stand for election. In the absence of AWS, which were important in ensuring women were selected for safe or winnable seats, prejudice can prevail against women candidates. Traditional attitudes regarding a 'woman's place' persist in areas that were once based around heavy industry. For the Liberal Democrat Party selection process, the problem of taking a gender-neutral approach is evident. The Liberal Democrat ethos is to not discriminate, so there is a reluctance to acknowledge the discrimination that women face in the selection process.

The 2001 campaign

I now turn to consider the role of women in the 2001 election campaign itself. How did the parties seek to appeal to 'Worcester woman'? Despite the potential importance of women voters, women politicians were largely invisible from the campaign and the policy agenda, although there were signs that women voters had been taken into account in the party manifestos.

The government set the tone of the election campaign when it announced in April 2001 that, if elected for a second term, it would introduce a 'baby bond' in the interests of tackling child poverty. Hence in looking to the

Table 13.2. Percentage of respondents (by gender) indicating which issues were the most important facing Britain at the 2001 election

	Men	*Women*
National Health Service	41	50
Education/schools	22	32
Pensions/social security	10	17
EU/European single currency	34	20

Source: MORI, November 2000, and B. Gill, *Where is Worcester Woman?* (London: Fawcett Society, 2001).

interests of the next generation it could be viewed as a forward-looking party concerned with the wellbeing of young people, with education, health and the economy. However, issues that are not prioritised by women (see Table 13.2), such as Europe and taxation, dominated the election campaign itself. This was despite the publication of research by Gill which suggested that the female vote is more volatile than the male vote, as women are more likely to be undecided in their voting intentions.[34] The research also showed that there was less satisfaction among women voters with the record of the Labour government, and that women's votes can be decisive in election outcomes because, since 1979, more women than men have turned out to vote. One particular issue was key to the Conservative campaign – 'save the pound' – but, as Table 13.2 shows, this had a low priority for all voters. Women appeared to emphasise their concerns about the state of public services and the perception that Labour had failed to deliver.

A review of the party manifestos reveals attempts to appeal to women voters. It was noted in the introduction to the chapter that equality has been a key gender issue since the 1970s. It relates to employment, reproductive rights, the family and child care. How were these issues, along with those given high priority by women, broached in the manifestos? The Liberal Democrats produced an additional 'manifesto for women', while pledges aimed at women in the Conservative manifesto were signalled in the policy consultation document *Choices* and the paper 'Common sense choices'. These provided more detail regarding women's needs and concerns on tax reforms, health, education, policing and transport, while the manifesto itself was couched in gender-neutral language. The Labour manifesto contained a number of policies specifically aimed at women voters.

To demonstrate its commitment to marriage and the family, the Conservative Party's manifesto pledged to introduce a 'new married couple's allowance' that would translate into 'a tax cut worth £1000'. It also proposed increasing the child tax credit, allowing unused personal allowance to be transferred to a spouse where the children were under the age of eleven years, and introducing family scholarships so that parents could train to get back to work after bringing up children. The manifesto promised to provide financial help for widowed parents and to reform the WFTC so it would be paid directly to the 'caring parent'. With regard to education, the Conservatives pledged an end to excessive bureaucracy in schools by introducing 'free schools', which would allow schools to set their own admissions policy and to exclude disruptive pupils, who would be sent to 'progress centres' for 'specialist help'. In addition, the party would sanction the establishment of schools by church and other faith communities, groups of parents, charitable foundations and companies. The manifesto also tackled tertiary education by proposing the setting up 'permanent endowment funds' for universities. Other pledges included a 'patients' guarantee' in the NHS, giving a maximum waiting time, and an increase in the pensioners' tax allowance and state pension.

It would seem that the concerns of 'Worcester woman' were firmly in mind when the Conservative manifesto was being drafted. With the promise of tax credits for children, a married couple's allowance providing a tax cut that could, perhaps, go towards the family holiday in Florida, along with policies to free schools and speed up access to the NHS, surely 'Worcester woman' would be persuaded to vote Conservative? Furthermore, the manifesto itself was replete with images of women of different ages, supposedly signalling the centrality of women to Tory policies. One woman sat contentedly with her partner and two children, while an older woman happily talked to two policemen on the beat. Other images showed a wheelchair-bound woman at work, an (Asian) mother and baby with their doctor, and a man and woman of retirement age out enjoying a coffee. Hence the manifesto suggested by its imagery that women of all ages and backgrounds were included in the Conservative vision.

The Liberal Democrat manifesto prioritised the NHS and pledged to cut waiting times by recruiting more doctors and nurses, increasing the pay of the worst-paid staff to retain them, and funding 10,000 extra beds. In education it proposed to reduce class sizes, recruit more teachers, provide funding for more books and equipment, cut bureaucracy and, at tertiary level, abolish tuition fees. The most interesting issues for women in the Liberal Democrat manifesto were 'pensions, wages and benefits'; 'reforming politics'; and 'civil liberties', which were also covered in the 'manifesto for women', along with health, education, and law and order. Under 'reforming politics' the party was committed to the introduction of proportional representation. It also expressed the intention to make Westminster more accountable by replacing the Lords with an elected Senate, enhancing the scrutinising powers of the Commons, and making its working practices more 'family friendly' and 'efficient' so that parliament could become more representative.

Notable pledges in the Liberal Democrat 'manifesto for women' were the replacement of the Sex Discrimination and Equal Pay Acts with a 'single, more effective and comprehensive Equality Act', which would cover all forms of unfair discrimination. Discrimination against part-time workers, many of whom are women, would also be addressed by ensuring that the Part-time Workers Regulations cover 'cleaners, cooks and retail workers', who are currently excluded. Other proposals included: an extra £200 per year to all families with children who have been on income support for more than a year; the Child Support Agency to be replaced with family courts; an increased basic state pension; and an 'Owned Second Pension Account'.

The policy pledges contained in the Liberal Democrat manifesto covered all the bases in terms of issues that concern women: equality, health, education, pensions and social security. The most radical element was the commitment to proportional representation and the reform of Westminster. How much this would appeal to the conservatism of the 'Worcester woman' stereotype is debatable. Presumably family concerns would take priority along with, perhaps, the question of part-time work, but the 'honest' approach of the Liberal Democrats – in stating that improved services require an increase in income tax – could be seen as a potential vote winner in a climate of political smoke and mirrors.

The imagery of the manifesto included a female nurse talking to a male doctor, a woman police officer in the community, women ballerinas, women at work and children in a playground. The images were less obvious than those in the Conservative manifesto but still attempted to convey inclusivity.

The Labour Party manifesto focused on a commitment to increase investment in public services, from a position of economic stability. This investment would translate into 20,000 more nurses, 10,000 more doctors, 10,000 more teachers and 6,000 more police officers. Labour also pledged to tackle child and pensioner poverty by an 'integrated Child Credit of cash support for children built on a foundation of universal child benefit' and a 'pension credit for lower and middle income pensioners'. In employment there was a pledge to increase the minimum wage to £4.20 by October 2002 and address the 18 per cent pay differential between men's and women's wages. There was also a commitment to increase maternity leave to £100 per week for six months, to introduce paid paternity leave of £100 per week for two weeks, and to provide 1.6 million child-care places. In recognition of the under-representation of women in politics, the manifesto stated that the Labour Party was 'committed through legislation, to allow each party to make positive moves to increase the representation of women'.

As with the Conservatives and the Liberal Democrats, Labour's manifesto contained pledges relating to the concerns of health, education, pensions and social security, prioritised by women. It also dealt with equality concerns regarding paid employment and the minimum wage. The manifesto showed many images of women, with their families, using public transport, as teachers, nurses, pensioners and police officers, hence also conveying that women are central to Labour's policies.

Overall the Liberal Democrats and Labour appeared, from their manifestos, to be making a more overt appeal to the female electorate than the Conservative Party. However, it is fair to say that the majority of the electorate acquire information about the parties via the media. In the third week of the campaign, Jackie Ashley of the *New Statesman* asked about the lack of women representatives in the election campaign at a press conference attended by Gordon Brown and the Schools Minister, Estelle Morris. To the amusement of the journalists present, Brown answered the question, speaking over Morris. On 24 May 2001, Natasha Walter asked, 'Where have all the women gone?'[35] She noted the lack of female politicians in the campaign and the lack of attention to women's concerns. Marney Swan, the chair of the Conservative Women's National Council, criticised the Conservative Party for not using women frontbench MPs on election platforms and argued that all the main parties were 'guilty of failing to give women a more prominent role in the campaign'.[36] She was also concerned that the 'keep the pound' campaign and attacks on Labour had dominated the agenda at the expense of issues such as child care and education.

The election outcome

The proportion of the electorate that voted was down by an average of more than 10 per cent. Whether the presentation of the parties' election campaigns had any influence on this is hard to say, but interviews with 1,000 women by *Good Housekeeping* magazine before the election provides an indication of dissatisfaction. That survey showed that 42 per cent of women aged eighteen to twenty-four and 25 per cent aged twenty-five to thirty-four had already decided not to vote. Furthermore, almost a quarter felt their interests were not represented by any of the parties.

Opinion polls conducted for the *Sunday Times* throughout the campaign showed little fluctuation in voting intentions, although by the last week the Liberal Democrats appear to have gained at the expense of the Conservative Party among women voters, as Table 13.3 indicates.

The election resulted in the number of women MPs declining for the first time since 1979. Christine Butler (Labour, Castle Point), Fiona Jones (Labour, Newark), Eileen Gordon (Labour, Romford) and Jackie Ballard (Liberal Democrat, Taunton) were all incumbents defending majorities of less than 6 per cent and were defeated by male Conservative candidates. There were 263 women PPCs standing for 'other' parties in the 2001 general election. Of these the Green Party had 26 per cent women PPCs; the UKIP had 14 per cent; the SNP had 24 per cent; the SLP had 16 per cent; the Socialist Alliance had 19 per cent; and Plaid Cymru had 15 per cent. Annabelle Ewing (SNP, Perth) won her seat and three of the parties competing for seats in Northern Ireland had successful women candidates. They were Lady Sylvia Hermon (UUP,

Table 13.3. Voting intention by gender in the run-up to the 2001 election (percentages of all those naming a party)

| | 10/11 May | | 17/18 May | | 24/25 May | | 31 May/1 June | |
	Men	Women	Men	Women	Men	Women	Men	Women
Conservative	30	33	29	31	27	33	29	30
Labour	49	50	48	51	51	47	43	51
Liberal Democrat	15	11	14	14	13	15	18	17
Other	7	5	9	4	9	5	10	3

Source: www.nop.co.uk/POLLS2001.

North Down), Iris Robinson (DUP, Strangford), and Michelle Gildernew (Sinn Fein, Fermanagh and South Tyrone). Three women MPs from Northern Ireland is significant insofar as politics in Northern Ireland is extremely male dominated. The last woman to be elected there to Westminster was Bernadette Devlin, at a by-election for Mid-Ulster in 1969. Overall the total number of women MPs is down from 120 in 1997, which included two SNP MPs and the Speaker, to 118 (18 per cent).

The government front benches will be populated by fewer 'grey suits', as seven women were appointed to cabinet posts (29 per cent) after the election.[37] There are eleven other women ministers, fourteen junior ministers, one whip and seven assistant whips. Hence there are women in key roles and at different levels of seniority in each government department.

Conclusion

This chapter has raised a number of issues regarding women and politics in Britain. It questioned how the political parties chased the votes of 'Worcester woman' given that there is evidence of a gender gap in political priorities and in voter turnout. It also considered whether the influx of women representatives at the 1997 election had made a difference to politics at Westminster, before moving on to examine the 2001 election campaign, in which women politicians were largely invisible and women's political priorities were sidelined in favour of debates about tax cuts and Europe.

The chapter has shown that women representatives along with the Women's Unit had been able to ensure a gendered dimension to policy. Although the new intake of Labour women after 1997 were mainly loyal to the party line, there is a perception that women politicians have a different style of politics, such as behind-the-scenes lobbying rather than open rebellion. While there have been attempts to change the masculine culture of politics, there is still no crèche and the hours of business are not family friendly. This failure resulted in the resignation of three of the new Labour women.

The 2001 election campaign was disappointing in that few women representatives featured in the campaign and, aside from the manifestos, the parties did not appear to spend much energy courting women's votes. It would seem that the development of policies designed to appeal to the average voter has led to spin, little innovative policy and the construction of stereotypes such as 'Worcester woman'.

The parties failed to build upon the high-water mark of 120 women MPs elected in 1997, as the number fell back to 118 in 2001. However, the new administration appears to be honouring the election pledge to introduce legislation that will allow parties to put in place positive measures to ensure more women are selected as PPCs. This was announced in the Queen's speech at the state opening of parliament. However, the dominance of white, male and middle-class MPs at Westminster will not be radically altered unless positive-action methods of selection are introduced along with a system of proportional representation. The present first-past-the-post system of election allowed a Labour landslide on the votes of 25 per cent of the total electorate.

The drop in turnout at the election suggests disenchantment, apathy, disengagement and that for many the outcome was a foregone conclusion. The Labour government has another term of office to deliver on its election pledges. If it fails to produce results on those issues that are prioritised by women, such as public services, the dissatisfaction with the government's record could be translated into lost votes at the next election, and a widening of the gender gap in favour of the Conservative Party.

Notes

1 D. Mattinson, 'Worcester woman's unfinished revolution: what is needed to woo women voters?', in A. Coote (ed.), *New Gender Agenda* (London: IPPR, 2000).

2 P. Norris, 'Mobilising the "women's vote": the gender-generation gap in voting behaviour', *Parliamentary Affairs*, 49:2 (1996), pp. 333–42, and 'Gender: a gender-generation gap?', in G. Evans and P. Norris (eds), *Critical Elections: British Parties and Voters in Long-Term Perspective* (London: Sage, 1999).

3 B. Gill, *Where is Worcester Woman?* (London: Fawcett Society, 2001).

4 *Ibid.*

5 J. Lovenduski, 'Introduction: the dynamics of gender and party', in J. Lovenduski and P. Norris (eds), *Gender and Party Politics* (London: Sage, 1993).

6 H. F. Pitkin, *The Concept of Representation* (California: University of California Press, 1967).

7 Brian Sedgemore MP (Labour) employed this comparison. Quoted in *The Times*, 7 February 1998, and cited by P. Cowley, 'An uncritical mass? New Labour women MPs in the House of Commons', paper presented to the Political Studies Association conference, Manchester, 2001.

8 S. Childs, 'In their own words: New Labour women and the substantive repre-

sentation of women', *British Journal of Politics and International Relations*, 3:2 (2001), pp. 173–90.

9 M. A. Stephenson, *Fawcett Survey of Women MPs* (London: Fawcett Society, 1997).
10 A. Perkins, 'So far, so what?', *Guardian*, 29 April 1999.
11 L. Ward, 'Learning from the "Babe" experience: how the finest hour became a fiasco', in A. Coote (ed.), *New Gender Agenda* (London: Institute for Public Policy Research, 2000).
12 According to Yvette Cooper MP, quoted in Perkins, 'So far, so what?'
13 Ward, 'Learning from the "Babe" experience'.
14 Perkins, 'So far, so what?'
15 F. MacTaggart, *Women in Parliament: Their Contribution to Labour's First 1000 Days*, Fabian research paper (London: Fabian Society, 2000).
16 Cowley, 'An uncritical mass?'
17 L. Ward, 'Brown shies from talking tampons', *Guardian*, 22 March 2000.
18 D. T. Studlar and I. McAllister, 'Candidate gender and voting in the 1997 British general election: did Labour quotas matter?', *Journal of Legislative Studies*, 4:3 (1998), pp. 72–91.
19 M. A. Stephenson, *The Glass Trapdoor: Women, Politics and the Media During the 1997 General Election* (London: Fawcett Society, 1998).
20 R. Sylvester, 'Smuts and taunts are the House rule, say women MPs', *Daily Telegraph*, 10 December 1997.
21 F. MacTaggart, 'Misogynists in the house', *Guardian*, 25 May 2000.
22 S. Schaefer, 'Blair to intervene on family-friendly hours for House', *Independent*, 28 June 2000.
23 Modernisation of the House of Commons Select Committee, *First Report: Programming of Legislation*, 2 April 2001, http://www.publications.parliament.uk/pa/cm/cmmodern.htm.
24 R. Sylvester, 'Speaker will not oppose breast feeding', *Telegraph*, 24 January 2001.
25 B. Gill, *Winning Women: Lessons from Scotland and Wales* (London: Fawcett Society, 2000).
26 L. Ward, 'It's the party of the family – shouldn't you be at home looking after the children?', *Guardian*, 25 March 1999.
27 Quoted in J. Hartley-Brewer, 'Tories "driving away" young women voters', *Guardian*, 26 November 1999.
28 *Sunday Times*, 4 October 1998, quoted in Cowley, 'An uncritical mass?'
29 T. Keswick, 'Second among equals: women and the Conservative Party', Centre for Policy Studies Lecture, Conservative Party conference, 5 October 2000.
30 R. Pockley, ex-Vice-Chair of the Conservative Women's National Committee, quoted by J. Knight and S. Midgley, 'Breaking glass', *Conservative Heartland: The Party Magazine*, 1 (2001), pp. 14–16. In a conversation with Michael Dolley, Conservative Area Campaign Director for Bristol and Gloucestershire (6 May 2001), he informed the author that selection committees for his area had been told there should be no discrimination on grounds of gender, race and sexuality.
31 N. Watt, 'Grassroots snub Hague plea for more women MPs', *Guardian*, 8 February 2000.
32 P. Norris and J. Lovenduski, *Political Recruitment: Gender, Race and Class in the British Parliament* (Cambridge: Cambridge University Press, 1995).
33 Conversation with Michael Dolley. N. Watt in the *Guardian*, 8 February 2000, quoted a Tory woman who noted, 'Some of the harshest questions come from women who often look down their noses at me'.
34 Gill, *Where is Worcester Woman?*
35 N. Walter, 'Where have all the women gone?', *Independent Review*, 24 May 2001, p. 5.

36 M. Woolf, 'Tory women accuse Hague of ignoring issues', *Independent*, 5 June 2001.
37 Margaret Beckett (Secretary of State for Environment, Food and Rural Affairs), Clare Short (Secretary of State for International Development), Helen Liddell (Scottish Secretary), Patricia Hewitt (Secretary of State for Trade and Industry), Estelle Morris (Secretary of State for Education and Skills), Tessa Jowell (Secretary of State for Culture, Media and Sport) and Hilary Armstrong (Chief Whip).

Upper Bann

The fault line within Ulster Unionism was perhaps revealed most starkly in the constituency of the UUP leader and First Minister, David Trimble. In 1997, Unionism's largest party had polled 20,000 votes, four times the level of support of the DUP, which had trailed in fourth place. Long before the 2001 contest, however, it was evident that Trimble's majority would be substantially reduced. As with several other intra-Unionist contests, the 2001 election in Upper Bann assumed the form of a further referendum on the Good Friday Agreement between the pro-Agreement UUP and the anti-Agreement DUP. The common assumption was that the closeness of the contest was a consequence of steadily increasing discontent among Unionists with the Good Friday Agreement. This may indeed have been true, but, as early as June 1998, a mere two months after the forging of the Agreement, the DUP had polled nearly as many votes as the UUP within the Upper Bann constituency. If that result was a product of increased discontent, such disillusionment had set in remarkably early. A more realistic interpretation of the 1998 referendum and Assembly elections and the 2001 result was that the fault line in Unionism remained largely unchanged. A narrow majority of Unionist voters continued to support the Agreement. The breakdown of pro-Agreement and anti-Agreement Unionist votes in 2001 nearly matched the 55–45 referendum split.

Meat factory owner and Orangeman David Simpson, the DUP candidate, inevitably campaigned on the issue of the need for the decommissioning of IRA weapons. He found a sympathetic reception in hard-line Unionist areas of Portadown and Lurgan, arguing the case that 'the real essence of terrorism is the threat of terrorism' (*Guardian*, 25 May 2001). Trimble drew some of the sting by issuing his threat to resign as First Minister by 1 July if progress on decommissioning was not forthcoming. Trimble acknowledged the existence of elements regarding him as another 'Lundy' (traitor), stating: 'I have difficulty canvassing Portadown.... But most of the town's going to vote for me' (*Guardian*, 25 May 2001).

In a constituency with a ratio of 61.5 per cent Protestants to 38.5 per cent Catholics, the battle between the Nationalist parties was always a secondary affair (*The Times*, 29 May 2001). Runner-up in 1997, the SDLP was comfortably overtaken by Sinn Fein's Dara O'Hagan, prominent in opposing the contentious Orange parade along the Garvaghy Road in Portadown. The main bout went to a recount, an overcautious measure criticised by Trimble. Decades earlier, an incumbent UUP leader, Prime Minister and reformer, Terence O'Neill, had been wounded by a close challenge in his constituency from Ian Paisley. In 2001, a UUP leader was again wounded by Paisley's party, although the new, post-conflict political context meant Trimble could yet survive as party leader.

Result

Upper Bann		
	No. of votes	% of vote
Trimble, D. (UUP)	17,095	33.5
Simpson, D. (DUP)	15,037	29.5
O' Hagan, D. (Sinn Fein)	10,770	21.1
Kelly, D. (SDLP)	7,607	14.9
French, T. (Workers' Party)	527	1.0
UUP majority	2,058	4.0
UUP hold		
Turnout		70.8

Conclusion:
implications of the apathetic landslide

Andrew Geddes and Jonathan Tonge

Although the 2001 general election contained very little of the drama of the 1997 contest, its outcome has far-reaching implications. The future of public services, the nature of the Conservative Party and the legitimacy of electoral contests are but three issues upon which the 2001 election will make a great impact. Labour's apathetic landslide was a consequence of an (often grudging) acceptance of the party as the only viable electoral choice. Labour failed to enthuse the electorate, but did enough to win comfortably, aided by the distortions of the first-past-the-post electoral system. Labour did comparatively well where it mattered. Although turnout fell most sharply in safe Labour seats, this was of no consequence to the party's fortunes. As David Denver has noted, however, Labour's vote share increased in its sixty-three most marginal seats, and the party enjoyed a swing in its favour in nine of its fifteen most marginal seats. Falls in turnout were lower in these seats. Voters were still prepared to record support for Labour where it looked as if the party might otherwise be harmed. If there was public disenchantment with Labour, it was because the party had not done enough during its first term in respect of the key issue of public services. A majority of the public were not hostile to Labour *per se*. This created a difficult campaign for Labour, in the sense that, although campaigning on the public services was sensible given the public's distrust of the Conservatives in this area, any failure to deliver by the governing party over the last four years was also highlighted.

Labour's campaign was the subject of much criticism. Indeed, the contest began with plenty of overexcited media talk of the Conservatives 'winning' the first few days of the campaign. A more realistic view of the campaign was that it reflected the positive and negative characteristics associated with New Labour. On the plus side, the party was seen as having the best leader; it had achieved governing competence and, crucially, as Mark Wickham-Jones has pointed out, Labour was now seen as the party best able to handle the economy. On most objective measurements, the 1997–2001 Labour government had performed at least satisfactorily on key economic criteria. Negatively, Labour had irritated with its seeming obsession with presentation, its double-counting of investment programmes, its introduction of 'stealth' taxes and its changes without mandate, such as the introduction of university tuition fees, curiously unmentioned in the 1997 manifesto yet presented soon after that election as the only way to save the university system. Generally, however, these negatives irritated rather than angered. Labour did not preside over anything calamitous during its first term, compared with the winter of discontent or the ERM debacle that had led to the two previous changes of government. The nearest Labour came to serious problems, the so-called 'fuel crisis' of autumn 2000, saw the party's opinion poll lead disappear. Nonetheless, the government's firm response saw the problem de-escalate quickly and the public's lack of faith with the Conservatives meant that any impact was short-lived.

Indeed, the Conservatives showed few signs of recovery between election defeats. The party has lost six million supporters in under ten years. Its ageing and declining membership, allied to a very weak parliamentary base (worse than Labour's in the 1980s), highlight the extent of disenchantment with the party. Recovery at local and European elections between 1997 and 2001, achieved on very low turnouts, could not mask the fundamental problems confronting the party. The debates over the strategic direction of the party and its inevitable modernisation were played out in the leadership contest following the resignation of William Hague. To blame the 2001 defeat mainly upon Hague would be crass. The Conservatives had suffered a calamitous loss in 1997, shipping over four million votes while offering, to their many critics, internal disunity and sleaze. Hague was, to use the kindest phrase, clearly not an electoral asset to his party. However, we have yet to see convincing evidence that the Conservatives would have polled substantially better if led by any of the other possible candidates.

This raises the question of whether the Conservatives could have performed better using an alternative electoral strategy. Again, we think that this was at least one election too soon to see a marked change in fortunes, although there were weaknesses evident in the 2001 campaign strategy. Rhetoric concerning asylum seekers and 'saving' the pound was likely to have a limited appeal. The latter appeared to be viewed by the Conservatives as a trump card, as the party attempted to turn the election into a referendum on the single European currency. At best, this strategy did no more than shore up the Conservatives' core vote. At worst, it insulted the intelligence of the British public, already promised a referendum by Labour if its economic criteria were met for joining the single European currency. To claim that such a vote would be 'fixed' by movement by stealth towards the euro, or through a loaded referendum question, simply did not sound credible. The Conservatives *could* have made at least some headway in their criticisms of the referendum by pressuring Labour with more cogent, intelligent points. Hague might have asked the Labour leadership for how long they would consider a 'no' vote binding. Would the Labour leadership accept that British entry to the single

European currency would then have been prohibited, or would a later referendum be held, based upon mysterious 'renegotiated' conditions, in a manner similar to the Danish Maastricht referendums? Any 'fix' on a euro referendum would come not from the question but from the frequency with which it was put to the British people until the 'right' result was obtained. Hague might also have asked whether Labour's cabinet would, as individuals, be allowed to campaign for or against the euro, in an attempt to flush out Labour's lingering divisions on the issue.

The most common criticism of the Conservative campaign was that it offered little on public services. There is much merit in this analysis. The Conservatives' preoccupation with less salient issues such as Europe and an increasingly dated obsession with tax cuts led to the neglect of a positive emphasis upon how the party might improve services. The Conservatives' approach reached its nadir when Oliver Letwin raised the prospect of a £20 billion cut in taxes, with its seemingly inevitable adverse impact upon the maintenance of public services. After this blunder, the Conservatives rowed back somewhat and declared their commitment to service provision, although the party's emphasis upon the private sector's role, or the need for 'choice' (i.e. private purchase) of services was never far away. It has long been difficult for the Conservatives to make improvement of public services the central plank of their campaign, given Labour's persistent lead in the polls on this issue. Those within the party favouring the promotion of other campaign issues could point to elections in 1987 and 1992 when public favouring of Labour on the 'most important' issues of health and education did not prevent Conservative victories. However, those elections had been fought against a background of Labour problems of division, image and competence, absent in 2001.

Fighting their first election under Charles Kennedy's leadership, the Liberal Democrats were widely credited with having fought the best campaign. We do not dissent, in that the party had a clear electoral strategy, after the Romsey by-election, of continuing to trade on anti-Conservative sentiment and targeting Hague's party in vulnerable seats, mainly in south-west England. Although a luxury of permanent opposition, the Liberal Democrats' insistence that higher taxes were a necessary downside to expanded public services chimed with the new public mood rather better than shrill calls for tax cuts. The advances of the Liberal Democrats ought not to be exaggerated. The most striking feature of the party's vote over the last three elections is its consistency, hovering around the 18 per cent mark. The party remains as reliant as ever upon a change in the electoral system to achieve its breakthrough. The party offered a social democratic version of politics arguably to the left (insofar as the term remains of value) of Labour. With the Conservatives in disarray and Labour sometimes seen as too timid, the strategy made sense.

If the modest progress of the Liberal Democrats proved unsurprising, the variable performance of the two nationalist parties was more curious. While

Plaid Cymru's vote share increased, the party lost a seat (though it gained another). The SNP performed moderately well but suffered a decrease in its vote share and lost a seat. For the SNP, elections to the Scottish Parliament may now take on greater significance, reflected in the number of retiring Westminster MPs and the relatively lacklustre campaign run with novice contenders in 2001. For Plaid, the weakness of the Welsh Assembly means the distinction between national and Westminster elections is perhaps less important, although the party leader's concentration upon the Assembly is again evidence of where the strength of future campaigning may rest. In Northern Ireland, meanwhile, a very different election was fought. The results, with gains for Sinn Fein and the DUP, did not jeopardise the peace process, but emphasised how intra-ethnic bloc rivalries have assumed an importance almost as great as the 'old' Northern Ireland politics of inter-communal division.

If Labour's historic second landslide provided the main story of the 2001 election, the decline in voting turnout came a fairly close second. The turnout was the lowest since the award of the universal franchise. David Denver provides a number of disturbing figures in his detailing of the 'catastrophic' decline in turnout in Chapter 1. A 59.2 per cent turnout represents a fall of 18 per cent since 1992, a trend that shows little sign of being reversed. Those wishing to excuse the low polling could turn to either of the structural factors outlined in our Introduction. The first, that national politics is increasingly meaningless in the face of global economics, is not entirely devoid of merit. The power of the Westminster parliament has declined and ideological debates between the parties have diminished (although such divisions were not great in the 1950s, a period of very high turnouts). Nonetheless, the 'irrelevance' thesis overlooks the substantial choices that national governments can still make. The second, that people did not vote mainly because they are contented, is exposed by Steven Fielding's reference (Chapter 2) to inner-city Liverpool, where Riverside was the constituency with the lowest turnout in the country. The 'culture of contentment' thesis lacks solid evidence. Although conditions in most poorer inner-city areas have improved, relative deprivation remains. Within inner-city constituencies over half of voters always turned out in elections until 2001. Now, the sense of legitimacy provided by contests in which a majority of voters took part has been greatly diminished in some areas.

The level of non-voting is disturbing and too easily excused. It would be interesting to hear from persistent non-voters (highlighted in Table 1.7 in David Denver's chapter) whether they somehow derived more meaning from voting in contests related to television shows such as *Big Brother* or *Stars in Their Eyes*. Non-voting has become to be seen as acceptable and somehow clever, as has the wider berating of elected public representatives. MPs, for example, have never worked so hard in representing their constituents, yet receive scant praise and much criticism for their (modest) salaries. Those sections of the electorate that simply abstain through apathy or indifference could be criticised for a gross dereliction of civic duty. If this sounds overly pompous, it is no worse than hearing the dreary litany of excuses for non-voting – 'all the same'; 'makes no difference' and so on, all too often indulged. Compulsory voting may be too illiberal a measure to be introduced in the UK and we do not recommend it – yet. Nonetheless, we are unconvinced that Australia is any less liberal a country in demanding that its citizens vote. Nor are we convinced that voting is any less a civic duty than, say, completing a census form. The politicians so derided by sections of the non-voting public presided, during the last ten years, over improved living standards, low inflation and greatly reduced unemployment. How much of this good fortune can be attributed to the politicians themselves is debatable, but their performance might at least be considered rather superior to that of those who, through a mixture of apathy, indifference and sheer idleness, do not bother to vote in general elections.

The contingent explanations of low turnout offer better excuses for non-voting. Most of the electorate believed that the election was a foregone conclusion. Indeed, the variation in turnout according to marginality of constituency offers some indication of people making rational choices about whether to vote. Labour's superior performances where it mattered indicate how this was a latent Labour landslide in addition to being an actual one. It suggests Labour had a 'reserve' army of support to call upon had the party's election victory appeared under threat. The belief that Labour's victory was a foregone conclusion thus affected the result in different ways according to constituency type. Equally, the perception of the inevitability of victory affected the campaign. Much of the discussion concerned Labour's imminent landslide and the respective standing of the parties in the polls rather than the merits of party policy. This is not to suggest that the polls determined the overall outcome, as such a suggestion would be preposterous. Polling firms cannot be blamed for the lack of a health warning accompanying their data. Furthermore, their final predictions of the outcome were accurate – within the 3 percentage point declared margin of error. We are concerned, however, that opinion polls distort national debate and affect individual constituency outcomes. In Italy and France opinion polls are banned in the immediate run-up to a general election. In Ireland a recent bill introducing a similar ban was lost due to technical incompetence. Reluctantly, given the illiberalism of the measure, we feel that it may be time to introduce a similar ban on opinion polls in the UK during election campaigns. The Representation of the People Act 2000 banished many of the old restrictions affecting television and radio election coverage. Nonetheless, a number of measures remain in place that are designed to prevent distortion of the outcome. The reporting of polls may be one such distortion. For part of the 2001 campaign, several opinion polls placed Labour at a 50 per cent poll rating. The figure was unrealistic, given that even Harold Wilson's 1966 victory, in a long-vanished era of two-party politics, was won on only a 48 per cent share for Labour.

Few would claim that a ban on opinion polls would act as a panacea, by which voter apathy would diminish and turnout would be restored to healthy, pre-2001 levels. Similarly, new methods of voting would induce only slight change. The introduction of postal voting by choice made scant impact in the 2001 contest and the limited experiments with electronic voting made little difference in the local elections in 2000. A much more fundamental change would be an overhaul of Britain's electoral system. The debate on such a change appears, if anything, to have dwindled, despite the perpetual distortions of first past the post. In a bid to retain the link between constituent and MP, 'AV plus' was recommended by the Jenkins Commission. There are serious reservations accompanying such proposals, in that they would do little to increase proportionality, although voting would become more meaningful in safe constituencies. The proposals appear to have been quietly shelved. A revival of the debate on proportional representation would be timely. The temptation for the Labour government will be to do nothing and await a third landslide, even more apathetic than the 2001 version.

Index

Page references for figures and tables are in italics; 'n' indicates an entry's appearance within a note.